A. S. Neill

Volumes of the *Continuum Library of Educational Thought* include:

Aristotle	Alexander Moseley
St Thomas Aquinas	Vivian Boland
Pierre Bourdieu	Michael James Grenfell
Jerome Bruner	David Olson
John Dewey	Richard Pring
Michel Foucault	Lynn Fendler
John Holt	Roland Meighan
John Locke	Alexander Moseley
Maria Montessori	Marion O'Donnell
John Henry Newman	James Arthur and Guy Nicholls
Plato	Robin Barrow
Lev Vygotsky	Rene van der Veer
Rudolf Steiner	Heiner Ullrich
Jean Piaget	Richard Kohler
Jean-Jacques Rousseau	Jürgen Oelkers
EG West	James Tooley
Mary Wollstonecraft	Susan Laird
Paulo Freire	Daniel Schugurensky
St Augustine	Ryan Topping
Loris Malaguzzi and the	Kathy Hall, Mary Horgan, Anna Ridgway, Rosaleen
Reggio Emilia Experience	Murphy, Maura Cunneen and Denice Cunningham
Robert Owen	Robert Davis and Frank O'Hagan

See www.bloomsbury.com for further details

Robin Barrow, Dean of Philosophy of Education, and former Dean of Education, Simon Fraser University, Canada.

Peter Gronn, Professor of Education, Department of Educational Studies, University of Glasgow, UK.

Kathy Hall, Professor of Education, National University of Ireland, Ireland.

Stephen Heyneman, Professor of International Educational Policy at the College of Education and Human Development, Vanderbilt University, USA.

Yung-Shi Lin, President Emeritus and Professor, Department of Education and Institute of Graduate Studies, Taipei Municipal University of Education, Republic of China, Taiwan.

Gary McCulloch, Brian Simon Professor of the History of Education,

Institute of Education, University of London, USA.

Jürgen Oelkers, Professor of Education at the Institute of Education, University of Zürich, Switzerland.

Richard Pring, Lead Director of the Nuffield Review of 14–19 Education and Training for England and Wales; Emeritus Fellow, Green College Oxford, UK.

Harvey Siegel, Professor of Philosophy, University of Miami, USA.

Richard Smith, Professor of Education and Director of the Combined Degrees in Arts and Social Sciences, University of Durham, USA.

Zhou Zuoyu, Professor of Education, Beijing Normal University, People's Republic of China.

A. S. Neill

RICHARD BAILEY

Continuum Library of Educational Thought
Series Editor: Richard Bailey
Volume 24

B L O O M S B U R Y
LONDON • NEW DELHI • NEW YORK • SYDNEY

Bloomsbury Academic
An imprint of Bloomsbury Publishing Plc

50 Bedford Square   1385 Broadway
London   New York
WC1B 3DP   NY 10018
UK   USA

www.bloomsbury.com

First published 2013

British Library Cataloguing-in-Publication Data
A catalogue record for this book is available from the British Library.

ISBN: HB: 978-1-8470-6087-7
PDF: 978-1-4411-0042-9

Library of Congress Cataloging-in-Publication Data
Bailey, Richard.
A.S. Neill/Richard Bailey.
pages cm. – (Continuum library of educational thought; volume 24)
Includes bibliographical references and index.
ISBN 978-1-84706-087-7 (hardcover) – ISBN 978-1-4411-0042-9 (pdf) –
ISBN 978-1-4411-1590-4 (epub) –
ISBN 978-1-4725-0489-0 (pbk.)
1. Neill, Alexander Sutherland, 1883-1973 – Influence. 2. Neill, Alexander Sutherland,
1883-1973 – Criticism and interpretation. 3. Education – Philosophy.
4. Education – Experimental methods. 5. Summerhill School. I. Title.
LB880.N382B35 2014
370.1 – dc23

Typeset by Deanta Global Publishing Services, Chennai, India
Printed and bound in Great Britain

In loving memory of my extraordinary mother, Betty Bailey.
The world is a darker place without you.

Contents

Series Editor's Preface   ix
A. S. Neill and Summerhill: Foreword by James Tooley   xi
Acknowledgments   xv

1   Introduction   1
2   Intellectual Biography of Neill and Summerhill   5
3   Key Themes of A. S. Neill's Work   105
4   The Reception and Relevance of A. S. Neill's Work   151
5   Conclusion   165

References   171
Appendix I: Reading Neill and Summerhill   185
Appendix II: Neill and Summerhill Chronology   187
Index   191

Series Editor's Preface

The books in this series take the form of what might be called "philosophical biography" in the area of educational studies. Their shared purpose, simply put, is to understand the thoughts and practices of certain educational philosophers.

Straightaway, this project is confronted with some potential difficulties. As even a cursory reading of the list of thinkers whose names provide the titles within the series will testify, many are not ordinarily considered to be philosophers. Some can be more sensibly located in other areas of the academy—sociology, economics, psychology, and so on. Others seem unsuited to the label because their contribution to education is primarily in terms of its practice. In the narrow, disciplinary sense, then, many of the subjects of this series are clearly not philosophers. In another sense, however, and this is the sense employed by Jean-Paul Sartre in his own attempts in the genre, a philosophical biography can be written about anyone whose thought is important and interesting. In this sense, I suggest, each of the thinkers acknowledged in this series are philosophers.

Implicit within the *Continuum Library of Educational Thought* is an assertion that theories and the practices that follow from them (and equally, practices and the theories that lie implicitly within them) are vitally important for education. By gathering together the ideas of some of the most important and interesting educational thinkers, from the Ancient Greeks to contemporary scholars, the series has the ambitious task of providing an accessible yet authoritative resource for a generation of students and practitioners.

It will always be possible to question the list of key thinkers that are represented in this series. Some may question the inclusion of certain thinkers; some may disagree with the exclusion of others. That is inevitably going to be the case. There is no suggestion that the list of thinkers represented within the *Continuum Library of Educational Thought* is in any way definitive. What is incontestable is that these thinkers have fascinating ideas about education, and that taken together, the *Library* can act as a powerful source of information and inspiration for those committed to the study of education.

Series Editor
Richard Bailey

A. S. Neill and Summerhill:
Foreword by James Tooley

Richard Bailey has written an engaging and important book on one of the educational giants of the last century, A. S. Neill, who still has, as Bailey highlights, a hold on the imaginations of educators today.

The first half of the book is a riveting read, as Bailey takes us through the life story of this extraordinary educator. There's the transformation of the young Neill, suffering the barbarism of Scottish schooling at the turn of the last century, through to the young graduate of Edinburgh University who knows one thing above all, that he doesn't want to end up teaching, to the "aged and frail man" (p. 107) who in his dotage became perhaps Britain's most popular media commentator on education and social trends. Above all, throughout his life, Neill espoused educational freedom. Unusually, he combined the qualities of being both a radical thinker and someone who put his ideas into practice, especially through the creation of perhaps the most famous "free school" of all time, Summerhill.

Bailey's engaging style presents us with a lively mix of biography and the history of educational thought of the last 100 years. All of humanity is there—or perhaps that should be narrowed to all of eccentric humanity. There is war and peace, love stories, and tales of huge egos falling out with one another, and with the world too. And here too are simple, fragile human beings, as when Neill himself grapples with the contrast of his own high ideals on what children are like with the trials of raising his own daughter Zoë.

In the second half of the book, Neill's ideas are encapsulated into key themes, contextualized, and critiqued within a broader intellectual framework, where Bailey highlights much of what is good about Neill's thought, and presents a critique of some of the weaknesses that he and others have identified. It's all very relevant for us as educators today, as Bailey acknowledges. A. S. Neill has had a considerable "soft" influence on the way things are now done in schools:

> the general tone of state schooling is significantly different from that even 50 years earlier . . . a form of progressivism is simply taken for granted by teachers in almost all schools. And such a dramatic change is due, in no small part, to the actions of thinkers like Neill. (p. 212)

Certainly, there is a huge contrast between the cruel reality of the schools Neill experienced as a child and those of today—at least in Europe and America. However, the Scottish school system of "ram it in, cram it in, little heads are hollow/belt it in, strap it in, more to come tomorrow" (p. 11), or the "Three Rs" taught through the "Three Bs"—Blackboard, Bible, and Belt (p. 11)—are not as absent as one might hope in some parts of the world today. Reading Bailey's descriptions of the methods of Scottish schools a hundred or more years ago chimes with some of what I see as I travel in parts of sub-Saharan Africa and South Asia. Neill's humanism still has much to offer to educators in countries emerging today as modern economies.

Neill's radical experiment—Summerhill—was not a complete success, Bailey concludes. But some of its shortcomings could be trivially solved today using technological advances. I was particularly struck by the descriptions of Neill's teaching methods (Chapter 3.5), which, as Bailey points out, seemed hopelessly misaligned with his ideals on noncompulsion and the voluntary nature of children's participation. If you're a student who decides you don't want to go to lessons one week, how do you catch up on the material when you do feel more inclined? And if you can't, doesn't that make a mockery of the supposed freedoms you've been given? Perhaps Neill's solution was implicitly that children should go back to the textbooks and teach themselves, as Neill himself had done throughout university. But not everyone thrives on that degree of autodidacticism. Nowadays, a child so inclined could learn, for free, through a patient, virtual teacher, online 24–7, on Khan Academy. Much of Salman Khan's approach would be anathema to A. S. Neill, I suppose; there's nothing in Khan's writings that suggest he would be at all sympathetic to the libertarian approach of Neill, particularly when it comes to questioning curriculum content. But nonetheless Khan's approach—where video lessons are available for children to learn from at any time, and where homework and classwork have been switched (so that children watch lessons at home in their own time, and come to school to do problems, more efficiently using teachers time)—might have appealed to Neill. Using technology in this way could certainly have made Summerhill a more effective learning environment.

Mention of technology reminds me of the one person today who perhaps most personifies Neill's approach, the prize-winning educator Professor Sugata Mitra—known as the Slumdog professor because he inspired the film *Slumdog Millionaire*. As his work becomes more internationally renowned, one can think of this as showing a continuing and powerful influence of Neill's ideas and practices. Known initially for his "hole in the wall" experiments, where Mitra showed how children in slums in India could learn to use the internet and computer software without any adult help, simply through trial and error through group peer-learning, his work has progressed to "Self-organised Learning Environments," and now the "School in the Cloud," where children's imaginations are allowed free reign to explore and marvel, all without any teachers in the equation. There are many similarities between Neill and Mitra—and Neill was an explicit influence on Mitra, whose formative years were in the 1960s when Neill's ideas were becoming popular. Both have "a powerful aversion to the common equation of schooling with teaching" (p. 70); Mitra would probably agree with Neill's statement: "I have decided to ostracise brilliant teaching forever. It is all wrong, fundamentally wrong." (p. 70). Mitra, like Neill, is all for "shifting the locus of control from the teacher to the children" (p. 69).

Above all, Mitra and Neill agree on self-organization, or "self-regulation": Reich's "Let the children themselves decide their own future" (p. 95) could be as much a motto for Mitra as it was for Neill. A. S. Neill had "a vision of people as self-regulated . . . an expression of . . . faith in the essential goodness and wisdom of human nature . . . qualities [that] will be stifled or corrupted by the impositions of external authority" (p. 88). Mitra's own vision is closely aligned to this. On a more prosaic level, they also seem to be somewhat similar characters: "I am much more interested in sunbaths, beer and baccy, than in all the new educational experiments under the sun" (p. 61), Neill once wrote. I read that and thought of Sugata Mitra's comparable bonhomie.

From the perspective of my own work, focused on the role of government in education, Neill's own views are ultimately somewhat disappointing. He seems to have changed his views on the role of government in education during the course of his life. Bailey points out that early on he is arguing "State schools must produce a slave mentality because only a slave mentality can keep the system from being scrapped" (p. 82), having in mind perhaps not only the German and Italian schools that were "preparing children for fascist states," but also capitalist states closer to home, which "also required a willing and pliable population" (p. 82). But later he seems to change his mind and think that the state could adopt more progressive ideas in education—indeed, he even apparently fantasized about creating a system of *state* Summerhills (p. 83). His later loss of faith with this idea does not seem to have come as a result of any philosophical or political realization, but only with a weariness of the difficulties of getting things done: In the end, he wrote, "I have to compromise . . . realising that my primary job is not the formation of society, but the bringing of happiness to some few children" (p. 204).

That's not the interpretation I would like to put on his work. I once wrote a book (*Reclaiming Education*) that was in part influenced by A. S. Neill, on the idea of seeking to reclaim *education* from the tyranny of *schooling*. The only way to do that I concluded was by first reclaiming education *from the state*. Only then could we hope to move forward to the ideals of educational freedom. That would seem to me to be precisely what Neill succeeded in demonstrating all too well. It was only by building a private school, Summerhill—that is, reclaiming in his own small sphere, education from the state—that he had any hope of realizing his educational ideas. And once you start down that road, I argued, then you don't want to stop at questioning compulsory lessons, but should move on to question compulsory schooling per se.

Reading Bailey's fine book brought alive again for me my own sympathies with the philosophy of A. S. Neill, and respect for him as a practitioner as well as a theorist, as well as a recognition of his shortcomings. Bailey has given us an excellent frame through which to view the life and ideas of this education colossus.

Acknowledgments

I would like to thank David Gribble, Mary Leue, and especially Zoë Readhead Neill and Danë Goodsman, for answering my questions about Neill and Summerhill. I am also grateful for the opportunity to visit Summerhill.

I would also like to express my gratitude to Anthony Haynes and Jo Allcock for early encouragement, and to Alison Baker and Rosie Pattinson for later patience.

Some good friends were cajoled into reading and commenting on parts of the manuscript of this book, and I would like to offer hearty thanks to Matthew Reeves, Gemma Pearce, Sara Loeffler, and Jennifer Leigh.

It is not possible to acknowledge adequately the support of some special friends and colleagues in recent years. Suffice to say, I shall be forever grateful. This may not be the place to name you all, but I hope you all know that I am aware of your kindness and generosity.

Chapter 1

Introduction

It has been 90 years since Summerhill School was founded by a gruff yet charismatic Scottish teacher. Summerhill—often called the most famous school in the world—continues to capture the attention of government, the media, and the general public. For some, the rather ramshackle little school is a holy place; for others, it represents all that is wrong in alternative or progressive or radical schooling. Whether its founder, Alexander Sutherland Neill, or subsequent Summerhillians intended it to be so, the school has become an emblem of a debate about the nature of education that has gone on for centuries.

There is an irony at the heart of the story. Summerhill is a very small private school in sleepy East Anglia, on the East Coast of England. Yet, its name and philosophy have been heard, at various times during the last 90 years, around the world. There seems little doubt that the "Summerhill experiment" was influential in the progressive educational revolutions of the 1920s/1930s and of the 1960s/1970s in the United Kingdom, the United States, and elsewhere, and the more gradual process by which classrooms became much more humane places for children. Yet, remarkably, despite the fact that the school has changed very little during its existence, it is still widely considered radical and controversial. The conservative educational writer Dianne Ravitch claimed that America is now a nation of Summerhills, and while not intended as a compliment, this sentiment certainly captures the sense of the school as representative of a particular tradition of education. Whether this impression is accurate or not is a matter for some debate. However, the power of metaphors and symbols lies not in their truth but in their potency.

This seems to explain, in part, the context of the events of 1999 and 2000, when the English government tried to close the school. State interest in Summerhill was not new: it is the most inspected school ever in the United Kingdom, and has hosted government inspectors almost from its inception. Most of the resultant reports reveal a sense of bewilderment on the part of the visitor. There is much about Summerhill that continues to stand in stark contrast to schools in general. Most decisions, including the most important ones, are made during an egalitarian meeting in which every young child has the same say as that of an adult. Attendance at lessons is voluntary. Relationships between adults and children are characterized by an almost total lack of authority. Generally, the school embodies values that, despite otherwise radical changes to most Western schools, would be shocking to most visitors.

Neill, himself, oversaw Summerhill for such a long time that the identity of the man and his school, many people argued, became merged. Such was the power of his personality that it was often simply assumed that Summerhill would not be able to survive his death. They were wrong. At the time of writing this book, Summerhill celebrated its 90th anniversary, and has survived nearly 40 years since its founder's passing.

Another common argument is that an analysis of Neill's thinking on education is doomed to failure. Neill the teacher, it is sometimes suggested, is an expression of a natural gift that is beyond theorizing. He was a gifted teacher, so the story goes, and his body of work was merely an extension of his personality. He also stood outside of any recognized educational school of thought. His innate understanding of the psyche of children extended beyond philosophy or psychology. Consequently, Neill's writings offer, at best, a crude picture of his thinking and practice. For his part, Neill usually encouraged this perspective. He often described himself as "a doer rather than a thinker", and much of his writing was prone to an affected disdain for abstract "theory." For example, in "The Problem Family," Neill wrote: "I am no thinker, no philosopher; I do hard work with children, doing mostly the right thing without thinking out the reason behind my action, working by intuition . . . whatever that may mean" (Neill 1949, p. 152). The implication of comments like this is clear: Neill was a savant; he was a gifted teacher who was guided by his innate wisdom, rather than the fluff and nonsense of academic theory. Not surprisingly, many commentators have taken Neill at his word and concluded that Neill lacked a coherent philosophy of schooling, and that Neill and Summerhill were educational oddities that defy analysis.

This book seeks to understand the Summerhill phenomenon. Following the pattern set by earlier volumes in the Continuum Library of Education Thinkers, the discussion begins with an intellectual biography that traces the origins of Neill's main ideas and practices, and the invention of Summerhill School. In doing this, it tracks Neill's progression from an academic failure to an educational celebrity, and Summerhill from a small school for a tiny group of students in Germany to a uniquely controversial school whose influence stretched far beyond its English home. It goes on to discuss the central ideas of Neill's work—Happiness and Interest, Freedom and Authority, Learning and Teaching—and in doing so, suggests a new way of understanding the underlying unity and coherence of Neill's thinking. Finally, the book evaluates the reception and relevance of Neill's philosophy of education.

I was first introduced to Neill and Summerhill while I was a student teacher, through his best-selling compilation "Summerhill" (1962). That summer, quite by chance, I stumbled across a copy of Neill's very first book, "A Dominie's Log," and read it in one sitting. The first book suggested to me the idea that alternatives to the normal way of running schools were not just conceivable, but also workable. The second book painted a beguiling portrait of a way of working with children that was entirely different from the rather brutal form of schooling I had experienced as a child, and was now expected to learn how to deliver as a teacher.

Later, while studying the philosophy of education, my initial infatuation with the Summerhill ideal changed increasingly to frustration as I struggled to get behind the plethora of rhetorical tricks and ticks that make up much of Neill's writing style. He was a uniquely funny writer on a usually very unfunny subject, but I was not sure if that was all there was to his work: entertainment. Or did Neill's gentle tales hide important lessons? Perhaps more importantly for me at the time, I wondered whether the philosophy of Summerhill could survive outside that rarefied air. Was there anything here for state school teachers? If not, was Summerhill no more relevant than "Swallows and Amazons" or "Billy Bunter"? It did not help that almost all of the books I was reading at this time either totally ignored Neill's contribution or used it as a case study in muddled thinking. More damage was done when a major television documentary represented Summerhill School in an extremely unflattering way. I know that I was not the only person painfully disillusioned by that portrait.

Looking back on those times from the vantage point of a few decades, I have no doubt that my early reading of Neill affected my teaching. The story of Neill's early attempts to find a more humane approach to his work as a "Dominie" within the draconian world of Calvinist Scotland seemed to reflect the struggles of many idealistic young teachers, but writ large. I am less sure how far it influenced my thinking about education. Writing this book has offered me an opportunity to consider precisely this question.

Chapter 2

Intellectual Biography of Neill
and Summerhill

A dominie's bairn

George Neill was the dominie, or parish school master, at the one-room, five-class village school in Kingsmuir, near Forfar, on the East of Scotland. His father was called MacNeill, but George had decided to anglicize the name to Neill on his way to lower-middle class respectability. Within the rigid hierarchy of Scottish village life at the end of the nineteenth century, the dominie was an important man. Normally placed below the Laird (the local landed gentry), doctor, and minister, in tiny Kingsmuir, the dominie was "head mon of the village" (Croall 1983a, p. 10).

George's wife, Mary (née Sutherland Sinclair), had trained and worked as a teacher, but propriety dictated that she abandon this career when she married. George and Mary had 13 children, of whom 8 survived.

Alexander Sutherland Neill was born on 17 October 1893. He was the fourth son. Allie, as he was known to everyone, was by all accounts a quiet, kind, and compliant boy, who nevertheless caused his parents to despair for his almost complete lack of interest and ability in academic matters. Looking back from a distance of 70 years, he wrote, "I never had any interest in lessons and could not learn" (1972a, p. 31). Yet, he was "obedience personified" (ibid., p. 61). He would stare at his books for hours, but nothing seemed to stick: "in the long run, my passive obedience backfired. Obedience made me stare at Allen's Grammar, but something inside me negatived my passive response by refusing to allow me to learn anything" (ibid.).

Allie Neill's childhood was characterized by fear and failure. It was not that he was not intellectually curious. On the contrary, he ceaselessly explored the local area with his mates: "my pockets were always filled with bits of string, chunks of old iron and brass, and nails, screws" (Neill, cited in Skidelsky 1969, p. 124). But these things were of no value in the education system represented by his father.

Allie's relationship with his father is difficult to judge. He used his autobiography to record: "My father did not care for me when I was a boy. Often he was cruel to me, and I acquired a definite fear of him" (Neill 1972a, p. 31), and "Father did not like any children; he had no contact with them. He did not know how to play, and he never understood the child's mind. The boy he admired was the boy who could beat the others in lessons; and since I never had any interest in lessons and could not learn, I had no hope of gaining Father's interest or affection" (ibid., p. 10). "Licks" of the tawse (a leather strap with two thinner "fingers" at one end) were common in George Neill's classroom, according to one of his ex-pupils (told to Croall 1983a). If there was no occasion to hit a child, Mr Neill would sometimes create one: "He'd sat a group of us to do some sums, and you had to put up your hand when you'd finished. The last one would get the strap—and you'd have a strapping for any you got wrong" (ibid., p. 17). Such behavior seems shocking, but perhaps it becomes more understandable when it is remembered that the dominie had to control and teach up to 139 pupils (with one assistant and one pupil-teacher) in a building that was designed for 25 pupils, and his income depended completely on his pupils' examination success (Hemmings 1972). George Neill was remembered rather fondly by many of his ex-pupils (Croall 1983a, p. 2). And his son's portrait in his early books is overall of a rather kind but pedantic man, strict in the classroom, but not excessively so (e.g., Neill 1916; 1932). He even hints as much in his autobiography, when he writes, "I am convinced that my father showed me how to be a good teacher. Though he had little humour, he had some imagination, and he could make history live for his pupils" (1972a, p. 166). It is the former image that has come to dominate in the literature on Neill's early childhood (e.g., Saffange 2000). His father, so the story goes, was a bully whose demands for obedience drove the young Allie toward radical ideas (e.g., Allender and Allender 2006). The difficulty with this view is that not even in the midst of his rhetoric flourishes did

Neill show his father behaving particularly badly toward his son, and compared to some of the dominies Allie met in later years, George was positively benign. Theirs was a drama created within a draconian, inhumane education system, in which both struggled to comply, and from which Allie Neill was ultimately purged.

The Scottish school system adhered to a pedagogy of "ram it in, cram it in, little heads are hollow/belt it in, strap it in, more to come tomorrow!" (Hendrie 1997, p. 1). Scottish teachers of his era, it used to be joked, taught the "Three Rs"–Reading, wRiting, and aRithmetic—with the help of the "Three Bs"—Belt, Blackboard, and Bible (Anderson 1995). The harsh and sometimes brutal teaching against which Neill later reacted was, therefore, reflective of Scottish educational practice of the time. Religion infused almost everything that took place at school, and the dominie was the revered figure responsible for ensuring that this was the case. While the Scottish school system developed what might be called a more "progressive" style, the dominie remained a revered figure well into the twentieth century, as is reflected in memoir, novel, and poetry (Holmes 2000). There was a playground rhyme chanted in schools which encapsulated the archetypal Scottish schoolmaster in very similar terms:

> Mr Rhind is very kind,
> He goes to Kirk on Sunday.
> He prays to God to give him strength
> To skelp the bairns on Monday.
> ("The Dominie's Happy Lot," Wingate 1919, pp. 60–1)

This verse captures in a few lines the key elements in the educational tradition represented by George Neill and hundreds of other dominies: the importance of religion and the central role played by the school in socializing and civilizing the children.

It is easy to imagine George Neill's exasperation at his wayward son. Allie was no "dunce" or fool, but he was unable to keep up with his classmates, and "He must have roared at me a thousand times, 'You've got no ambition! You'll end in the gutter'" (Neill 1953, p. 156). Scottish classrooms were dominated by arithmetic, spelling, Latin, and teachers were paid for their results. Young Allie's predicament was recounted some years later in the semiautobiographical novel "Carroty Broon":

> He turned his attention to the blackboard with its tiresome requests to find the Lowest Common Denominator, but his interest was elsewhere; he was wrong in every sum, because his interest lay in a folding pair of nail scissors he had found in the gutter in Tarby. They were very rusty, and his whole soul longed for a free hour and a sheet of emory-cloth, with bath-brick to finish up with. (Cited in Croall 1983a, p. 15)

Allie had great affection for his mother, who was a busy homemaker, but she was also a snob: "Lower-middle-class respectability was perhaps the keynote of [the Neill's] family life" (Skidelsky 1969, p. 123). Mary Neill was even more ambitious for her children than was her husband. As the family of the village dominie, "We sons of the school house had a difficult role to play. We spoke broad dialect among our peers, but when we crossed the threshold of the house we automatically broke into English proper" (Neill 1931, p. 12). Mary Neill insisted on standards of behavior that inevitably and deliberately set her children apart from their peers, who were "mostly children of farmworkers, poor, ill-fed and many of them, often ragged, mischievous" (1953, p. 92). Allie's inability to perform at a level that would be expected of a dominie's child brought embarrassment on the family, and that, Mary Neill made very clear, was not acceptable.

Just as the young Allie disengaged from his classroom studies, so he was repelled by the severity of his moral upbringing that took the shape of the harsh Puritanism of Scottish Calvinism: "The general idea . . . is the conception that man is a sinner by birth and that he must be trained to be good" (Neill 1926, p. 139). The Scottish poet Edwin Muir—who, decades later, was to become a friend and ally of Neill—said of John Knox, the great Calvinist reformer: "As I read about him in the British Museum I came to dislike him more and more, and understood why every Scottish writer since the beginning of the eighteenth century had detested him" (Muir 1993, p. 226). Calvinism, according to Muir, "turned Scotland into a Puritan country, to remain so until this day" (Muir 1929, p. 100). It had no place for the merciful or the generous and "Judged by the best in humanity, its figures seem narrow, sick and almost pathological" (ibid., p. 116). The potency of the peculiar melancholy of Calvinism lay not in its formal expressions, like the Kirk (church), the sabbath, or religious training in school; it was more subtle and more pervasive: "It was in the air, an atmosphere of negation of life . . ." (Neill 1972a, p. 44).

The Calvinist insistence on denial of the body, the importance of the intellect over the imagination, and, above all else, the moral obligation of obedience, was harsh medicine for young Allie. In later life, he frequently spoke and wrote about the joys of play and friendship spoilt by the ever-present threat of divine retribution. This fear was fostered as much by family life as at church: "We were not specifically taught religion; it was in the air . . . an atmosphere of negation of life" (Neill 1972a, p. 44). He recounts a dramatic experience when he was 6 years old, for example, when he and his younger sister Clunie stripped and were examining each other's bodies. The two children were caught by their mother who beat them severely and made them kneel down to ask God's forgiveness. When their father came home, he beat them again, and locked Allie in a dark room: "So I learned that of all sins, sex was the most heinous" (Neill 1972a, p. 80).

All in all, Allie's time at school became progressively uncomfortable, saved only by the opportunities to play that were available to him and his friends once the school bell rang. His schooling did not so much end as fade away. When they reached 14 years of age, pupils left George Neill's village school to attend the Forfar Academy in the next town. The Academy had a strong academic reputation, counting among its alumni J. M. Barrie, and it was simply taken for granted that all of the Neill children would attend and that they would benefit from the associated career enhancement. When the time came, all moved up to Forfar except Allie: "My brothers and sisters moved on to Forfar Academy when they had passed the Fifth Standard, but I never got there. I was rather a poor student most of the time, and it was felt that the Academy would be a waste of time and money" (Neill 1931, p. 12). Instead, he was sent out to work. As he recalled in his Autobiography, there was no doubt that his father saw him as a failure:

> I was obviously the inferior article, the misfit in a tradition of academic success, and automatically I accepted an inferior status. If there was a particularly hard and unappetizing heel to a loaf, my father would cut it off with a flourish; with another flourish, he would toss it over the table in my direction, saying: "It'll do for Allie" (1972a, p. 35).

Armed with the flawless handwriting drilled into him by his father, 14-year-old Allie traveled 80 miles to the capital city, Edinburgh, to begin his working life as a junior clerk at a gas-meter factory. Any satisfaction he felt in the freedom from schooling was offset by the difficulty of surviving on a bread-line salary, a dull job, and homesickness.

"For once, his parents were sympathetic, and brought him home, arranging a job as a draper's apprentice in Forfar, in a shop that was "only a few yards from the house where he had been born fifteen years before. In more than one sense, he had not come far" (Croall, 1983a, p. 25)."

The boredom of the 12-hour-days of menial work in the shop ended when, by happy ill-fortune, Allie's feet became seriously inflamed.

In making his case to his father to return from Edinburgh, Allie had suggested that he could take the Clerk's examination, which would have increased both his salary and his career options. However, when faced with his books, he found himself no better able to apply himself than he had at school. On leaving the draper's shop, Allie tried again to study; this time for entry to the civil service, and once again, he was incapable of sticking with his studies. Given the choice, Allie would have opted to become an inventor or a craftsman, but practical work was out of the question. The social status of the dominie's boy meant that his mother summarily dismissed all such plans. Instead, and no doubt to the horror of both father and son, she decided that Allie (still only 15 years of age) would cut his losses and become George Neill's "Pupil Teacher." For George, the proposal at least had the virtue of relieving him of difficulty of teaching four classes at Kingsmuir School. For Allie, the benefits were not at all evident.

A young dominie

Allie Neill's main role at Kingsmuir was to supervise the youngest two classes. With only a chalkboard between his and his father's groups, he would have been under continual surveillance. During break times, however, he chatted with and sketched the children. He was popular, but his skills as a pupil teacher were initially rated "barely fair" and then "weak" by a school inspector (Croall 1983a). With time, the young teacher became more confident and competent, and taught a wider range of subjects. This led him to start taking some mathematics classes, himself, which, contrary to all expectations, he enjoyed. His pleasure in mathematics was largely attributable to the quality of the tutoring he received from Ben Thomson, the mathematics master at the nearby Forfar Academy: "I think he had a genius for teaching, and I have never seen a teacher who took so much pains with his pupils. I know that I was a dull pupil, but he sacrificed hours of his time to make me understand" (Neill 1931, p. 12).

Allie worked at Kingsmuir for 4 years. As was the custom, he sat the entrance examination for teacher training college: he came 103rd out of 104 candidates. Despite this disastrous failure, Allie seems to have found enough satisfaction in his experiences as a pupil teacher to wish to continue in the role. He worked briefly at a school at Bonnyrig, near Edinburgh, but was appalled by the severity of the headmistress' discipline, and after only 8 weeks he resigned and moved back to rural Fife. The discipline at his new school, Kingskettle, was, in anything, stricter than before. The headmaster, James Calder, modeled his practice on the military, even making the children march between lessons! Neill was expected to follow this disciplinary approach himself:

> Kingskettle remained a horror to me. There must have been times during those three years when I was happy, but the main memory is one of fear; fear of being late in the mornings, fear of having my class examined by Calder, fear of him when he leathered the poor ones who could not learn. I realized that if I had been his pupil, I would have been strapped every day. My father had never been that strict. True, he had strapped often and sometimes hard, but there was in

his school a certain freedom, freedom to laugh and chat and carve your name on the desk. We never had to match in or out like soldiers. (Neill 1972a, p. 98)

Calder was a monster and his methods were barbaric, but Allie's free time was his own, and he made good friends in the local community; he even joined the army volunteers. The young teacher also met a man who was to become his first mentor, Aeneas Gunn Gordon, minister: "He was a Canadian, tall, straight, distinguished, with a strong beard and a nose like an eagle's beak. He took me under his wing . . ." (ibid., p. 101). Neill had started to have thoughts of becoming a priest, himself, and in support of this ambition, Gordon taught him Greek. In exchange for regular attendance at the Kirk and showing respect on the Sabbath, Gordon taught his protégé every morning before school. Surprisingly, Allie started to enjoy academic study, and his interests broadened to include literature, too. His ambitions slowly changed from a career in the church to attendance at University. This change of heart was no doubt inspired by his new-found love of learning, but was also helped by witnessing the social life of his older brother at St Andrews. With the support of Gordon and Ben Thomson, his old mathematics tutor, Neill passed a preliminary University entrance examination. Soon afterward, he also passed a Preliminary Acting Teacher's Certificate, and he moved a step closer to an academic life.

After 3 years of the miseries and joys of Kingskettle, Neill resigned to take up a post as Assistant Teacher at Newport Public School. This episode is barely mentioned by Neill's commentators, which is odd as it warrants discussion for a number of reasons. First, the affluent Newport offered the young teacher new and exciting experiences that had previously been denied him: he learned to dance, attended the theater, and his headmaster introduced him to musical appreciation. Second, Neill fell in love: "I fell violently in love with a pupil. Margaret was about sixteen; I, twenty-four" (1972a, p. 106). The object of Neill's affection seems to have been lukewarm about the attentions of her teacher, but Neill was obsessed, and remained so for many years: "The remarkable thing about Margaret was her persistence in my mind. While other girls faded from memory, she continued to haunt my dreams for years" (1972a, p. 107; the strength of Neill's affection for

Margaret is revealed in an outburst shortly before his death 67 years later: "Och, Margaret lassie, I should never have left you behind. I should have had the courage to think that you could grow with me" (cited in Croall 1983b, p. 409). Third, it was during his tenure at Newport that he seems to have first actively sought to explore relatively progressive teaching methods (Limond 1999). He rejected the use of the tawse (the leather strap), but stuck with nonphysical disciplinary methods. Generally, though, he was friendly and relaxed in his dealings with his pupils, he chatted with them outside of classes, and arranged extracurricular nature walks. Neill's confidence to examine his own pedagogy was no doubt fostered by the atmosphere engendered by his headmaster: "Willsher [his new Head Master] could not have been more unlike Calder. His discipline was easygoing—he did not care how much the children talked—and from the first day I loved the school. My two years in that southern suburb of Dundee were perhaps the happiest of my life thus far" (Neill 1972a, p. 105). Neill took and passed his remaining University examinations, and the Acting Teacher's Certificate: "thus he was finally qualified at the very moment when he decided to move away from teaching" (Croall 1983a, p. 39). In fact, Neill's teaching career had largely been one of convenience, and whatever pleasures he got from being with children were not enough to compensate for his unhappiness working in the harsh—at times brutal—Scottish education system.

Neill entered the next phase of his life aged 25 in 1908, when he enrolled as a student of agriculture at the University of Edinburgh. He did not choose this subject himself: his ever-concerned father had made the selection, based on advice that it would ultimately ensure well-paid work. Neill did not object, primarily because he had no better ideas of his own to offer, and also because the curriculum was the least of his motivations for moving away from the glare of his parents' disapproval. He returned to Edinburgh scarcely better off than during his ill-fated attempt to work as a factory clerk a decade earlier, and his meager funds (partially supported by a grant as a poor student) barely covered his accommodation, fees, and food. So, unable to experience the wealth of activities offered by the capital city, he turned instead to University clubs. He played sports, maintained his interest in military training, and wrote for the University magazine,

The Student, and for the *Glasgow Herald* newspaper. Such was the extent of Neill's contributions to *The Student* that he became its editor during his final year. In addition to the vocational benefits accruing from his appointment, he found his social opportunities greatly increased. He had led, during his first 3 years in Edinburgh, a rather sober and restrained life, in which his poverty led him to feign lack of interest in the theater, and other entertainments. Suddenly, this was all changed. As editor, he had the pick of Edinburgh's nightlife, with free tickets to concerts, plays, and films. This was the period not coincidentally, when the naive, sexually repressed mature student was able to explore more active relationships with women.

By the end of his first year, and remarkably having passed his examinations, Neill decided to change his course of study to English. So, chemistry and physics gave way to Anglo-Saxon, Chaucer, and Shakespeare. However, the excitement of a course change was to be short-lived as, whatever virtues lay in literature, Neill (and his fellow students, by his account) found the lectures, and the examination system that lurked ever-presently behind them, tedious in the extreme. Neill used his magazine editorials to vent his frustration, built up over the last 2 years: "we are all apathetic and disinterested" (Neill 1912a, p. 295); "Speaking generally, we say that most exams . . . test knowledge, not thinking ability. Indeed, independent thinking is discouraged . . . In short the system corrupts the morals of not only the pupil, but of the master" (ibid., p. 315). Then, Neill turned to a theme that was to emerge repeatedly during his later educational writing: "a teacher must first make friends with his pupils before they will listen to him . . . you must like a man before you can respect him" (ibid.). In a later issue, he laid the blame for the situation squarely with the academics: "We have reluctantly decided that our Profs. are far from being ideal teachers. Indeed many of them are not teachers at all, they are merely lecturers. Now in the twentieth-century lectures are an anachronism. The system dates from a time before to the invention of printing, and our University education is not dissimilar from the education in vogue a few centuries ago. . . . Our Profs. have been too long on pedestals, and pedestals are not popular in these days of strikes and heretics. Besides Statues are cold things" (Neill 1912c, p. 335). Clearly enjoying his chance to put his teachers in their place, and apparently forgetting his own miserable childhood experiences, the editor went on to suggest that lecturers should only be allowed to teach in universities if they had served an apprenticeships in schools. There is a passage in "The House with the Green Shutters" that describes students' treatment of a weak lecturer:

> it was a bear garden. The most moral individual has his days of perversity when a malign fate compels to show the worst he has in him. A Scottish University class – which is many most moral individuals – has a similar eruptive tendency when it gets into the hands of a week professor . . . This was a morning of the kind. The lecturer, who was an able man, but a weakling, had begun by apologising for the condition of his voice, on the grounds that he had a bad cold. Instantly every man in class was blowing his nose. One fellow, of a most portentous snout, who could trumpet like an elephant sent his handkerchief across the room . . . Then the "roughing" began, to the tune of "John Brown's body a-mouldering in the grave" – which no man seems to sing, but every man could hear. They were playing the tune with their feet . . . At last the lecturer plunged wildly at the door and flung it open. "Go!" he shrieked, and pointed in superb dismissal.
>
> A hundred and fifty barbarians sat where they were, and laughed at him; and he must needs come back to the platform, with a baffled and vindictive glower. (Brown 1901, p. 397)

Neill witnessed similar behavior, concluding that "a learned neurotic is not any different from an unlearned neurotic" (1960a, p. 28), and that the students in this prestigious and privileged setting "have been taught to know but have not been allowed to feel" (ibid.). Aside from any inherent interest, these comments are noteworthy as they signal Neill's first explicit statement of the problem of authority and the first signs of his disaffection with the traditional educational system (Swartz 1984).

It was at Edinburgh that Neill started to articulate some of his ideas about teaching and learning, and it is not difficult to see how these ideas became embodied years later in Summerhill. He argued that learning cannot be forced: learners might put on a show of obedience to the teacher, but this is worthless if interest is elsewhere, as interest is a function of a specific aim (Skidelsky 1969, p. 128). Once a purpose has arisen for the learner, then learning takes place as it allows the achievement of that purpose. In other words, Neill's emerging theory of learning, the essence of which remained largely unaltered during the rest of his life, was that learning was the consequence of an individual's attempt to meet some aim or goal. Such goals arise spontaneously, so learning is impossible to predict or plan.

Three writers gave shape to Neill's growing distaste for authority while at university. He devoured the works of H. G. Wells, George Bernard Shaw, and Henrik Ibsen. As a young teacher, Neill's few political interests had leaned toward Toryism, but Shaw's writing, in particular, quickly killed such conservatism, replacing it with a zeal for social reform, along with a vocabulary for his budding contempt for class divisions, social conventions, and authority. For Neill, as for countless other young people at the time, Shaw was an inspiration (Pearson 1961).

Neill graduated from Edinburgh University in 1912, and was forced again to think about careers: "All I knew was that I didn't want to teach: to think of going on all my life as an English master in some provisional secondary school or academy made me shiver. No, teaching would be the last resort, if every other line failed" (cited in Croall 1983a, p. 51). His ambitions clearly lay in journalism, but with those jobs hard to find, Neill settled for a position editing one of the many home encyclopedias that were popular at the time. Shortly after starting this task, and much to Neill's delight, his publisher moved to London. His next editorial project was entitled "Popular Educator," a self-help guide that sought to encapsulate in one volume, in Matthew Arnold's memorable phrase, "the best that has been thought and said" (Collini 1993, p. 190). At least, that was the claim; in practice, the book was a rushed hack job. As editor, Neill commissioned himself to write the sections on English Language, English Literature, and Mathematics, which he managed, thanks to judicious paraphrasing of commentaries he found in the British Library Reading Room. All the while, he was applying for jobs in journalism, and he was eventually successful when he was offered the post as Art Editor of the new *Piccadilly Magazine*, on Fleet Street. Circumstances conspired against his ambitions, however, as the first edition was due to be published in August 1914.

Like many young intellectuals of the day, Neill was ambivalent about the case for war. His conviction that Germany had been in the wrong by entering Belgium was undermined somewhat by the position of his personal hero, George Bernard Shaw, who maintained that Britain had no place intervening. His eventual and reluctant decision to enlist became moot, however, when problems with his feet meant that he would not have been accepted, anyway. So, in a few short months, both Neill's journalistic ambitions and his sense of patriotic duty were subverted, and he was forced to head north and return to his family in Scotland. Fortunately, any humiliation he might have felt were short-lived, as he was almost immediately offered the job of headteacher at a school in the village of Gretna on the Scotland – England border.

The dominie's logs

Gretna School had 130 students aged between 5 and 14 taught by three teachers in two poorly heated and poorly maintained classrooms. Neill would later recount his frustration at the poor state of repair and was sometimes forced to close the school. His predecessor had sought to civilize his pupils, using the standard tool of the dominie: the tawse. The new headteacher had a different philosophy, although Neill's own experiences and teacher training meant that, on the first signs of disobedience, he still found himself resorting to beatings.

Neill was not acting from an explicit or worked-out theory of education at Gretna School. Nor was he articulating a personal educational philosophy. He later described it as "groping" (Skidelsky 1969). He seemed to have been reacting to feelings associated with memories of his father's school at Kingsmuir, the miseries of Kingskettle, and the sense of freedom he acquired up at university. Also, he seems to have become profoundly influenced by the children themselves at the school. His initial position was as a somewhat traditional dominie, but his observations and reflections led him to abandon the social codes he had taken for granted because the children had no sense of manners as he understood them. His dealings became progressively more direct and honest with the children. Neill gradually gave up the traditional curriculum in favor of the more hedonistic pleasures of play.

As Hemmings (1972, p. 15) notes, "It was not studied forbearance on his part, but rather the result of his coming to see things more and more from the child's point of view."

The tension between Neill's growing reluctance to use the tawse and his acknowledgment that it was an expected part of his job was a dominant theme during his time at Gretna. He noted: "I have not used the strap all this week and if my liver keeps well, I hope to abolish it altogether . . . I see that it is only the weak man that requires it" (Neill 1915, p. 23). The eventual decision to destroy the tawse was a source of both anxiety and relief: "It was difficult, because they had been accustomed to being beaten up. Still I got over it . . . When I lost my leather tawse forever I lost my fear of my pupils and they lost their fear of me" (ibid.). These words were recorded in Neill's first book, "A Dominie's Log," which was his attempt to reconcile his journalistic aspirations with what he assumed to be his temporary predicament as a teacher.

The book took the form of the teacher's log, provoked by the rule that: "No reflections or opinions of a general character are to be entered in the [school's] log-book" (Neill 1915, p. 13). "A Dominie's Log" could, therefore, be considered his private log. Some commentators (e.g., Stewart 1968) have described Neill's first book as a work of fiction, but this is probably inaccurate. Neill, himself, says that the book sets out to provide an accurate account (albeit with synonyms) of Neill's working life at Gretna; it was "told more or less truly" (Neill 1972a, p. 97). The book reveals an idealistic teacher searching for an alternative to the old ways: "My work is hopeless, for education should aim at bringing up a new generation that will be better than the old . . . What is the use of anything?" (Neill 1915, pp. 14–15). Building on his tentative experiments at Newport, it was while teaching at Gretna School that Neill began to build his confidence in the core educational ideas for which he would later become known. He quickly abandoned physical punishment in the hope of promoting habits of self-discipline among his pupils. He encouraged creativity and introduced an early form of self-government among his children, though not without doubts as to the value of either: "O! the people are poor things. Democracy is the last futility . . . Yet the only way is . . . to strive to convey some idea of my ideal to my bairns" (ibid., pp. 61–2).

"A Dominie's Log" offers a collection of comments and reflections on Neill's everyday experiences, but not a coherent or well-worked-out critique of the Scottish education system. Nevertheless, it was in this book that he first openly questioned the relevance of the traditional approach to school curriculum: "I began to challenge the system ... When I began to wonder what learning decimal fractions, the Long Parliament, bean exports of Peru had on the lives of children who were destined to go out as farm-workers and blacksmiths" (Skidelsky 1969, p. 132). This was a familiar complaint at the time. However, the rationale for the curriculum for mass education in both England and Scotland was not primarily concerned with the intellectual development of children. In the words of one textbook of the day, its purpose was to "train the poor to an honest and industrious poverty which knew its place and was duly appreciative of any favours received" (cited in Barnard 1961, p. 62). Education, then, was an exercise in social stability; it was a process through which the classes were taught to accept their places in life. The precise knowledge that was put to memory was relatively insignificant in comparison to the process by which they were acquired. Memorization developed good habits of hard work and compliance with the labor force. The job of the schools for the working classes was to break and civilize the savage children in their care, and make them fit for the world of mainly manual labor (Skidelsky 1969).

In principle, the Scottish school system had a second function: to provide an escape route for bright working-class children. This had been the mechanism by which George Neill had stepped up from the coal-miner's son to a teacher. And it was his ambition that each of his children would benefit in the same way. However, as his son Allie noted rather pointedly, meritocracy in such a system was unrealizable because poverty and lack of parental opportunity made progress futile. So, such gestures toward a superficial meritocracy were merely variations within a redundant system that aspired to little more for its pupils than "wage slavery" (Neill 1915).

"A Dominie's Log" garnered a great deal of attention when it was published. Reviews were mostly favorable, and Neill's relaxed and quirky writing style even became the subject of an affectionate parody in the satirical magazine *Punch* (Croall 1983a). Whatever qualities it may have had, the book's success might be explained partly by the timing of its publication. The themes that dominated the book reflected the struggles that were preoccupying society at the time, such as between creativity and tradition, authority and emancipation. The book seems to have cemented Neill's educational convictions and built his confidence to the extent that he started giving lectures to the people of Gretna. One of his lectures was entitled "Children and their Parents." The villagers attended, but did not take the young schoolmaster's insights very seriously: "I can not flatter myself that I made a single parent think on Friday night. Most of the villagers treated the affair as a huge joke" (Neill 1915, p. 154). It was not difficult for Neill to learn that he would never be able to realize fully his ideals while working as a Scottish dominie. It was obvious that the community was not ready for him: "Were I to carry my convictions to their natural conclusions I should be an outcast" (ibid., p. 98). Indeed, by the end of the "A Dominie's Log," it is something of a surprise that Neill has not been dismissed. His summary of his relations at Gretna, its School Board and parents was that: "That school board did not care very much what I was doing . . . [and] general opinion among the villagers, [was that] I was quite a nice chap but, of course, half daft" (1972a, p. 96).

If "A Dominie's Log" was a predominantly factually based account of Neill's school life, its sequel, "A Dominie Dismissed" (1917), was "pure fiction" (1972a, p. 97). Like its predecessor, the book was a popular success, and it set a pattern of writing that was to continue throughout Neill's career: humor, anecdote, controversial statements, and a certain looseness with the facts. Perhaps driven by his journalistic ambitions, or perhaps attempting to follow the path of his literary heroes like Shaw, Wilde, and Ibsen, Neill decided to frame his ideas within the form of a story. This relatively uncontroversial fact has eluded many writers on Neill (e.g., Freedman and Marshall 2011). Even his American publisher Harold Hart seems to have been thrown by Neill's shift from (mainly) fact to fiction, and his introduction to the 1975 collection of the Dominie books gives a peculiarly inaccurate accurate of Neill's early teaching career (Limond 1999). About this stage of Neill's career, Hart writes: "The community [at Gretna] was, to put it mildly, benighted, and the parents were dedicated strictly to a teaching of the three R's. They expected that a good dominie would certainly whack the kids around and enforce strict discipline" (Hart 1975, pp. 8–9). This summary might be best described as misleading. When he turns to the autobiographical account in "A Dominie Dismissed," though, Hart completely misrepresents events:

> we learn that the inevitable has happened. The parents . . . [have been] unable to fathom this strange young man who refuses to pummel their children, or to abide by a set curriculum.

So, Hart tells us, "Neill is fired, and for a while becomes a farmhand" (ibid., p. 9).

Neill was never dismissed from his post as headteacher. The extent of the misreading of this aspect of Neill's biography is revealed by its reproduction in other books, including the highly regarded "The History of Scottish Education": "Neill, the apostle of freedom for children, was dismissed when he tried his ideas in an elementary school in Angus" (cited in Limond 1999, p. 304).

"A Dominie Dismissed" is presented as a sequel to "A Dominie's Log," and describes the young teacher's further adventures. Following his departure from the school, the Dominie leaves for London in pursuit of work and adventure, but he soon returns and takes up employment as a farm laborer. That, at least, is his official job. In fact, the book recounts the battle for the hearts and minds of the children between the Dominie (who is obviously supposed to represent Neill, himself) and his replacement, the arch-traditionalist, MacDonald. One of the literary devices used is to follow the imagined development of one of Jim Jackson, who first appeared in "A Dominie's Log" (where he had taken Neill prisoner). When the Dominie returns to Gretna, he is dismayed to see that Jackson's imagination has been stifled, or more accurately beaten out of him by the new dominie. He sets out to save his soul: "I'll do all in my power to help the lad preserve his own personality" (Neill 1917, p. 25). However, his efforts ultimately end in failure. He tries to understand the cause of his failure at Gretna, and concludes that he, as a simple, single teacher, was simply unable to counter the social forces of conservatism in education and the wider society: "I am losing Jim Jackson. The battle for his soul is unequal. MacDonald has him all day, while I see him only at intervals . . . His father and mother are people after MacDonald's own heart. They are typical village folk, stupid and aggressive." (ibid., p. 61). In other words, his failure with Jim Jackson was due to his inability to resist the forces of society.

"A Dominie Dismissed" is a rather more serious read than its prequel partly because it gives voice to Neill's budding educational philosophy. Using the contrived debates with MacDonald, Neill outlines his views on the true nature of education and learning, which, not surprisingly considering his predicament, he sees as taking place outside of the classroom. In doing so, he acknowledges the inspiration of someone who was to have a pivotal influence on his professional and personal life: "There are two ways in education: MacDonald's, with authority in the shape of School Boards and magistrates and prison to support him; and mine with the Christ-like experiment of Homer Lane to encourage me" (Neill 1917, p. 53).

Despite their differences in style and verisimilitude, a common tension that runs through the Dominie books is Neill's attempts to reconcile his professional responsibilities to prepare his children to earn a living with his personal commitment to teaching them how to live. It was in the context of his attempts to ease this tension that he came to conclude that educational reform was impossible without social change. And so he was led, for the first time in his life, to seek out fellow travellers in his pursuit of alternatives in education.

Homer Lane

Most people saw activities during the Great War as temporary annoyances since it was widely assumed that it would end in a matter of months (Arthur 2003). Of course, it did not, and Neill found himself spending much of the war years teaching and writing in Scotland, until he was eventually called up for service in March 1917. He was, perhaps not surprisingly, a dreadful foot soldier: military training was not well suited to idiosyncratic individuals with a fierce resistance to discipline. Fortunately, a fortuitous combination of his physical inadequacies and intellectual achievements led to him being removed from the tortures of drill to Office Cadet Training. This was much better suited to Neill's temperament, and by March 1918, he found himself traveling to Aldershot as a commissioned officer awaiting deployment. He never was called up, as severe nightmares and insomnia meant he was judged incapable of service. Once again, Neill returned home to Scotland as a failure.

The war years were not entirely wasted for Neill. He had heard about an unusual home for delinquent children run by an American in Dorset from one of the readers of "A Dominie's Log," and he used the relative proximity of the Artillery School at Trowbridge, Wiltshire, to visit one weekend. It was during this visit that he first met Homer Lane, who was to become his close friend and most influential mentor: "That weekend was perhaps the most important milestone in my life. Lane sat up till the early morning telling me about his cases. I had been groping for some philosophy of education but had no knowledge of psychology" (Neill 1960b, p. 3).

Homer Lane has become an almost mythical figure in progressive intellectual circles of his day. For his followers and admirers, he was a figure held in almost reverential esteem (Stinton 2005). Yet, his name rarely appears in textbooks and he is hardly well known to the general public. For some time in the early parts of the twentieth century, Lane was cited as an authority on the "new psychology" that was coming from Continental Europe (Selleck 1972), and he and his ideas were heard in discussions of schooling, therapy, and the care of delinquents (Bazeley 1928; Wills 1964). In fact, Lane's teaching was a "Freudification" of the theories he had developed from his own practice and reading (Stinton 2005). Many progressive educational thinkers of the 1920s and 1930s referred to Freudian psychoanalytic theory in their own philosophies. Homer Lane (and later Neill) was among the most explicit in this regard, but Freud also appeared throughout the writings of advocacy groups like the New Education Fellowship. However, as Carr (1984) points out, many of the educational prescriptions that were deduced from Freud were identical to those from thinkers influenced by other psychological theorists, like Skinner, Montessori, and Pavlov. However, Freud held a particular appeal for many progressives, none more so than Neill who, in addition to Lane, met and had extensive analysis with

Wilhelm Stekel, one of the original Viennese group. He later judged this analysis to be of little value to him, but maintained his conviction that Freud offered a guiding light:

> Freud showed that every neurosis is founded on sex repression. I said, "I'll have a school in which there will be no sex repression". Freud said that the unconscious was infinitely more important and more powerful and the conscious. I said, "in my school we won't censure, punish, moralise. We will always allow every child to live according to his deep impulses." (1962a, p. 294)

Neill was clear about his intellectual debts: "Homer Lane gave me more inspiration than anyone else gave me" (in Child 1962, p. 146), and largely thanks to Neill, some modern educational writers continue to draw on Lane's ideas (Carr 1985; 1988; Purdy 1997; Swartz 1982; 1999). Some years after progressive education discovered him, Lane became something of a guru to a group of writers that included W. H. Auden and Christopher Isherwood. For them, his appeal lay in the emancipatory power of Lane's version of Freudianism in which the individual needs to—first and foremost—examine himself. In his autobiographical novel "Lions and Shadow" (1977, p. 299), Isherwood summarized the central axiom of Lane's teaching like this: "There is only one sin: disobedience to the inner law of our nature."

Lane had trained in Sloyd, a method of handicraft training and, as a student, had come under the influence of the idea of John Dewey. From Sloyd, he learned the importance of "a taste for a love of labour in general; to inspire respect for labour; to develop independence and self reliance; to train in habits of order, exactness, neatness and cleanliness. To train the eye and the sense of form; from accustom to attention, industry, perseverance and patience; to promote the development of the physical powers" (cited in Stinton 2005, p. 13). From Dewey, he acquired a dissatisfaction with the contemporary educational system, and a commitment to aims focused on shared interests and social interaction. Working as a wood-work teacher with delinquent children at a Sloyd School and then as a Superintendent of Playgrounds, Lane became progressively convinced of the centrality of play in children's lives and the need for self-government, which he understood in terms of both the self-government of the community and the self-regulation of the individual. These experiences led him to a cautious interest in the ideas of Maria Montessori and her theories on the relationship between work and play.

Lane eventually found himself Superintendent of the Ford Republic (later the Boys Republic), where he initiated a series of reforms similar to those that had been made famous by the George Junior Republic in New York State, which had modeled itself on the United States political system, with its own courts, police force, prisons, and punishment. Lane later denied that he had known anything of the George Junior Republic, but the similarities between the two settings make this seem implausible. However, Lane's "style" of self-government was more democratically and organically shaped by collective decisions than by any structure imposed upon it (Stinton 2005). Lane came to believe that the young people sent there had simply learned ways of behaving badly. Lane maintained that the first thing he needed to do was to help the children regain their self-respect. Once self-respect was firmly established, the child could go on to develop self-reliance, and finally self-restraint (Bazeley 1928; Wills 1964).

Homer Lane's stewardship of the Ford Republic attracted a great deal of attention both within the United States and overseas, and the institution was visited by groups from around the world. Some of the Republic's board members had concerns about Lane's radical methods, and asked the sociologist Charles Cooley to observe Lane's methods in action. Cooley became an instant advocate, writing:

> Of Lane's remarkable natural aptitude for boys' work there can be no question. His sympathy with them and faith in them, and freedom from all insincerity or formalism are such that he needs only to be among them to ensure their devotion. I have never seen a better man in this regard . . . his main principal is that the way to bring out the best in them is to inculcate an ideal or group tradition by personal influence and let it work itself out without interference [even if the process] seems slow and disorderly . . . His ideas are in harmony with the best psychological and pedagogy. (Wills 1964, pp. 78–9)

Another visitor to the Republic was George Montague, later Lord Sandwich, an influential benefactor. Montague was impressed by Lane and by the Ford Republic, and was interested in getting advice to inform his own pet project in England, a home for delinquents called the Little Commonwealth. When Lane was forced to resign his post after making a fellow teacher pregnant, he was invited to England to act as a consultant, and almost immediately thereafter, Superintendent of the new venture.

Lane's arrival in England in 1913 was seen by many to be a turning point in the history of progressive education in England (Wills 1964). His contemporaries spoke and wrote of freedom, but he put it into practice to a degree that no one else dared. So, Lane became an enigmatic figurehead of the new progressives, drawing admiration and suspicion in equal measure. The Little Commonwealth quickly became inextricably tied to Lane's personality and his philosophy. His practices were based on three key principles: first and most fundamentally, the Law of Love, which was his view that love is motivated not by pity but by love; second, the necessity of Freedom from Arbitrary Authority; and third, Self-government in both accommodation and the school as a whole (Bazeley 1928). From his experiences in the United States, Lane had concluded that people basically just wanted to love and be loved; that every human being possesses an inborn goodness that is "Love" (Hemming 1972). In one of his published lectures, Lane said, "The only true authority is love, and the only true discipline is founded upon hope. The authority that is based upon force will transform love into hatred and hope into fear" (Lane 1928, p. 177). Lane believed that the perversion of young children was the result of their loss of freedom, of the training given to them from infancy, and that the perversion might take the form either of a loss of power or of delinquency (Hemmings 1972). Christopher Isherwood interpreted Lane's philosophy this way: "the disobedience is never, in the first instance, our fault – it is the fault of those who teach us, as children, to control God (our desires instead of giving him room to grow ... Conventional education ... inverts the whole natural system of childhood" (Isherwood 1977, pp. 299–300). Lane maintained that it is through the imposition of arbitrary, external authority that children begin to manifest dysfunctional behaviors. External constraints, rather than self-restraint, he argued, will always be flawed. He likened outside restraint to splinting up a perfectly well leg for a few weeks: "It would be useless when they are removed. It [will be] weak and [unable to] perform its natural functions from disuse." Lane concluded: "Surround a boy with restrictions and routine which prevent him from using his self restraint and judgement for a year or two, and these virtues, which are absolutely necessary in a community of human units, are not present when an occasion for their use arises" (cited in Wills 1964, p. 89).

Neill's visit to the Little Commonwealth in 1917 was 4 years after Lane had launched his radical experiment:

> I arrived in time to see a self-government meeting, and a breezy one it was. The Little Commonwealth was divided into four houses, and one house was attacking another on its disorderliness, saying that the rest of the Little Commonwealth was kept awake late at nights by the unseemly noise coming from the unsocial house. I forget how the meeting ended: all I remember is my surprise to see a company of delinquent children manage their social affairs so easily and cleverly (Neill 1921a, p. 109).

This was a revelation for Neill who had found his first, and most significant, mentor. He observed that "most of [the young people] had been court cases at one time, but to me they seemed quiet, social, gentle young men and women who without the Commonwealth, I am sure, would have been in prison" (cited in Lamb 1992b, p. 209). Lane introduced Neill to the "new" child psychology coming from Europe, and gave a form to his groping for freedom. What Lane said about freedom "was the gospel I had been looking for; a scientific foundation for the vague yearnings shown forth in my Dominie's Log" (1972a, p. 157). And what was it, exactly, that he learned from Lane? "I feel certain now that Lane's chief contribution to my life lay outside the field of analysis altogether – in his treatment of children. His immortal phrase was: 'You must be on the side of the child'" (ibid., p. 184). This would have been music to Neill's ears. In fact, 3 years before he met Lane, Neill had written: "I find that I am on the side of the bairns. I am against law and discipline; I am all for freedom of action" (1915, p. 117). Thus, what Lane taught was not something new to the young dominie. Rather, Lane served as a living example for Neill's own emerging ideas to their logical conclusion and under real conditions. In particular, he became converted to two ideas that were to become central to his own educational philosophy: self-regulation, and the notion of education as applied psychology. The philosophy of the Little Commonwealth enthralled him and struck a chord that resonated within him and the two men parted on the basis of an intimate alliance and friendship, and a commitment from both that Neill would work at the Little Commonwealth when he finished his army service.

As it turned out, Neill never did work at the Little Commonwealth. By the time he found himself heading back to Scotland, the decision had been made by the School Board to close the Little Commonwealth. Lane had been accused of inappropriate behavior with two of the young women in his care. The accusations were eventually retracted, but not before Lane's reputation had become mired in controversy and the authorities had demanded that he be replaced. The Trustees thought it inconceivable that the Little Commonwealth could carry on without Lane, so in July 1918, the home closed. Many of Lane's followers saw the girls' accusations as a mere smokescreen, behind which lay a more sinister threat: Home Lane's teachings were simply too dangerous to tolerate.

When one reads of the Little Commonwealth and its legacies—in particular, of course, Summerhill, but also more generally its influence over progressive educational thinkers between the wars (Selleck 1972; Skidelsky 1969), it seems astonishing that it only operated for little more than 5 years. Looking back on the situation in his autobiography, Neill wrote that, "The tragedy of Lane's life was that he was associated with social scandal and not with the great work he did with problem children" (Neill 1972a, p. 188). Nevertheless, Lane's influence continued to be seen for years after the closure of the Little Commonwealth, thanks to Neill:

> I myself owe much to Lane ... It was from Lane that I obtained the idea of self-government at Summerhill ... Forget the idea that education means learning school subjects, conditioning children, moulding character. The only true education is in letting a child grow in his own way, in his own time, without outside fears and anxieties. Homer Lane showed the way. (Neill 1969, p. 5)

Neill took Lane's demise badly; they had become close friends, and this had only intensified after they both found themselves living in London. Neill was a frequent guest at Lane's house and followed his lectures on psychoanalysis. He also undertook sessions of analysis, or "private lessons" as the unqualified Lane had to call them. With the wisdom of hindsight, Neill judged many of Lane's interpretations to be highly arbitrary, but at the time his opinions and claims were all taken at face value (Neill 1964a). At one point, Lane accused Neill of misrepresenting his views during a public lecture, and the two quarreled. Neill temporarily stopped this psychoanalysis with Lane, and started with a Jungian therapist. But before long, the pair overcame their differences and resumed their mentor-student/therapist-patient relationship. Indeed, Neill wrote an article entitled *Psycho-Analysis in Industry*, in which he briefly summarized the main theories of psychoanalysis before concluding in favor of Lane's concept of self-government as a solution to all of society's problems (Neill 1919b).

The end of the war had presented Neill with a dilemma. Homer Lane had converted him to the philosophy of the Little Commonwealth, but its closure meant that career path was now unavailable. The most attractive alternative was to found a school or home himself that reflected Lane's philosophy, but there were obvious financial difficulties with such a plan. Instead, he recalled that a reader of "A Dominie's Log" had invited him to visit King Alfred's School in Hampstead, London, passing on a report of a talk given there by Homer Lane. Neill visited the school and found it "a delightful place . . . The tone of the school is excellent: the pupils are frankly critical and delightfully self-possessed" (1919, p. 75).

At the time, King Alfred's was generally regarded as the freest school in England (Child 1962; Selleck 1972). Indeed, Homer Lane chose to send two of his own children there. It placed great emphasis on children's freedom and moral decision-making, and none at all on religious teaching. The school also operated a form of self-government, in which an "Advisory Council" made up of representative staff and students formulated and enforced rules. Within the English progressive tradition of Abbotsholme and Bedales Schools, focusing upon the development of reason, ethical behavior, and healthy development, the school was progressive to the extent that it tried to

blur the boundaries between school subjects, encouraged nature study
and manual work, and abolished marks, examinations, and corporal
punishment (Skidelsky 1969). Neill was also attracted to the fact
that its parents were intellectual enough to recognize the value of a
free education, and had chosen to send their children there. With no
acceptable alternatives open to him, Neill wrote to John Russell, the
headmaster, and was offered a job; he started teaching in December
1918. He found that he enjoyed working at the school and was generally
popular with the pupils. He even started to experiment with different
teaching methods, such as drama (Hemmings 1972). However, his
zealous advocacy of Lane's methods led to tensions developing with
other teachers, and it became increasingly obvious that King Alfred's
school was less radical than he had let himself believe. In what seemed
to be an attempt to show his fellow teachers the error of their ways,
Neill invited Lane to give talks on his psychology to the staff at that
school, but these were not well received. Neill wrote that Lane had
sat "with a face like vinegar" and afterward declared that the school
was full of hate (1972a, p. 156). Disputes centered on the issue of self-
government, with Neill rating the Advisory Council a poor imitation.
He made a case for a more thoroughgoing version, but his colleagues
objected: "under Homer Lane's influence, I became a heretic assistant.
I kept asking for self-government, stupidly of course, for what self-
government can one practice in a day school?" (Neill 1960d, p. 4).
Matters came to a stalemate until the headmaster suggested that Neill
experiment with self-government first in his own class. Even this
provoked the ire of his fellow teachers, due to the increase in noise:
"Naturally, all self-government meant to them was a chance to let off
steam in my room for an hour ... At the next staff meeting, they all
said it was obvious, of course, that self-government didn't work" (1972a,
p. 158). There were, however, the occasional worthwhile experiences:

> One day a class was holding a self-government meeting, and they sent
> for me. I was annoyed because I was having my after-dinner smoke in
> the staff-room. However I went up, "Hullo!" I said as I entered, "what
> do you want?" Eglantine the chairman said: "A member of this class
> has insulted you." "Impossible, "I cried. Then Mary got up "I did," she
> blurted out nervously, "I said you were just a silly ass. ""That's all right!

"I said cheerfully," I am, "and I made for the door. Then the class got excited. "Are not you going to do anything?" Ian asked in surprise. "Good Lord, no!" I cried. "Why should I?" "You're on the staff," said Ian. "Look here," I said impatiently, "I hereby Authorise the crowd of you to call me any name you like." (Neill 1921b, p. 385)

The rest of the teachers objected to the eccentric Scottish dominie, and eventually John Russell is claimed to have said to him: "One of the two of us must go Neill" (Neill 1961c, p. 4). So, Neill left.

Despite the disagreements, Neill departed from King Alfred's School on good terms with John Russell. He had gone there hoping to realize Homer Lane's vision in education, and had failed. Years later, he expressed the lesson he had learned from this experience: "You can have true self-government only when living in a community all the time" (Neill 1964b, p. 363). His problem, of course, was that he had no community.

A new era

In December 1918, US President Woodrow Wilson expressed the hopes of many when he said, "Men are beginning to see, not perhaps the golden age, but an age which at any rate is brightening from decade to decade, and will lead us some time to an elevation from which we can see the things for which the heart of mankind is longing" (cited in Mowat 1955, p. 1).

The First World War had seen the old world die. The horrors of the war had hardened many British people to idealized notions of "the golden age," but there were few who did not hope that the suffering that had taken place might inspire movement toward a better world: a safer, fairer society at home, greater co-operation between countries. According to Mowat's reckoning, "The history of the twenty years between the two world wars is the history of the disappointment of these hopes" (ibid.). The idea that Western civilization was tottering, and that one last push might send it crashing to the ground, was the product of deep anxieties, shared by many in the interwar period. Albert Schweitzer gave a lecture-series in Oxford, where he announced that "it is clear now to everyone that the suicide of civilisation is in progress" (1923, p. 3). The English translation of Oswald Spengler's treatise on the rise and fall of civilizations, "The Decline of the West," convinced many readers that they were living through the dying days of a civilization that had lost all creativity and power (Overy 2010).

The social and intellectual liberation, which the war had hastened, supported hopes that this really would be the start of a new era. Norman MacMunn (1921, p. 1) wrote, "Educational ideas that seemed startling in 1914 are hardly likely to perturb the world of 1920 . . . [People are ready to accept] the failure of courses hitherto considered good and wise and safe . . . and to examine more closely, and with less confidence, the foundations of their own judgements." Many people concluded that the most plausible solution for ensuring that nothing like the war could ever happened again would begin with young people and children and their education.

The romantic conception of childhood as a separate and special phase of human development was already well established in progressive minds by the early twentieth century (Steedman 1990). An interest in applying theories of psychology to education, however, was a recent development, and so the calls from Neill, Lane, and others were seen as both exciting and controversial. Earlier thinkers like Friedrich Froebel, and movements like Child Study, had reinforced the legitimacy of discussions of child development, play, and experiential learning (Whitbread 1972), and they had created an appetite and audience for psychological ideas among teachers and parents (Wooldridge 1994). Britain, specifically England, was at the forefront of the development of these sorts of ideas (Thomson 2006). At the time, there was a relatively decentralized education system and a strong emerging tradition of progressive independent schools (Child 1962), and this context encouraged experimentation, debate, and change.

There were also ideological changes taking place. There was, according to Thomson (2006), a strong utopian impulse during this period whose most important and lasting legacy was in educational reform. The educational systems of England and Scotland had been quite stable since payment by results had been introduced in 1852. George Neill had worked successfully within this system, and to some extent, the differences between him and his son reflected those that were being argued out across both countries from the turn of the century. Edmond Holmes' "What Is and What Might Be" (1911) epitomized this spirit of the age, and sounded a clarion call for change. Holmes' radicalism was made all the more striking by the fact that he had been very much an insider: he had previously been the Chief Inspector of the Board of Education in England (Selleck 1972). Holmes had progressively become disillusioned by an education system that lacked any interest in the mental and spiritual lives of working class children: "blind, passive, literal, unintelligent obedience is the basis on which the whole system of Western education has been reared" (Holmes 1911, p. 50). It was during his period of disenchantment with the existing educational system that Holmes became interested in Theosophy. The Theosophical Society was founded in 1875 by a diverse group led by the enigmatic Madame Blavatsky. Their aim was to create an exotic synthesis of Eastern and Western spiritualism that became attractive to writers and artists, and also a much wider educated public who were seeking meaning in the post-Darwinian world (Heelas 1996). Theosophy taught that God or "the truth" lies within every self, and is waiting to be discovered or released (Brehony 1997). Like many other new age movements of the day, the society taught that only the inner circle had access to secret knowledge; for Theosophists, this meant perfection, immortality, and the ability to perform astonishing occult acts (Washington 1993). Also, like other spiritual groups of the day, the Theosophical Society was riven by recurrent internal controversies and scandals (Campbell 1980). Probably the best-known split (at least from an educational perspective) was that associated with Rudolf Steiner in 1913, which was related to issues around the succession to Blavatsky (Brehony 1997).

The Theosophists' views of education read like an oriental translation of the Rousseauean Romantic movement, which in many ways is what they were:

If we had money to found schools, children should above all be taught self-reliance, love for all men, altruism, mutual charity. And more than anything else, to think and reason for themselves. We would reduce the purely mechanical work of the memory to an absolute minimum, and devote the time to the development and training of the inner senses, faculties and latent capacities. We would endeavour to deal with each child as a unit, and to educate it so as to produce the most harmonious and equal unfoldment of its powers, in order that its special aptitudes should find their full natural development. We should aim at creating free men and women, free intellectually, free morally, unprejudiced in all respects, and above all things, unselfish. And we believe that much if not all of this could be obtained by proper and truly theosophical education. (Blavatsky 1893, pp. 270–1)

The history of Theosophy's ventures into education is closely associated with the figure of Beatrice Ensor. A former teacher and School Inspector, Ensor had a Pauline conversion to a new gospel of education. In fact, she drew on Holmes' articulation of the case against the instrumentalism, inflexibility, and memorization of traditional schooling in her own work (Selleck 1968). Ensor resigned her post as Inspector to found the Theosophical Fraternity in Education. Later she wrote, "From the moment of the inception of the 'Fraternity in Education' in 1915 it was a dedicated spiritual movement and in my view has always remained so" (World Education Archive 1967, unpaged). Under her leadership, the movement founded a number of schools characterized by parent-teacher co-operation, an international outlook, coeducation, versions of self-government, a caution regarding discipline and punishment, the abolition of competition as an incentive to learning, and vegetarianism (Snell 1975). To these practices were later added the Montessori Method and Dalcroze Eurhythmics (ibid.). In 1921, the Fraternity evolved into The New Education Fellowship, but despite its change of name there is no doubt that the New Education Fellowship was an initiative led by members of the Theosophical Society and above all of Ensor, as can be seen from its stated first goal of education: "The essential aim of all education is to prepare the child to seek and realize in his own life the supremacy of the spirit. Whatever other view the education may take, education should aim at maintaining and increasing spiritual energy in the child" (Boyd and Rawson 1965, p. 73). This goal was as clear and unapologetic a statement of the Theosophical agenda in education as is imaginable. The Fellowship was not, however, entirely made up on Theosophists, and included a broad range of progressives.

The central theory of Fellowship was initially expressed in quasi-Jungian language: every child possesses a life force that thrusts him/her toward achievement and perfectibility. This force is deflected by the pressures exerted by the unconscious, which is the home of that part of the life force's great expression that has been repressed by bad parenting and education. The New Education Fellowship's motto was "making the unconscious conscious," which effectively meant removing the repressive forces of the old parenting and education, and in their place guiding the life force toward authentic forms of expression. This, they believed, was the route to realizing individual potentialities (Skidelsky 1969). Later, the Fellowship spoke of the "Inner Self," which Adolf Ferrèire, the editor of the French version of *New Era*, defined this as "the angel within us, trying to overcome our instincts" (cited in Skidelsky 1969, p. 146).

In 1920, Ensor founded a journal entitled *Education for the New Era: an International Quarterly Journal for the Promotion of Reconstruction in Education*. In the Spring of that year, ready to commence work on the second issue of the new journal, she appointed a coeditor, Alexander Sutherland Neill. The extent to which Neill supported or had even been aware of the New Education Fellowship when he took up this position is unclear. He was certainly an admirer of Holmes's "What Is and What Might Be," and he paid tribute to and agreed with its criticism of the traditional school in "A Dominie's Log" (1915, pp. 125, 236). The Fellowship was the main meeting point, and the *New Era* aimed to become the clearinghouse for progressive educationists at the time. In principle, then, his interest in the journal was predictable. His tenure at *New Era* gave him an opportunity to step back and reflect on his own experiences and ideas, and to learn more about the ideas and practices of other educational reformers. Perhaps the most important lesson learned was that, far from being alone in his criticisms of traditional schooling, there was a thriving community. It would be inaccurate to describe this community as allies; their main point of agreement was their opposition to the old ways of education.

His role as coeditor of the movement's journal also offered Neill another chance to test his authorial hopes. For years, he had oscillated between his dream of being a full-time writer and what he saw as settling for work as a school teacher. His first two books—"A Dominie's Log" and "A Dominie Dismissed"—were commercially successful, although some reviewers were not sure whether the author was a humorous teacher or a humorist writing about teaching (Croall 1983a). Neill, himself, struggled with this issue: "The worst of being called a humourist is that everybody seizes on your light bits, and ignores your serious bits" (Neill 1917, p. 122). Matters became further confused when he wrote two books that were only marginally related to educational topics. Neill claimed that this change in focus was due to pressure from his publisher. However, it is unlikely that he offered much resistance, as the publication of these books also realized Neill's ambitions as a writer (Hemmings 1972). The results were Neill's least well-known and least successful books: "The Booming of Bunkie" (1919a) and "Carroty Broon" (1921). The first of these books is a rather lightweight tale set near Neill's family home in Forfar. He described his next book, "Carroty Broon," as a "fictional autobiography of my boyhood" (cited in Croall 1983a, p. 171). The novel tells the story of the childhood of the red-haired Peter "Carroty" Brown (which would have been pronounced "Broon" in Neill's Scottish accent). Although it is fiction, the story is clearly inspired by Neill's life and experiences, and the eponymous hero is a thinly veiled disguise for Neill himself. The starkest, most shocking character in the book is a dominie, "the sadistic tyrant," who is clearly inspired by James Calder, the vicious headmaster from his days at Kingskettle.

During his time at *New Era*, Neill wrote his books, as well as editorials, attended conferences, and took part in the exchange of ideas that formed the heart of the Fellowship. He also had enough personal fame to undertake a lecture tour in England and Scotland (Hemming 1972). The topics of these talks—mechanisms of thought, psychoanalysis, the subconscious of the child, the psychology of teachers who spanking, self-government and mass psychology (Croall 1983a)—are evidence of the hold Homer Lane continued to hold over Neill. These topics would have been familiar to members of the Fellowship, as would the Lane's name; despite his dramatic fall from grace at the Little Commonwealth, he was still a Messianic figure for many progressives.

Neill dedicated "A Dominie in Doubt" (1921a) to Home Lane: "Whose first lecture convinced me that I knew nothing about education. I owe much to him, but I hasten to warn educationists that they must not hold him responsible for the views given in these pages. I never understood him fully enough to expound his wonderful educational theories" (Neill 1921a, p. 224). "A Dominie in Doubt" reveals a more cautious, less evangelical author/teacher. As before, much of the book is taken up with fictional dialogues between the Dominie and his successor, this time relying more on Neill's mixed experiences at King Alfred's School. He writes about the importance of the new psychology of Freud, Jung, Adler, and others, and infers from them scientific support for self-government and coeducation (Neill 1921a; cf. Kühn 2002).

In the following years, he visited other progressives, although the effect of these occasions was mainly to corroborate what he already knew. For example, he reported a visit to Edward O'Neill at his primary school in a Lancashire Mill Town: "I walked into the school and two seconds after entering I said to myself: 'E. F. O'Neill, you are a great man!' ... a young man came forward, a slim youth with twinkling ... I wanted to tell him that his school was a pure delight ..." (ibid., pp. 237–8). Like many progressives, O'Neill based his work and theories on beliefs that went beyond reason and evidence; instead, he relied on intuition, or on personal conviction: "I don't think he has any theoretical knowledge ... anyone could trip him up over Freud or Jung, Montessori or Froebel, Dewey or Home Lane. But the man seems to know it all by instinct" (ibid., p. 238).

Two theorists dominated Theosophical thinking in education during this period, alongside Holmes and Lane. Rudolf Steiner was not formally linked to the New Education Fellowship at all, but was a powerful influence over both Theosophists and progressive educationists across Europe, nonetheless. He had been invited to act as General Secretary of the German section of the Theosophical Society, and held this position from 1902 until he resigned in 1913. Unlike many of those within the New Education Fellowship who sought to build their educational methods on findings from empirical child psychology, Steiner based his educational plan entirely on his idiosyncratic "spiritualist anthropology" (Ullrich 2008). The most prominent intellectual influence over the New Education Fellowship, though, was Maria Montessori, whose systematic approach appealed to the scientific pretensions of the movement. She became its intellectual figurehead, and many of the early issues of the *New Era* contained articles on the Montessori Method; an editorial decision based on

Ensor's view that it was "a most valuable element in the forward movement in Education" (Ensor 1920a, p. 113).

Neill did not comment on Steiner in his Dominie books at all. He did, however, meet many of Steiner's students and followers and, presumably based on their recommendation, proclaimed him one of the great educators (1921a), specifically praising Steiner's movement form of eurythmy. Elsewhere, though, Neill seemed to have been rather suspicious of Steiner, his spirituality, his attempts to mold and guide children, and his disapproval of self-government.

Neill was introduced to Montessori's ideas by Homer Lane, and it seems likely that this framed Neill's subsequent considerations of Montessori. The Little Commonwealth had been the home of one of the first trials of the Montessori method in England, although Lane's biographer, Wills (1964, p. 124), doubted that Lane would have found the "relatively cold, scientific, academic personality of the Italian woman" appealing. Montessori placed an emphasis on the acquisition of manual skills, like Lane and Neill. However, Montessori teachers would also, unobtrusively, prearrange their groups of children and shape any problems in ways that minimized disruption. Lane and Neill, on the other hand, prescribed as little as possible. Lane, in particular, relied on his instincts to dictate his actions; Montessori's approach in comparison would have appeared rigid and overly intellectual. Neill disliked the Montessori approach even more than Lane. Any admiration he held for the ingenuity of the system was more than counterbalanced by his distrust of it lack of creativity and spontaneity. He wrote that: "The Montessori world is too scientific for me; it is too orderly, too didactic" (1921a, p. 146). Likewise, in a letter to the less critical Bertrand Russell in 1926, he cautioned:

I do not share your enthusiasm for Montessori. I cannot agree with the system set up by a strong church woman with a strict moral aim. Her orderliness to me is a counterblast against original sin. Besides, I see no virtue in orderliness at all. My workshop is always in a mess but my handwork isn't. My pupils have no interest in orderliness until they come to puberty or there abouts. You may find that at the age of five your children will have no use for Montessori apparatus. Why not use the apparatus to make a train with? (Croall 1983b, p. 30)

Neill's rejection of Montessori's teachings would have put him in direct conflict with many members of the New Education Fellowship for whom Montessori was a savior, and, most problematically, with his colleague Beatrice Ensor.

A third influence on Mrs Ensor and the New Education Fellowship is also worth mentioning at this point. Émile Coué was a hugely popular advocate of self-improvement at the time. His "suggestion theory," with its repeated mantra of "Tous les jours à tous points de vue je vais de mieux en mieux" ("Every day, in every way, I am getting better and better"), remains a familiar cultural reference to this day. Coué's psychology appealed to the progressive educationists because, for all their talk of natural laws of growth, most simply assumed that their job was to improve children, albeit in a more humane version than traditional approaches (Hemmings 1972). For the new educationist, it was up to the teacher to supply the suggestions and reinforce them by surrounding the students with a positive environment. The teacher decides which are the right messages.

Neill had developed many disagreements with the New Education Fellowship, not least for its support and promotion of the ideas of Montessori. But the advocacy of Coué's theory of autosuggestion simply appalled him. Teaching by suggestion was as far from Neill's vision of education as it was possible to be. It embodied in one simple package much of what he thought needed to be exorcizes from schools: "It is all suggestion, and it is not one whit better than the suggestion of the old Puritans who told the child he was born in original sin" (cited in Skidelsky 1969, p. 158). Following Homer Lane, he argued against any external interference in children's development. In response, to Neill's frequently expressed concerns about the imposition of adult authority and influence, the redoubtable Mrs Ensor made an argument that was to be repeatedly made against Neill's ideal of interference-free upbringing: "Mr Neill, himself, is a constant suggestion to the children around him ... The teacher is bound to influence his pupils" (ibid.; cf. Barrow 1978; Punch 1972).

Neill saw a common theme in the philosophies of Steiner, Montessori, and Coué: the teacher knows best. He argued that the benign authority of the progressive was more dangerous than that of the old-fashioned School Master because it was hidden (Neill 1960a).

This is why he said: "I had rather see a child educated by a drill sergeant than a higher-life person" (Hemmings 1972, p. 37). "Higher-life" was Neill's dismissive nickname for the goals of the progressives within the New Education Fellowship). The drill sergeant was at least explicit in his aims. The higher-lifers' ambitions were harmful, it seems, because of their veneer of progressivism. Authoritarian and progressive authority are both forms of repression, and were, therefore, unacceptable. Neill thought that children were innately wise and good, and that they had lives of their own to lead, and adults should not direct them, or shape them: they should not impose rules or sets of expectations to which children would feel obliged to aspire. Later, he would wonder whether adults exercised power just for the pleasure of feeling powerful, or because they wanted children to achieve something that they wished for themselves but could not acquire (ibid., p. 145).

The extent to which Neill differed from his peers became apparent in the July 1920 issue of *New Era*, which he edited alone. If "A Dominie's Log" was Neill's first formal statement of his dissatisfaction with traditional methods, this editorial was, perhaps, his first published statement of some of the core elements of the positive aspects of his philosophy and the foundations of what would become his vision for Summerhill School. He also took this opportunity to repeat his critique of traditional approaches to schooling, and including within his aim the alternative offered by the progressives of the New Education Fellowship. The endlessly energetic Mrs Ensor found herself committed to other work, and merely added a short preface to the issue: "Owing to the fact that I have had much to do in my capacity of Secretary to the Children's Famine Area Committee the editing of this number has been left entirely to my co-editor Mr A. S. Neill. As his interest is in the psychological side of education the main portion of this issue is devoted to the new psychology" (Ensor 1920b, p. 67). In fact, only one article about psychoanalysis appeared in the issue. However, what did appear was an extended editorial. Neill wrote about the necessity of students' self-government, but warned that it required a commitment from a type of teacher who saw all authority as dangerous, and reflecting his infatuation with psychotherapy, he located the sources of this danger in the repression of the child's ego and the resultant hatred of authority. "There is no such thing as the lazy child" (Neill 1949, p. 211), he wrote. "The word is used instead of 'lack of interest'" (ibid.). So, punishment is wrong, because it leads to fear when love is needed, and confuses results and causes. For the sake of the child's libido, Neill wrote, the teacher needs to let the children choose their own studies. Neill's editorial also included a direct attack on what he called "Crank Schools." This was his teasing nickname for the self-described "progressive schools" that made up the membership of the Fellowship and whose supporters formed the core readership of the *New Era*. The main target of his attack was one of the founding principles of the New Education Fellowship: the inculcation of "higher" values and tastes in children.

Mrs Ensor and her Theosophical friends, of course, had a quite different view, and the reaction to his comments is hinted at by the tone of Mrs Ensor's words in the following issue of the journal, when she took back editorial control in October (Ensor 1920b), and by the selection of letters that were reproduced. Almost every aspect of Neill's editorial inspired strong disagreement and sometimes anger: his rejection of authority and respect; his advocacy of self-government (or, at least the radical form he advocated based on Homer Lane's practice). But the topic that inspired the great response was Neill's denial of the importance of teaching children values. Ensor revealed nothing of the frustration she surely must have felt on discovering that her newly appointed coeditor had effectively positioned himself as her movement's official opposition. Her response was to reframe the matter into a virtue: "Mr Neill does us great service in stressing the danger which may entrap the new idealists in trying to impose their views of life on children who are not ready for them, or are not along that particular line of development" (ibid., p. 125; emphasis added).

Around this time, Neill produced "A Dominie Abroad" (1921), which was a sequel to "A Dominie Dismissed." The timing of the book's publication seems designed to assert the author's independence from this employer. The book was also his opportunity to state his intellectual and practical debts to his mentor:

To Homer Lane, whose first lecture convinced me that I knew nothing about education. I owe much to him, but I hasten to warn educationists that they must not hold him responsible for the views given in these pages. I never understood him fully enough to expound his wonderful educational theories. (Neill 1921b, p. 224)

The book is made up of a series of anecdotes and reflections on education, psychology, and life, in general, structured around the Dominie's continued battle to persuade other teachers about the error of their ways. Like its predecessor, "A Dominie Abroad" is loosely autobiographical, although it included more actual events from Neill's life, such as his visit to Holland to fetch orphans to England (which was on behalf of Beatrice Ensor), and his search for a suitable school of his own in London. Mainly, though, the elements of the book's plot served only as pedagogical tools to highlight Neill's educational messages. So, the Dominie's successor is given no space to respond as he is told about the urgent necessity of self-government and coeducation, and of the psychological revolution brought about by the insights of Freud, Jung, Adler, and Lane (Neill 1921b).

Disagreements between Neill and most of the other members of the Fellowship only intensified when Ensor organized the first of what was to become a regular series of international conferences for progressive educators. The New Education Fellowship had become the clearinghouse for progressive education, and since progressive education was really only an umbrella term for a wide range of beliefs, the Fellowship included a very diverse group. An idea of the extent to which the conferences succeeded in capturing the spirit of the progressive education age can be gathered from a list of some of the participants: Jean Piaget, John Dewey, Maria Montessori, Adolphe Ferrière, Susan Isaacs, Carl Jung etc. The first meeting took place in July 1921 in Calais. It was during this conference that the participants formally established the New Education Fellowship and adopted Ensor's journal, as its official magazine. Although the New Education Fellowship refused to adopt a constitution, the members accepted some core principles as a basis for co-operation that clearly reflected the Fellowship's origins in Theosophy, including that "education should help children increase their spiritual energy," "competition must disappear," and "children should develop senses of their own dignity and of loyalties to humanity" (Jenkins 2000).

Neill attended this event, and it is unlikely that he would have had much opposition to these principles, apart from the first. The topics addressed by the speakers reflected the eclecticism that characterized the New Education movement, with a particular emphasis on psychology, which was starting to become equated with progressive ideas (Brehony 2004). He contributed a lecture entitled "The Abolition of Authority" that summarized many of the ideas that were starting to take shape in his writing, like the danger of moral education and those who seek to promote it and the need to reject adult authority, all couched in Neill's idiosyncratic version of Freudianism. One observer wryly commented: "For a good many of those present, and especially for continental people who have not had chance to learn from the Dominie books, how much wisdom and lay behind the occasional extravagance, this appeared dangerous doctrine" (cited in Boyd and Rawson 1965, p. 72). Neill left Calais the "enfant terrible of extremist educational ideas in England" (Ferrière 1922, p. 384).

Neill used his short European trip over the English Channel as an excuse to explore the continent nominally on behalf of *New Era*. He traveled to Brussels and then to Salzburg, Austria, to attend a conference on "Psychology, Education and Politics," where the highlight for him was a presentation by Franz Cizek (Neill 1921a). Cizek had revolutionized thinking in Europe about the power of children's creative art (Viola 1936). For Neill, Cizek's work confirmed his own views about the importance of creativity and expression in children's development: "The child creates subconsciously. What originates from the conscious is thought out, what comes from subconscious is touching. Everything great has originated from the subconscious" (Viola 1944, p. 33). It is obvious why Neill was attracted to the ideas of Cizek. His philosophy of art reflected many of the principles that were to become embodied in Summerhill. For example, while being ambivalent about whether or not children's artistic ability improves, Cizek maintained a quasi-Freudian stage-like view of their process of creative development. And in words that could have been spoken by Neill: "No child . . . should . . . enter a new stage before the previous one is finished. Only a child who has completed all the early stages has a good basis for his whole life" (Viola 1944, p. 46).

Neill's visit to Germany was even more significant; in fact, it was life-changing. He had been sent to find out about new schools but seems to have spent his time at just one (Neill 1921c). He had been invited to visit a Dalcroze School near Dresden by a friend he had met while teaching her son at King Alfred's School. An Australian by origin, German by marriage, Lillian Neustätter had become one of Neill's closest friends in London, where the two of them had spent many hours imagining an utopian school: "I had already planned one day to have a free school, and she shared my enthusiasm, but we had no money" (1945, p. 157). By the time of Neill's European tour, Lillian was living with her husband in a place that seemed well suited to house utopia: Hellerau Garden City. Garden cities were a socialist concept originating with the town planner Ebenezer Howard, which sought to develop new co-operative towns on what was previously agricultural or waste land (Kamp 1994). Howard had established two garden cities in the south of England, at Letchworth (1903) and Welwyn (1920). Hellerau had originally been designed as a home for artists and craftsmen. Its original "Jacques-Dalcroze School" for Eurythmics had been derelict since the start of the 1914 War. It had been named after the founder of the method, a Professor of Music at the Conservatoire in Geneva who had devised a new system of training in movement. Dalcroze saw Eurythmics as far more than a form of dance or physical training: he believed that the ability to express rhythm in free movement could assist in a harmonious development of personality (Small 1987). Neill had actually met Dalcroze in 1912 when he visited London to demonstrate his Eurhythmics. Later, when teaching at Gretna School, Neill commented on his excitement to find an illustrated article about the Dalcroze School: "The photographs were beautiful studies in grace, the school is apparently full of Pavlovas. I think I should set up a system based Eurhythmics of the photographs . . ." (1916, p. 57). The rhythm and flexibility of Eurythmics was an appealing alternative to the drills that represented the physical education of his youth, and embodied the freedom he sought to foster in other aspects of education. There were two other aspects of the Dalcroze approach that immediately appealed to Neill: the first was that its teachers seemed to operate relatively autonomously, not "waiting for guidance from the fountainhead" (Neill 1921c, p. 221); the second was the lack of apparatus (ibid.). In other words, Dalcroze had managed to avoid the double standards that led Montessori to use the language of freedom while maintaining a desire to control and mold children, a tension that Neill thought doomed it to become "a dead, apparatus-ridden system" (ibid.; cf. Neill 1939; 1967).

The joys of Hellerau made all of his other commitments pale into insignificance, and Neill teased his coeditor with claims of never returning (a prospect she might not have found entirely upsetting):

> Dear Mrs. Ensor, I know you picture me spending my time running round visiting the schools of Germany. The truth is that I spend the day lying in the sun, clad in a pair of bathing drawers that would not satisfy the critical eye of Councillor Clark. Of course the dishonest explanation is that the schools are all closed for the summer vacation, but the real truth is that at the present moment I am much more interested in sunbaths, beer, and baccy (*sic*; tobacco), than in all the new educational experiments under the sun. I warn you solemnly that I am not coming back to London until I have taken a full course here. (Neill 1921c, pp. 220–1)

The Dalcroze School in Hellerau was run by Christine Baer-Frissell, who had been a student of Dalcroze himself. Neill and Baer-Frissell struck up an immediate friendship, and started planning a new venture. The Eurythmics School was flanked by two wings. On one side was a "Neue Schule" (New School) that had been founded by parents dissatisfied by the German state system. Neill enjoyed the relaxed and informal approach to teaching adopted by the mainly young teachers, and especially the central place given to creative activities. The second wing at Hellerau was unoccupied, and Baer-Frissell proposed that Neill take it over as an "International School" and operate it on his own terms (Neill 1923; Muir 1968). Neill enjoyed finding himself in the unusual position of being relatively well-off, thanks to the favorable exchange rate in postwar Germany: "I had £400 saved and that made me a rich man in a country where the Mark had little value" (Neill 1960a, p. 4). So, at the age of 37, Neill decided to start his own school:

> In August 1921, Mr A. S. Neill, M.A., author of the Dominie books, joined Mrs Baer-Frissell, an American lady, in the directorship of the Dalcroze-School Hellerau ... The centre of school life will

be social life. There will be no dictatorship from above. Already democratic government from within has begun, and the school is really a self-governing body. The pupils and staff have begun to make constructive experiments in education ... Psychologically the school is founded on the belief that the child is good, and no punishment or rewards will be given. The school is also founded on the belief that creation and self-expression are of more importance than mere learning. (cited in Croall 1983a, p. 113)

This notice announced the establishment of a new type of school based on Neill's ideas of self-government, freedom, and children's innate goodness. Despite its location and name, the founding of the International School in Hellerau is considered by many (including the current members of the School) to be the birth of Summerhill School (Goodsman 1992; Neill 1953).

Summerhill marks I and II

Neill's decision to stay at Hellerau and establish his own school did not coincide with his resignation from his position as coeditor of *New Era*. In fact, Neill stayed in that post for more than a year. It is not clear why he chose to do this, and presumably the establishment of a new school in a foreign country would have required a huge commitment of time and energy on his part. Neill certainly felt little loyalty toward the New Education Fellowship. As he acknowledged years later, "I was always critical of this body; to me it seemed too much to sit on the fence ... I thought it became too timid" (Neill 1960d, p. 4). His disagreements with the progressives were recorded publicly through the pages of *New Era*, and through his public lectures. The most plausible explanation for Neill's actions is that he stayed out of a sense of duty to Beatrice Ensor, although the small salary that accompanied the post of coeditor might have been supplementary factor. Ensor, herself, was often the focus of his polemic attacks in the *New Era*, but his relationship with her was underpinned by affection and mutual respect: "I soon saw that the more outrageously I attacked pedants and schools, the more delighted she was ... I liked her and ragged her most of the time" (Neill 1972a,

167). Ensor seems to have reciprocated affection for her coeditor, encouraging his expression and tolerating his occasional outbursts of frustration. So, despite the controversy caused by Neill's first attempt to lead the journal's editorial agenda, she agreed to hand over another edition to him. Ensor wrote in the preface: "It may serve a useful purpose if occasionally a whole issue of the magazine is devoted to some particular phase of the new ideals in education. Thus this number deals with Self-Government in Schools" (Ensor 1921, p. 156). Self-government was both a timely and risky subject for the discussion: drawing on ideas about children's freedom, adult authority, and the aims of education, it touched on each of the most hotly contested issues in the progressive school movement. By coincidence, the eighth edition of *New Era* was published in the Autumn of 1921, the same month as the International School opened. It included several articles about self-government, although few garnered Neill's approval: "Most of our contributors to this issue have declared against a sudden introduction of self-government. I disagree. I am all for the dramatic moment, the abreaction of the repressed emotions" (Neill 1921, p. 157). Ensor, in words apparently designed to check Neill's zeal, responded: "Any scheme for self-government must come as a demand from the children themselves and not be imposed upon them by authority" (Ensor 1921, p. 155). While Ensor was happy to tolerate alternative views, Neill was not. He continued to rail against Montessori and the "higher-lifers," using his contributions to the journal and his opportunities for public speaking to question their claims to offer a genuine alternative to traditional schooling. Matters came to a head in October 1922, though, when Beatrice Ensor dedicated a whole issue of *New Era* to the ideas of Émile Coué, supplementing with an enthusiastic editorial. Neill cautioned that suggestion theory was a superficial solution to children's real problems, and that its practice was open to abuse. Ensor disagreed, and argued that Coué had provided a valuable tool that teachers could use to guide children on their spiritual journey toward perfection. Neill, of course, thought that teachers should do no such thing, and that Coué's mantras and suggestions were morally indistinguishable from the religious indoctrination that had been taking place in state schools for years. For him, this was just another case of his so-called progressive peers failing to free themselves of the authoritative shackles of traditional schooling. A fist in a velvet glove is still a fist.

For their part, the majority of progressive thinkers rejected Neill's vision. He was criticized as a "Dogmatic defender of freedom, provocative and sentimental..." (Selleck 1972, p. 37), and many of Neill's contemporaries shared the opinion of J. H. Badley, an active member of the New Education Fellowship and headmaster of Bedales School, who thought that Neill's ideas were dangerous (Badley 1923, p. 29). With a very few exceptions—Dora Russell at Beacon Hill and William Curry at Dartington Hall—Neill had become isolated from his most obvious potential allies.

Perhaps Neill was looking for an excuse to end his involvement with the New Education Fellowship anyway, and their disagreement about Émile Coué provided it. Or perhaps it was Ensor who was looking for a time to end their editorial relationship. Either way, the January 1923 issue of *New Era* included a short notice:

> Mr Neill has very definite views on psychology and education, and it is probable that I print many opinions with which he would not agree. This has occurred in connection with my October editorial on Suggestion and Auto-Suggestion, and therefore, in fairness to "The Dominie", I think his name must be dropped from the magazine as co-editor. (Beatrice Ensor, cited in Croall 1983a, p. 109)

Meanwhile, the International School quickly developed a reputation as a center for progressive education in Germany. Neill's experiences in Hellerau are reported in some detail in his next book, "A Dominie Abroad" (1923), which seems to have been conceived partly as an advertisement for the school (Kühn 2002). After his dalliance with fictionalized accounts, he decided to return to a more factual description, using a diary format. The book shows that Neill depended on two people as he started to realize his vision: Lillian Neustätter and Christine Baer-Frissell. Between them, they started to envisage a new type of school, "where creation will be the chief object, where the child will do further than learn, where he will spend a month making a ship if he wants to" (Neill 1923, p. 65). For Neill and Baer-Frissell, three strands of the curriculum were key: Art, Crafts, and Eurythmics.

For Neill's part, these subjects made perfect psychoanalytical sense: "We concentrate on creative education, that is the release of the unconscious" (ibid., p. 67).

Part of Neill's rationale for establishing a school of his own seems to have been to avoid the frustrations of dealing with those who were unwilling or unable to share his vision. As he, Christine Baer-Frissell, and Lillian Neustätter planned their utopia, a vital assumption had been their choice of handpicked teaching staff. Such luxury quickly became impossible in a financially crumbling Germany. Nevertheless, the small group was remarkable in other ways: "It is impossible to find a staff that will agree to my views of education, and it is well that it is so" (Neill 1923, p. 133). An additional difficulty seems to have been Neill's reluctance to appoint men who might rival his dominant role within the school (Hemming 1972). The eventual staff was a diverse group, as is revealed by an interesting, if unlikely story from another European intellectual. Franz Kafka's sister and her husband had debated whether or not to send their children (a boy and a girl) away to a boarding school (Small 1987). Kafka wrote to his sister offering advice:

> There are schools in Palestine which are more akin to us and perhaps more important. But for proximity and minimal risk there is probably nothing except Hellerau. Too young, because he is a few months short of ten? But seven- year-olds are taken there; there are three elementary grades, you know. One can be too young to be put to work, too young to marry, too young to die. But too young for a gentle, unconstrained education that brings out the best in a child? (Kafka 1977, p. 290)

When the family eventually did make a visit to the International School, it was not a successful occasion. Kafka wrote to a friend in September 1922, reporting the outcome:

> My little niece will not be sent to Hellerau, of course. I did succeed in having my sister, brother-in-law, and the children pay a visit to Hellerau, but through this partial victory I lost all hope of the eventual victory. Frau Neustgdter [sic] frightened them off, for

she malignantly contrived to have both sniffles and boils on her face the day they were due. Herr Neustadter [sic], the Englishman [sic], a teachers' aide, and a Dalcroze student made a very good impression, but could not prevail against the sniffles. (ibid., pp. 361–2)

The person described as an "Englishman" is almost certainly the Scottish Neill (Small 1987). The incorrectly spelled Frau Neustätter had appointed herself housekeeper/matron at the school, and quickly established herself as the children's mother figure. She also provided a much-needed sense of order and organization to balance Neill's capricious management style (Neill 1923). The "teachers' aide' was probably Willa Muir, who had known Neill since 1912, when they were students in the University of Edinburgh. By extraordinary serendipity, she and her husband, the poet Edwin Muir, had met Neill at a tram stop in Dresden, just as he was setting up his International School. Willa Muir had experience of running an experimental school in London (Kamp 1994); she had, in fact, been dismissed from that role on the grounds that she was a subversive influence (Hemming 1972). Her reputation alone would have attracted Neill to her a potential collaborator, and, according to Muir, as soon as Neill saw her he had decided that she was the person he needed to help him: "It was, I suppose, a foregone conclusion that I should yield to Neill's entreaties . . ." (Muir 1968, p. 69). Finally, the "Dalcroze student" would have been Christine Baer-Frissell, the director of the conjoining Eurythmics School. There was one more teacher on the staff at the International School who seems not to have met the visiting family. Prof Zutt was a Swiss arts and crafts teacher, and a friend of the radical art educator Franz Cižek. He and Neill became friendly, with Zutt encouraging the new headmaster to learn metal and wood working (Neill 1923).

While Neill and his band hatched their plans, tensions started to build with the third school of the Hellerau complex, the Neue Schule. Circumstance meant that the two schools had to work together: the Neue Schule was financially unsustainable and required a new source of revenue; Neill needed school buildings (Neill 1924). However, it was not happy marriage. Neill's assessment was that "It was really a conflict between freedom and asceticism" (ibid., p. 8). Elsewhere, he wrote:

> The Neue Schule was run by idealists, most of them belonging to the Jugend movement of Germany. They disapproved of tobacco, alcohol, fox-trots, cinemas; they wore Wandervogel clothes. We on the other hand, had other ideals; we were ordinary folk who drank beer and smoked and danced fox-trots ... Our intention was to live our own lives while we allowed children to live their own lives. We intended that children would form their own ideals. (Neill 1923, p. 119)

The Jugend movement was the post-War manifestation of the Wandervogel, a popular scouting movement that that offered a wholesome expression of romanticism and anti-industrialism (Stachura 1981) that might have appealed to the sensibilities of the rebellious and socialist Neill. However, the movement was also infused with a commitment to character-building and virtuous living that would have amounted to much the same in practice as the moral instruction he so loathed. So, despite a superficial friendliness between Neill and the Director of the Neue Schule, Carl Thiel, meetings and collaborations between the conjoined schools were fraught with difficulties, and became very rare. Postwar Germany was not, perhaps, the most welcoming place for Neill's evolving ideas. While his German colleagues in the neighboring school were relatively progressive within the context of Germany, they were still authoritarian by disposition, by Neill's judgment. These teachers maintained an allegiance to the character-building philosophy of the Jugend, which left little room for the creativity that Neill, Baer-Frissell, and their colleagues so valued. Neill came to despair of the German teachers' seriousness and puritanism, in their preference for "serious" literature over pulp fiction, and for worthy educational programs over comedies. The writer Peter de Mendelssohn (1955, p. 56) was a student at the German school, and recalled the difference between the two teachers' styles:

> Neill's pedagogical principles were much more modern; any convention was unhesitatingly pushed aside ... It was fascinating to see – or to track as the young boy was not yet able to see clearly – such

as the mystical, almost mythical authority that radiated towards us children of Carl Theil, from the keen pragmatism of the metaphysics-averse Scottish educator. (De Mendelssohn 1955, p. 56; translation by author)

It was while in Germany that Neill experienced a growing sense of uncertainty about the role of the teacher. Neill's account of his own teaching at the International School shows of a series of experiments with teaching methods and approaches that resulted in an ill-defined eclecticism: "I refuse to run a German school, my idea is to take all that is best from all traditions" (Neill 1923, p. 148). His experiences at King Alfred's School, and his infatuation with the ideas of Homer Lane, certainly gave him plenty of ideas. One interpretation of this time is that Neill was exploring ways of shifting the locus of control from the teacher to the children (Hemmings 1972). There is, however, an alternative explanation: Neill was experimenting with methods and using the children in his care as his sample, much as a scientist might. Decisions to switch from one approach to the other did not appear to originate with the children; they came from a restless, bored schoolteacher: "It has come to me with something of a sudden shock that I am no longer interested in teaching. Teaching English bores me stiff. All my interest is in psychology" (1923, p. 196). Whatever the reason, Neill developed a powerful aversion to the common equation of schooling with teaching, resulting in a radical conclusion that was to become one of the defining characteristics of his educational approach: "I have decided to ostracise brilliant teaching forever. It is all wrong, fundamentally wrong" (ibid., p. 72).

While his German colleagues based their pedagogy on an explicit philosophy, Neill based his practices on an ad hoc mix of intuition, trial and error, and his interpretation of, and experiments with, the new psychology. With a group of young and inquisitive minds at his disposal, not to mention the young ladies from the Eurythmics School who tended to pool together, Neill found a captive and largely willing audience for his analysis. Up to this point, his engagement with psychology had been largely theoretical, gleaned from his voracious reading and conversations with Homer Lane. But in Germany, Neill was able to draw toward him a diverse group of young disciples, ready and willing to place themselves in his therapeutic care: "I became not only the substitute for father and mother, but I became a sort of Christ who helps people without thought of reward" (Neill 1923, p. 507).

In "Dominie Abroad," Neill recounted a series of psychotherapeutic encounters with students. His approach was idiosyncratic, as one might expect from a self-educated therapist. His language wandered between Freudian complexities and Jungian unconsciouses, all set within a practical philosophy given both form and content by Homer Lane. Neill's stated aim in this treatment was not to psychoanalyze the children per se, but to make the unconscious conscious, so that the children would be able to feel the effects of their unconscious mind on their actions. He believed this to be a primary educational aim. Neill's main mechanisms for bringing about such a change were self-expression through artistic activities, and day-to-day social interactions with other children. And, of course, both of these methods required a certain type of school. Discussing the apparent positive changes witnessed in his most challenging pupil of this period, David, Neill writes: "I am willing to give much credit to the influence of his free environment. Indeed I have much more faith in that than in psychological treatment, and if he were not such a difficult problem I should certainly allow the environment to do all the work" (Neill 1923, p. 207). In distinctly Jungian language, Neill wrote about his treatment of a young woman called Rita who had a very strong personal unconscious (i.e., the conscience). Neill interpreted the personal unconscious as the result of one's environment: it is "first formed by mother and father and later teacher and parson add their quota to it" (ibid., p. 44). A second form of unconscious was the impersonal or collective unconscious, "Which is a radical inheritance inborn" (ibid.). Neill believed that unhappiness and neurosis originate from a tension between these two parts of the child's mind. There is no doubt which side Neill believed would ultimately win, and which ought to take precedence: "The impersonal conscious comes from God, while the personal unconscious comes from people who think God didn't know his job when He created man" (ibid.). Rita was caught in a struggle between these two sides of her unconscious. She had initially fought him, but gradually weakened until she finally announced that she had lost her consciousness with the aid of wine and cigarettes.

It is at the International School that Neill's educational philosophy began to take shape, changing from a largely negative set of criticisms of other positions, such as the Scottish dominie or the English progressive, to a more positive stance, albeit laden with criticisms or alternative views of all varieties. In hindsight, it is remarkable that all of these events took place in less than 3 years, as in 1923 the school was forced to shut. Economic and political troubles in Europe inevitably reached Dresden, where shots were fired in the streets. Nationalism and anti-Semitism were becoming increasingly common, and high inflation had made Neill's savings worthless (Muir 1968). When some of the parents took their children home, Neill finally decided to leave Germany. He and Lilian Neustätter led a small group of students first to Vienna and then on to a youth hostel in the mountainous lower Austria, in a village called Sonntagberg. Neill and six pupils were rejoined later by Willa and Edwin Muir and a new teacher, creating a small, close-knit group. This group tried to continue the work begun at Hellerau. Struck by the evident beauty of this new setting, Neill was filled with hope: "Sonntagberg will be a Paradise for the children, but I fancy that many a time they will talk about dear old Hellerau and its joys" (Neill 1924, p. 12). However, peace was not to last long as tensions soon emerged between these outsiders and the local villagers. According to Willa Muir, they discovered that there was "a dark side to the Austrian peasantry and that whatever came out of the unconscious was not necessarily good" (1968, p. 104). For Neill, "The Roman Catholic peasants were the most hateful people I had ever met. To them we were pagans and unwelcome foreigners. They were priest-ridden" (Neill 1966a, p. 3).

Local people thought that Sonntagberg was a holy mountain, and this was a source of the villagers' income, attracting pilgrims from around the area. The pupils from Hellerau behaved in ways that were bewildering to the local villagers. One of the largest causes for concern was that the students had no formal classes, so they were often to be seen wandering around the village during the day. Suspicion eventually turned to hostility and even violence against the children. Willa Muir (1968, p. 102) simply wrote, "A less suitable place for a 'free' school could not have been chosen." Before long, the local authorities became concerned about the strange goings-on at Sonntagberg. Their requests for information about curriculum and professional responsibilities were repeatedly ignored by Neill, and his position quickly became unsustainable.

In Austria, Neill completed the last of his five Dominie books, "A Dominie's Five" (1924), a children's adventure story in which the remaining Hellerau pupils featured as the principal characters. The stories were originally improvised for the children. A later collection, featuring a different generation of students, was published as "The Last Man Alive." The October 1924 issue of *New Era* published a notice that read:

THE DOMINIE RETURNS TO ENGLAND WITH HIS SCHOOL

A. S. Neill, the Dominie, has brought his International School home, and has set up at Summerhill, Lyme Regis. He is specialising in problem children and says that he wants boys and girls that other schools find troublesome, lazy, dull, antisocial. He steadfastly refuses to compromise . . . "There is my school" he says to parents "absolute freedom to work or play. Take it or leave it."

Lilian Neustätter had remained with Neill in Austria, and, in 1924, the couple married. "Mrs Lins," as she came to be known, owned a house in Lyme Regis, a small, wealthy town in the South-West of England. It offered an open and altogether more welcome home for Neill's school, which found its home on the "Summer Hill": "it is to be delightful to think that only one inhabitant of Lyme Regis has ever had to complain about the conduct of my problem pupils" (1926, p. 223). The writer Edith Mannin knew Neill at this time, and recalled, "The good Lyme Regis people must have been very shocked, but the local people always regard Neill's community as 'queer'. The Lyme Regis people had a theory, I believe, that the school was composed of bastards, mentally deficients, and orphans . . ." (Mannin 1930, p. 220).

It is unlikely that the school's genteel neighbors would have been so welcoming had they known about the ideas of its eccentric headmaster. Aside from the degree of informality encouraged among the students, it is likely that they would have been horrified to discover his attitudes toward sex. Neill's Lanean conversion meant that in the 10 years from

"A Dominie's Log" to "The Problem Child," Neill has changed from a confused and repressed product of a Calvinist upbringing to a libertarian advocate of the Freudian revolution. Noting in "A Dominie's Log" that most of his contemporaries' views of sex were soured by a conspiracy of silence, the best alternative Neill could envisage was to encourage children to believe in the "Stork Theory of Birth" (1915)! Lane led Neill to the conclusion that complete openness and honesty were the only valid approaches, and guilt about sexual thoughts, and especially masturbation, only caused further difficulties. So, it is hardly surprising that a headmaster who wrote that, "I write it without blasphemy – that a child is nearer to God in masturbation than in repenting" (1927, p. 46) might draw calls of alarm from some quarters. The Lyme Regis years marked a step change in Neill's public status. According to Croall (1983a, p. 153), "the three years he spent at Lyme Regis marked a change in his reputation, from an eccentric, pipe-smoking dominie who wrote humorous books, to a serious, zealous, and – to some people – dangerous proselytiser and seducer of children's minds."

Neill was a strange sort of zealot. While his writing style has settled into a combination of humor and provocation, most accounts of him in person tended to stress how likeable and quiet he was. Edith Mannin (1930) recalled meeting a man quite at odds with his public figure:

> The school was then at Lyme Regis, in a big square house at the top of a hill. The gates were painted black and orange, which I thought encouraging ... I pulled the bell-broke and the bell went clanging through the house, but some time nothing happened. Finally a black-haired, stockingers, sandalled young woman came round the corner and looks surprised to see me, although her smile was friendly enough. I explained who I was and said that I was expected. She said she would see if she could find anyone-she thought everyone had gone bathing "except a few of the kids" ... The girl, I afterwards learned, was Homer Lane's daughter ... Finally A. S. Neill came in ... a tall, thin, slightly stooping figure, with a lean, clever, sensitive face. (Mannin 1930, pp. 216–17)

Whatever was the reality, Neill's reputation served to ensure a high public profile, and an increasing demand for places at his school. The five pupils who had traveled with him to England had grown to only 10 two years later (Hemmings 1972), and demand seemed to be on the rise. A school of this size was obviously not enough to secure its future. His writing came to the rescue, both by offering financial support and by raising awareness of the new school. The books in the 1920s were all about "problems"—Child, Parents, School. His decision to focus on these special cases was as much influenced by his residents at Summerhill at the time as by the intellectual influence of Homer Lane. Selling his wares as a specialist at helping difficult children was Neill's solution to the problem of income generation.

"The Problem Child" (1926) became a best-seller, and secured Neill's reputation as an expert in caring for and educating disturbed children. The book was written in a more serious tone than the earlier Dominie series, and was dedicated to the question of human nature and development. Neill wrote a whole chapter on the "philosophy of freedom," in which he claimed that he is "interested in freedom began as a protest against the authority of my childhood" (Neill 1926, p. 225). He argued that the natural way for children to be brought up was also the most effective. By this he meant that children should grow up without adults imposing their wishes and ideas on them: "Hating persuasion and suggestion, I arranged that no child in my school shall be persuaded to do anything" (ibid.).

This book also explored sex and masturbation more seriously and explicitly than before. Sexual repression and the suppression of power explained a host of personal and social problems: "Too little importance is attached to the power theories of Alfred Adler ... [the motivation for delinquency lies in] trying to express power that has been suppressed ... the anti-social boy, the leader of a gang of stone-throwers, becomes, under freedom, a strong supporter of law and order" (1926, p. 66). Bertrand Russell's book "On Education" (1926) was published in the same year as Neill's "The Problem Child." He wrote to the philosopher Bertrand Russell in enthusiastic tones:

I marvel that two men, working from different angles, should arrive at essentially the same conclusions. Your book and mine are complementary. It may be that the only difference between us comes from our different complexes. I observed that you say little or nothing about handwork in education. My hobby has always been handwork, and where your child asks about stars my pupils asked me about steels and screw threads. Possibly also I attach more importance to emotion in education than you do. (Croall 1983b, p. 30)

It seems to be that this letter was Russell's introduction to Neill and his ideas. The strategy obviously worked, as it sparked a respectful relationship that lasted some years.

The lease to Summerhill expired in 1927. Sales of "The Problem Child" and increased student numbers meant that Neill and his wife went looking for new accommodation. They eventually found what they were looking for in the small market town of Leiston in Suffolk, on the East coast of England. They decided to keep the same name of the school, and, apart from a break during World War II, this new site was to become the permanent home of Summerhill School.

The free school and free family

According to Jonathan Croall, Neill's biographer, "To most of those involved with Summerhill, the 1930s represented a kind of golden age, a time when the school stopped being an experiment and became a demonstration – that freedom worked" (1983a, p. 156). The move to Suffolk signaled the end of Neill's wandering and searching, and the beginning of his opportunity to put his ideas into practice. It was during this period that Summerhill became established as a center for radical, left-wing, and other progressive ideas in education. Socialist families began to send their children to the school, and whereas the school had initially been promoted as a center for dealing with problem children, it was increasingly drawing families attracted to positive aspects of Neill's philosophy. So, Summerhill had become a welcoming place for progressive parents and teachers who felt alienated from the mainstream, which was a feeling well captured by the writer Edith Mannin: "There is no room for the intelligent man or woman in the orthodox education system, and increasingly thinking men and women are coming out of it and going over to the ranks of radicals like A. S. Neill and Bertrand Russell" (Mannin 1930, p. 34).

The year 1932 saw the publication of "The Problem Parent," which opened with the words: "There is never a problem child; there is only a problem parent. That may not be the whole truth, but it is nearly the whole truth" (p. 9). Neill had made numerous references to the problems caused by parents in his previous books, and his attitude toward them seemed to alternate between antipathy and contempt. They were the cause of many of children's problems and were the main obstacles for their improvement. He told Bertrand Russell: "I am getting weary of clearing up the mess that parents make" (cited in Croall 1983b, p. 3). Elsewhere he wrote: "To the teacher the parents is the enemy" (1921a, p. 175); and, "This eternal imposition on children of adult conceptions and values is the great sin against childhood . . . I grant that I cannot write dispassionately, for I have a grievance against the parent" (Neill 1926, p. 116). His feelings toward parents seem to have originated from his experiences as a teacher at Gretna, and given shape by his developing quasi-Freudian view that all problems originate in childhood. In "The Problem Parents," he wanted to resolve these issues by educating parents in the new psychology.

"Is Scotland Educated?" (1936) was part of a series by the publisher George Routledge and Sons, which focused on a range of aspects of Scottish life (Hemmings 1972). The editor of the series, the novelist Lewis Grassic Gibbon, gathered a group of leading Scottish writers and thinkers. Gibbon was an admirer of Neill (and later sent his son to Summerhill), and sought him out for the education volume. However, despite the fact that Neill was arguably the most famous Scottish teacher and educational writer of his time, his selection as author of the volume on education was somewhat surprising as he had not taught in the country of his birth for many years. At the least, Neill did not have a strong sense of the situation in Scotland and the dominant issues. The irony was not lost on Neill, himself, who repeatedly reminded the reader that he was not really qualified to write the book at all! As it turned out, many of the topics of his commentary—which was generally scathing—were relevant because Scottish schools had not progressed from his days at Gretna and Kingskettle, such as the beating of students (Wells 1985). Neill also used the book as an opportunity to bemoan the reluctance of Scottish teachers to engage with his ideas. He was "a prophet without honour in his own country," he complained, and he was able to fill lecture halls in London, Oslo, and Stockholm, but not in Aberdeen or Edinburgh. Scotland's refusal to accept the wisdom of its prodigal son was further evidence for Neill that the country was backward, both educationally and culturally.

His next book, "That Dreadful School" (1937), was largely written as a corrective of the sensationalist media attention that had started to be attracted to Summerhill. This book was the first explicit and relatively organized statement of the Summerhill philosophy, including a clear statement of unconstrained vision. It explained and justified the emphasis on self-government, and argued that it was central to Summerhill, where authority is distributed evenly among the members of the community, including children. Neill's justification was both philosophical and practical: "when there is a boss, freedom is not there" (p. 31). It also explained the necessity of the School Meeting: "one weekly meeting is, in my opinion, of more value than a week's curriculum of school subjects" (ibid.). "That Dreadful School" was widely reviewed in the National press, even in Scotland, giving an indication of Neill's growing celebrity. Generally, commentators recommended the book as an important, if challenging and controversial read. For some, Neill's books had become stimuli for challenging the readers' own assumptions about education and its methods (Croall 1983a).

A consequence of Summerhill's fame was that there were numerous visitors from around the world who wanted to see the value of Neill's ideas in action. It also became a center for various counter-culture groups, including artists, academics, left-wing groups, and especially those anxious about the rise of fascism in Europe. The philosopher Bertrand Russell and his social activist wife Dora became close friends of Neill, and often visited Summerhill. In preparation for the establishment of their own school, Beacon Hill in the south of England, the Russells read the works of the great educators and psychologists, and visited many of the educational pioneers. This was why, in 1927, Bertrand Russell spent a week living and studying at Summerhill.

Russell and Neill are probably best described as allies rather than as collaborators as their points of agreement on educational matters tended to be with regard to the flaws of traditional schooling rather than with any positive philosophy. That this was the case was revealed in Neill's account of an occasion when he and Russell were walking, and started to discuss the differences between their views.

> I remember once walking with him to a cinema in Lyme Regis one starry night. I said to him, "You know Russell; if we had a boy with us now I would leave him to think his thoughts and you would give him a lecture on the stars." I think that that really sums up our differences of approach. He, Montessori and most of the others attached a great deal of emphasis on learning in education, whereas I have never done so. Then, again, I never knew what Russell thought of Freud and the psychoanalysts. (Neill, in Philpot 1985–86, p. 148)

For all of his proclamations of anti-intellectualism, the tone of his letters suggests that Neill was in thrall to the philosopher (Croall 1983b). However, it was Dora Russell with whom he developed a closer professional affinity. She placed much greater emphasis than her husband on play, and was open to explore Summerhill-style self-government (Gorham 2005). Dora Russell, then, was a rare exception: a progressive educator who Neill admired. The rest were either "higher-lifers" (such as the New Education Fellowship Schools) or "compromisers" (like King's Alfred's School), or both.

Another educator who managed to escape Neill's contempt was the psychologist and teacher Susan Isaac from Maltings House in Cambridge. Isaacs ran the school for the first 4 years of its brief existence. Her ideas spread not directly through her work at the school but through her books on child development, and through her role as Head of the Department of Child Development at the Institute of Education, University of London (Darling 1988). While he lacked the scientific approach of Isaacs, Neill saw a lot to admire, especially the central place she gave to freedom in education.

Neill's writings during the 1930s reveal a greater political awareness, and for the first time he started to associate the concept of freedom with wider social concerns (Spring 2006). "The Problem Teacher" (1939) is, perhaps, his clearest statement of the shift in his thinking, and his debt to the psychotherapist Wilhelm Reich. Neill discusses at length the relationships between education and political and economic systems, and states bluntly: "State schools must produce a slave mentality because only a slave mentality can keep the system from being scrapped" (p. 21). Neill was writing this, of course, as German, Austrian, and Italian schools were preparing children for fascist states. But his sights were also set closer to home: capitalism also required a willing and pliable population. For Neill, slave mentalities take different forms, but they always rob the working classes of their freedom. Echoing Reich, he came to define schools as products of direct class interest which discipline the workers in such a way that they are symbolically castrated for life, the aim being to continue the privileges of the rich, who would remain safe with an under-class that had been unmanned and therefore did not have the courage to rebel. He also thought that English schools robbed the working class of effective leadership: "The master stroke in . . . education policy was the secondary school . . . that took children of the working class to white collar jobs in . . . the professions. Thus it robbed the workers of its best men and women" (ibid., p. 24).

He drew a parallel between the father as head of the family and the teacher as head of a class of children. But the situation might be worse at school, since the teacher does not necessarily feel the love of a father for his children. So, the teacher represents only the hostile side of the father, "and this is true of the disciplinarian, for he has no love to give out, only hate. No, the school does nothing to counter-act the evils of home" (p. 27). The only solution he could imagine to this dire situation was Summerhill and the free family.

"The Problem Family" (1949) continued Neill's analysis of the institution of the family, and made a fundamental distinction between the free and unfree family. In contrast to the unfree family (which is the patriarchal family), the free family is characterized by equality between husband and wife, which eliminates the chain of authority and repression from the father to the mother to the child. By breaking this chain of command, the child escapes the internalization of authority produced by moral discipline. And since such discipline is the source of hatred and violence, the spread of the free family (and with it the free school and the free workplace) will have a positive impact on society. Until this transformation happens, Neill argued, children will have to attend a free school like Summerhill. Indeed, he once dreamed of a state system of Summerhill Schools. In "Hearts not Heads in the School"

(1944), Neill wrote: "Naturally, I want to specify that such a school will be a free school, with self-government and self-determination of the individual child ..." (p. 19). His vision of a world of self-regulated individuals who are intolerant of authoritarian repression owed a debt to his second mentor, after Homer Lane: Wilhelm Reich. Despite significant differences in terms of their characters and backgrounds, the two men shared a conviction that the evils of the world would disappear when child-rearing and educational practices changed (Spring 2006). Their friendship was preoccupied with precisely this issue.

Wilhelm Reich

Neill's greatest ally in the Summerhill era was the quirky, controversial, and somewhat difficult Austrian – Jewish psychiatrist, Wilhelm Reich, whom he met in 1937. Reich had been a brilliant, but rebellious disciple of Freud, from whom he split in 1933. Such were the differences between the temperaments of the two men that their close friendship seems implausible. Reich was a fierce and arrogant intellectual who knew he was a man of destiny, loudly proclaiming his philosophy of personal and political salvation through sexual orgasm. Neill, by contrast, presented himself as a doer, not a thinker, was distrustful of abstractions and theories, and was still rather uncomfortable even talking about sex (Placzek 1982). On the other hand, Neill needed a new guru—"Reich, I have so complete a faith in your genius" (ibid., p. 79)—and Reich needed a disciple to spread his gospel. And Neill's experiences with his problem children meant that that he was well prepared for the occasional tantrums of his highly strung friend. So, one way or another, they developed an intimate, albeit tempestuous relationship in the 1930s after Reich settled in America that was intensely close and, for Neill at least, influential, that lasted until Reich's tragic death in 1957.

Neill first met Reich while teaching in Norway. From that meeting, a friendship quickly developed. Neill recalled his first encounter:

We sat till far into the morning. If I remember aright his English was just as bad as my German, so that he spoke his language and I mine.

On departing I said, "Reich, You are the man I've been looking for years, The man who joins up the somatic with the psychological. Can I come to you as a student?" (cited in Boadella, Appendix III)

Whether or not Reich initially refused Neill's request is unclear, but Neill followed his meeting with a warm letter:

As you probably know I am called the most advanced child psychologist in the country, but I realise that I can learn much from you, and I think it splendid that you are giving me the opportunity to come and do so. Your character analysis is the finest thing I have come across for many years. (Neill in Placzek 1982, p. 6)

Reich agreed, and in 1937 Neill (14 years his senior) became his private therapy patient.

Neill's motivations for having therapy with Reich almost certainly included his wish to ease his own psychological distress. He had long been a sufferer of mental illness, which came to a head while waiting to be deployed in World War I. His psychological difficulties frequently expressed themselves in physical distress and pain. His Dominie books were littered with comments about his painful liver, migraines, and constipation. As a young teacher, he was frequently absent due to ill health. By 1929, his illness became more serious, with a kidney disorder and the urinary infection. He thought that mainstream medicine was unable to treat his condition, so he visited an alternative practitioner who made a cleansing description of a vegetarian diet, exercise, massage, and hydrotherapy. This treatment seemed to work, as Neill quickly returned to reasonable health.

Neill's experiences with Homer Lane had convinced him of the connection between the body and the mind and his firsthand experience of that happening simply served to strengthen this conviction. Reich was the leading contemporary writer on the relationship between the body and the mind, or in his terminology between the soma and the psyche. Neill was Reich's student for 2 years—between 1937 and 1939—and underwent periods of intense therapy 3 times a year during the holidays to Oslo. According to Neill's account, Reich confronted Neill's difficulties with dealing with emotional conflict, especially with adults. Over time, Neill started to make some progress and, to his surprise, some of his physical ailments like neck and stomach pain, started to improve, too. Later, in "The Problem Teacher," he interpreted these events in a characteristically quasi-Freudian way: "I have found something very vital, namely that I was allowing my petty ego to stand in the way of my progress. It was one of the most important discoveries of my life" (1939, p. 36). Reich's somatic treatment was a revelation to Neill, who felt it was more effective than any of the "talking therapies" he had received from Stekel and even Lane (Neill 1972a).

Reich worked on other aspects of Neill's complex psychology. Perhaps the most important was Neill's anxieties about sex. His marriage to Mrs Lins was not sexual, and he had had some guilt-ridden affairs in the past. Reich taught Neill to let go of his fears. The result appeared to be that Neill sought intimacy outside of his marriage; but he was at least relaxed about it!

Reich integrated Freud's psychology with Marx's social analysis. To Marx, the exploitation of the masses by a small ruling elite was a social fact. This social reality was only sustainable so long as the masses accepted the capitalist ideology. So, any attempts to enter this exploitation required an intellectual emancipation of the masses concerning their true interests (Skideslky 1969). Reich's contribution was to offer an explanation of how the elite managed to transfer their ideology to the masses. He built on Freud's theory that the patriarchal family created the child's social reality. Demands for obedience and moral rectitude, and the child's need for parental approval and love, resulted in external suppression becoming internal repression. However, whereas Freud framed this process in terms of the maintenance of "culture," the more radical Reich understood it in terms of a repressive social order. The family, the school, and the church were institutions that socialized the child into accepting and absorbing the interests of the ruling class. They achieved this by making the child feel shy, anxious, and afraid of authority: "In brief, the goal of . . . suppression is that of producing an individual who is adjusted to the authoritarian order and who will submit to it in spite of all misery and degradation" (Reich, cited in Sharaf 1994, p. 163).

Reich extended Freud's notion of the libido into a new type of physical energy that he called "orgone energy." Neurosis is caused by a blockage of the orgone energy, which prevented its natural outlets in sexual gratification. Neill's therapeutic experiences with Reich would have probably focused on releasing the physical "armourings" that trapped this energy, and on restoring his sexual potency. Reich's therapy led Neill to rethink his commitment to working with "difficult" children. Reich's view was that prevention was for preferable to cure, and then concluded that this meant he should invest his energies saving children from problems rather than patching them up once they were damaged: "Years of living and dealing with all sorts of crooks, swindlers and liars showed me that they were one and all inferiors" (Neill, cited in Skidelsky 1969, p. 178).

The extent to which Reich's teaching directly influenced Neill's educational practices is difficult to judge. Neill's extended and intimate contact with the psychoanalyst certainly provided him with a broader theoretical base for his arguments, not to mention a new vocabulary. Reich's discussions of the relationships between individuals and the authoritarian state also presented a powerful metaphor for understanding his own intentions in establishing Summerhill as he had: "Reich's arguments . . . provide a method of analysing the linkage between political structures and educational and child rearing patterns" (Spring 2006, p. 96). It also held out the hope for an education system that would lead to the end of aggression and authority.

Reich and Neill shared a vision of people as self-regulated, which was an expression of their faith in the essential goodness and wisdom of human nature. They also shared a fear that these qualities will be stifled or corrupted by the impositions of external authority. Reich argued that the patriarchal family is the primary institution for training children to live in an authoritarian state. The father administers authority over the mother, who in turn exerts authority over the children. The combination of the repression of sexuality, particularly in children, with the strict hierarchical authority structures, means that, According to Reich, "children play the role of household pets whom one can love but also torture" (Reich 1969, p. 77). Neill drew parallels between the father as head of the family and the teacher. However, the situation might actually be worse in school because the teacher will not necessarily feel love for the students in the same way as a father will. So, the teacher ends up in representing just the hostile, authoritarian side of the father:

"And this is true of the disciplinarian, for he has no love to give out, only hate" (Neill 1939, p. 27).

In most respects, the spell of Reich over Neill was similar to the influence of Homer Lane: such was the depth of Neill's personal vision that most of Reich's psychology and spirituality may have had the primary functions of adding a theoretical foundation and language to Neill's work, and for confirming Neill's suspicions that he had been right all along (Kühn 1995). It is almost certainly not the case, as is sometimes claimed, that Neill's practice at Summerhill, primarily self-governance by children, was "an implementation of Reichian principles" (Leue 1989, p. 65). Neill did not even meet Reich until 1937, 16 years after he had first implemented self-governance at Summerhill. But inevitably, some insights did start to seep into Neill's educational philosophy. For example, his earlier rejection of moral education became reframed in Reichian terms:

> When the child is corrected morally he stiffens his stomach. I took that with a large grain of salt when I first heard it from Reich, but on examining the small children at Summerhill I was astonished to find out that the ones who have been brought up without morality has soft stomachs, while the children of the religious and moral had stiff stomachs. (Neill 1939, p. 57)

While Neill accepted much of Reich's controversial teaching about adolescent sexuality at a theoretical level, he was resistant to allow it enter Summerhill. Adolescent sexuality was one of the few issues on which Neill compromised his beliefs, putting above them the one thing that mattered to him more, namely the continuation of Summerhill (Croall 1983a). Reich dismissed Neill for pandering to public opinion, and Neill uncharacteristically lashed back at his mentor: "To me the big thing in my life is my work . . ." (Neill, cited in Skidelsky 1969, p. 178).

He accepted Reich's teaching about the evils of capitalism much more readily. In fact, Neill had already embraced the version of socialism presented by George Bernard Shaw from when he was a young teacher in Gretna. So, Reich's contribution was really just to add a psychosexual dimension to Neill's politics (Spring 1975): that sexual repression was a deliberate strategy designed to make the workers impotent before their masters:

> If Reich's analysis of society is right, and personally I think it is, what harm is being done by the teachers acceptance of conventional sex morality? The schools are producing not only wage slaves but sex slaves ... What is the use of smashing capitalism if we are retaining capitalist sexuality? (Neill 1939, p. 62)

Neill traveled twice to the United States (in 1947, 1948) to give lectures, and took the opportunity to visit Reich on both occasions. He even considered moving Summerhill to the United States in order to escape the draconian inspection regime in England, although he eventually decided against that plan. When Neill wanted to travel back to see Reich in 1950, he found that his youthful dalliance communist thought was to return to haunt him when he was denied a Visa. His application had apparently been rejected for his advocacy of subversive views, since he had once written in sympathy of the Russian October revolution and socialist education (Kühn 1995). This was a disaster for both men, as they had developed a close friendship. Neill resented being denied contact with his mentor. For Reich, the situation was even worse, as Neill was the only person willing and able to tolerate his increasingly bizarre and confrontational behavior. This meant that their friendship became one of letters (Placzek 1982). Even to Neill, Reich's letters were almost entirely devoted to work. His letters make almost no mention of his personal life, his relationship with his wife, his feelings about his colleagues and students, other than rather dispassionate evaluations of them as workers. The foci of their correspondence were education and social – political issues. Neill's, on the other hand, were full of personal details, and conveyed a sense of love for Reich.

War years

Neill wanted to stay with the pupils at Summerhill during the war, but this became progressively less plausible stop as Hitler's forces moved through Europe and began air raids on England. Summerhill was located quite near a military engineering works, which made it a potential target for German bombing. Nevertheless, Neill remained unsure about whether or not to evacuate the school as late as the Dunkirk landings, when the army took the matter out of his hands by requisitioning his property. Of course, staff and pupils had already begun to leave the school, so numbers were dwindling. So in 1940 he reluctantly took the remaining members of the school to Ffestiniog, a village in North Wales, and away from danger. He told Reich that he had considered relocating the school to the United States: "I've played with the idea to try to bring them to America, but there was something in me, however, I suppose, a kind of refusal to run away from danger" (Placzek 1982, p. 73).

The Summerhill community settled into an old, cold mansion that had been empty for some time (Croall 1983a and 1983b). Almost immediately, Neill started to regret his decision to move to Wales. He later reflected on his time in North Wales as the most miserable period of his life. He disliked the climate and isolation of North Wales, the scarcity of supplies, and the chronic shortage of cash. The chapel fundamentalism of the locals reminded him of the village he grew up in Scotland, and the war filled him with pessimism (Placzek 1982). He wrote to a Scottish friend shortly after arriving: "Here we are so out of things, seldom see a movie, for it means queuing for the buses, usually in heavy rain. Visitors cannot come. One gets tired of the staff, one exhausts one's and their conversation" (Croall 1983a, p. 53). Neill hated the dampness and isolation, and especially the chapel fundamentalism of the locals, which reminded him of the Calvinism of his childhood (Neill 1945; Placzek 1982). He reflected in his autobiography: "I came back to the atmosphere of my native Scotland village churches and hymns, anywhere – with the associated hypocrisy" (Neill 1972a, p. 154). In addition to the personal dramas being acted out, the scarcity of supplies caused by the war and the chronic shortage of cash meant that the school became a dire place. Ironically, this was one of the few times in the school's history in which it was overflowing with pupils, as parents' fears for their children led them to evacuate or look to safe schools for the duration of the war.

In many ways, the war years were business as usual. The children who had left the school were replaced in even greater numbers by new a crop, some new teachers were recruited, and Summerhill carried on its work. As had happened at its earlier bases, there were tensions between the school and its local community. For example, some of the locals objected to the school pupils gardening on the Sabbath. The influx of new teachers, mainly conscientious objectors, did present a new challenge to Neill. His letters to Reich, Curry, and others reported that he felt his position as headmaster to be under threat as some of the younger teachers openly criticized his management of the school. Although he had turned 60 in 1943, Neill made it very clear that he had no intention of stepping down or changing any of the principles on which Summerhill operated.

If Neill remained vigorous in advancing old age, his wife, Lillian Neustätter—Mrs Lins—did not. Her deteriorating health was no doubt worsened by the stresses of being a German in war-ravaged Britain. She withdrew from the life of the school and from life more generally. Eventually, she went to a mental health institution.

Not surprisingly, Neill found the whole experience deeply unsettling, and turned to Reich for support: "my wife files and is most pathetic to see you now ... it is a grim life to see one who was so energetic and capable go downhill like that" (Neill, in Placzek 1982, p. 64). Lillian died in 1943. A grief-stricken Neill immersed himself in his work and especially in trying to complete his next book, although, as he confessed to Reich, "what worries me, that I am unable to write" (Neill, in Placzek 1982, p. 135). In an attempt to break his writer's block, he started to plan a biography of George Douglas Brown, the author of Neill's favorite book, "The House with the Green Shutters." He knew the book by heart, and used to visit Edinburgh's National Library to read the 1901 original, as well as Ayrshire where Brown based his book (Neill 1972a). Sadly, for Neill, the book was not to be, due to low predicted sales (Croall 1983a; Neill 1953). So, he returned to writing his educational books.

"Hearts Not Heads in the School" (1944) offered an expression of Neill's hopes and fears for the future of education. It included his now-familiar criticism of learning from book, as well as of the strict examination system of the day. There was a new element to his argument, too: a national network of free boarding schools (free both in terms of cost and character) that would prepare and protect young people away from the manifold potential harms of the family. The book also contained a touching acknowledgment to his late wife's contribution to Summerhill in the form of the final chapter, "Mrs Lins."

He continued to write and give public lectures, and his view was that the philosophy of freedom was becoming more and more popular among both teachers and the general public. Yet, there was little sign that his vision was influencing those in charge of policy. His letter to Reich was written shortly before the 1944 Education Act, and "Hearts Not Heads in the School" was littered with pessimistic comments about the educational establishment and its inevitable decision to cling to the certainties of "pre-Freudian schools in a post-Freudian world . . ." (Neill 1945). As it turned out, the 1944 Act was rather less draconian than Neill had feared. In fact, there were signs of a move toward progressive practice in state and independent schools, although these hardly resembled the transformations that Neill envisaged.

Neill's greatest influence at this time was on the young teachers who visited Summerhill. The best-known example of this was another radical Scot, R. F. Mackenzie. He had learned of Neill while working as a teacher in the Forest School, a quirky and distant relative of the Scouting movement in which children learned about the outdoors within the context of a melange of invented rituals and ceremonies (van der Eyken and Turner 1969; Mackenzie 1970). Mackenzie was never openly a follower of Neill, yet he was open about his admiration of Summerhill and of what he saw as Neill's courage. As he became a well-known writer himself, Mackenzie railed against many of the same concerns as those voiced by Neill. For example, inspired by Reich's teaching, Neill used to say that conventional education started at the neck and worked upward, without touching the rest of the body (Darling 1986). Mackenzie had similar concerns, as is revealed when he characterized pupils in the prevailing system of thought as "intellectuals to be trained" (Mackenzie 1970, p. 18). He also reflected Neill's assertion that children are far more capable, considerate, and responsible than was generally assumed by schools, and consequently authoritarian approaches to teaching were unfounded. One of the remarkable things about Mackenzie was that he tried to apply ideas like those that operated at Summerhill in state schools, and in doing so, tried the ultimate test of Neill's ideas and practices.

The end of the war brought with it a welcome return to Leiston. Neill had recently remarried—to the school matron Ena Wood—and this gave the school another capable woman to balance his more idiosyncratic approach. At the same time, so strong was the association between Neill and Summerhill that some found it difficult to adapt to the thought of another woman blocking their access. A second female entered the Neill house not long after the wedding: a baby girl, Zoë Sutherland. Zoë gave Neill an opportunity to test his ideas in the crucible of his own family. He had long believed that many of the problems that caused unhappiness originated from the parental home, so he was committed to avoiding the traditional repressive practices and deadening hand of religious and moral upbringing. His mentor Reich taught that no one can adequately understand the energetic concept of functioning unless he had worked with, and carefully observed, babies (Baker 1967), so the birth presented an ideal opportunity for learning. He had also been influenced by the work of the child psychologist, Dr Benjamin Spock, who popularized the idea that infancy was the period of development when the child's destiny was set, "long before the teacher has anything to do with him" (1932, p. 213).

Neill wanted Zoë brought up according to what Reich called "self-regulation" (Reich 1969; cf. Carleton 1991). For Reich, self-regulation was first and foremost a condition of the individual's character structure, and the ability to function with a genuine openness, and spontaneity, and rationality. The emotionally healthy, self-regulated individual does not adjust to the irrational part of the world and insists on his or her natural rights. For Reich, self-regulation was not a concept at all, but a biologically observable fact (ibid.):

> The newborn infant is not, as so many erroneously believe, an empty sack or a chemical machine into which everybody and anybody can pour his or her special ideas of what a human being ought to be. It brings with it an enormously productive and adaptive energy system which, out of its own resources, will make contact with its environment and will begin to shape it according to its needs ... LET THE CHILDREN THEMSELVES DECIDE THEIR OWN FUTURE. Our task is to protect their natural right to do so. (Reich 1983, p. 20)

The postwar years

World War II and the period of austerity that followed it devastated many of the comfortable myths and certainties about the inevitability of progress that had characterized Britain in the past. In many respects, these were difficult times at Summerhill. Neill was overjoyed to be home, but Summerhill had suffered during the war: "Perhaps the most joyous day of my life was the one in 1945 when I set off on my return to Leiston with my second wife Ena and a cat. In the five years the Army used the school; it had done more damage to the premises than my kids had done in twenty-five. But nothing seemed to matter; we had come home to dear old Summerhill" (Neill 1972a, p. 183).

The school was in a precarious financial condition, too, and Neill's ideas had started to fade in the public perception. The postwar shock has stimulated an exceptional rise in interest in educational innovation, as tends to happen following social trauma (Skidelsky 1969). But Neill was becoming increasingly detached from educational debates, and reverted to a crude Manichaeism in which the world of educational ideas was divided between friends and enemies. The group of friends became progressively smaller with time, and the *enfant terrible* had started to become *l'etranger*.

Somebody who he certainly saw as a friend, albeit from a distance, was George Bernard Shaw. Neill had been invited to write an essay on "Shaw and Education" (1946) in an anthology in honor of Shaw's 90th birthday. Neill's was a rather playful piece, teasingly rewording Shaw's motto that those who can do and those who cannot teach, "No, it is the teacher who is dangerous Shaw. He who can, teaches, he who can not, writes about teaching" (Neill 1946, p. 143). As for the importance of Shaw's ideas, Neill was unsure. On the one hand, "I claim that his educational theories are ultimately derived from his own schoolmasters, and therefore are of no great value" (ibid., p. 145). On the other, he maintained that Shaw's ideas might still be suitable for conventional teachers and parents. Ultimately, though, Shaw failed because he did not pass the stringent criteria of throughgoing nonauthoritarianism required by Homer Lane and Neill. Almost everyone did.

Neill's first opportunity to visit Reich after World War II occurred in the summer of 1947. Neill had arranged a visit to America that included a lecture tour and a stay with Reich. His second wife, Ilse, described the visit thus:

Neill and Reich talked deep into the night over a glass of whiskey and innumerable cigarettes. All their favorite topics were taken up: criticism, recognition, socialism, communism, sex-economy in pedagogy, and especially the new born child ... Neill saw some of the experimental work that was going on at Organon [Reich's home] but he maintained that he did not fully understand it ... One incident that Neill remembers very clearly is that one afternoon, during which we all sat together talking about cars and other mundane matters, Reich told Neill that such drawing-room conversations about nothing were sheer agony for him, they took him out of his sphere of thinking and he could not participate. This was always true for Reich, and was mentioned as a part of his character by many others to whom I talked. He could not and would not participate in chitchat and small talk. (Ollendorf 1969, p. 111)

At the same time, the US government began its formal investigation into Reich's work, especially into his "orgonon accumulator." Years of investigation followed, resulting in his imprisonment for ignoring an order not to sell accumulators or their parts. As his life's work was questioned, rubbished, and then destroyed, Reich gradually slipped into mental illness, and this led to the end of his friendship with Neill, who refused to believe Reich's claim that President Eisenhower had sent aeroplanes to fly overhead specifically to protect Reich and his family members. Reich's appeal to his sentence was rejected, and he started undergoing a 2-year term in a federal penitentiary in March 1957. In November 1957, he was found dead in his cell.

It was also around this time that Neill and his wife Ena decided to have a child. Earlier, Neill had written to Reich about this, seeking his advice: "Ena, my wife does not seem to get pregnant I wish that they will soon come to a specialist ... you do not like doctors, but ... We are both very happy together in love and experience the ultimate fulfilment" (Neill, in Placzek 1982, p. 224). Eventually, Ena did become pregnant, and give birth in October 1946, when Neill was 63 years old.

"The Free Child" was published in 1953 and included a description of the natural growth of his daughter, Zoë, during the first 6 years of her life. The book was essentially a defense of Reich's concept of self-regulation, which was a biological principle that allowed the infant to develop in the most natural and healthy way possible, and without developing neuroses. Reich's discovery of the principle of self-regulation, he argued, had revolutionized child psychology: "Self-regulation is the answer, Reich's answer, to the arresting questions arising out of Freud's discoveries" (Neill 1953, p. 105). Even very young infants should regulate themselves, Neill argued, and parents should step back and limited themselves to providing physical requirements like food, bedtimes, and clothing.

The continual demands of a young child can challenge the worldview of anyone, and Neill soon realized that self-regulation was an ideal, and one that can sometimes be difficult to follow in real life. Zoë, herself, believed that her father remained true to his convictions:

I have always felt a dual role as Neill's daughter. First, I was the little girl that he loved, and second, a kind of work-in-progress, a chance to test his ideas on child rearing and education. In my experience as his daughter, Neill always remained true to his ideals. I don't know whether he ever thought in depth about parenting, whether he and my mum ever planned how I would be reared, or whether, like me with my kids, it all came naturally, bearing in mind that they were following the Summerhill idea every day at school. (Readhead, in Vaughan 2006, p. 68)

Neill seems rather more ambivalent on this subject. His letters suggest that he struggled to meet his commitment to raise Zoë as a "self-regulated child" (Croall 1983b; Placzek 1982). In a letter to Reich, whose own son's behavior was causing concern, Neill wrote, "self-regulation can be too damned difficult sometimes" (Croall 1983b, p. 189).

Of course, the criteria for problem behavior in early childhood can be difficult to define, but there is little doubt that Neill the parent acted in ways that Neill the author would have found reprehensible, ranging from being overly licentious in some cases to overly disciplinarian in others (Neill 1972a). He also discovered that self-regulation did not offer a child protection from the toxic influences of the outside world. Living in the relatively enclosed community of 70 middle-class children meant that, while the truly neurotic influences of adults were kept to a minimum, Zoë still picked up childhood mythologies and a joy in swearing from the older children. She was also the subject of resentment by some pupils and even some of the teachers, and was a victim of bullying.

Neill's solution to Zoë's problem behavior was surprising: he sent her to another school. Even more surprising was his choice of school. Despite his apparent admiration for a small number of his contemporary progressives, Neill was unwilling to send his daughter to another British school. This was, perhaps, indicative of the limited extent of Neill's sense of shared values with even his closest allies. However, his motivation may have been more personal than ideological, as the school he eventually chose, in many respects, represented the principles and practices against which he had fought for many years.

L'École de l'Humanité in Switzerland was the very embodiment of German high culture, and the "high life" of the *New Era* progressives. Pictures of Goethe, Schiller, and other grand men hung around the school to inspire the children, whose daily routine included early rising, cold showers, long walks, and early bedtimes. However, the school did have a regular School Meeting that was somewhat similar to Summerhill's (Geheeb 2009). In addition to the obvious differences in Summerhill and l'École, as educational institutions, Neill's response to Zoë's behavior was often inconsistent. For example, he routinely responded to antisocial behavior among Summerhill's students through a combination of giving them time and space, and the strictures of the Meeting. The misbehaving Zoë, however, was sent away to a more disciplined school. Similarly, homesickness was normally casually dismissed by Neill as caused by a "bad home," merely requiring time to adapt to the new school environment, until his own daughter suffered, when he traveled to Switzerland to bring her home. Of course, such judgments lack the acknowledgment that a parent's decisions for his child are laden with emotion. And Neill acknowledged himself that he struggled to respond rationally where Zoë was involved.

Nevertheless, Neill did find the experience of parenthood profoundly insightful. He told one of the Summerhill parents that he had never learned so much as when he had a child of his own (Croall 1983a). Yet, remarkably, such learning seems to have been short lived, as the tenants of Summerhill remained unchanged by his experiences as a father.

Neill entered his 70s in 1954, and spoke about his thoughts of giving up his role as headmaster at Summerhill. Such talk was probably the stuff of fantasy, rather than serious discontents: "I should retire, but know that if I did I die" (Neill, cited Croall 1983b, p. 325). Whatever his dreams of retirement, Neill remained opposed to any changes to his philosophy and approach. Criticisms and suggestions, even from other teachers within the school were treated with resistance or suspicion. These responses were fairly well-established expressions of Neill's insecure character, but their intensity seems to have increased under the paranoid mentorship of Reich. Indeed, Reich's most long-lasting and damaging influence over Neill may have been is reinforcement of Neill's distrust of outsiders. Reich, meanwhile, was suffering badly through what he saw as the persecution of him and his work. As public support diminished (as much due to his own behavior as anything done to him), Reich became convinced that he was at the center of a great conspiracy.

Neill had already shown this tendency toward manichaeism, and was generally open to Reich's division of the world into friends and enemies, insiders and outsiders. Indeed, Neill started to see conspiracies at Summerhill, too. Tensions developed between Neill and some of the teachers, and Neill's blanket refusal to engage in serious discussion about Summerhill's practices and principles only served to make matters worse.

There is an irony at the heart of Neill's attitude toward his fellow teachers. He gave a remarkable degree of freedom and control of his environment to the young people in his care, but his fellow adults generally worked in a much more restrictive place. In classic Freudian style, Neill blamed the disagreements on his opponents' neuroses. One man's conspiracy is another's shared criticism, and Neill had repeatedly shown himself unable to take criticism about his work at all. He became obsessed with threats from the outside, especially from government inspectors. Neill was also resentful of some of the male teachers at school who were able to grab the affection of students. His justifications for disliking these teachers varied considerably, and often contradicted themselves. For example, despite his widely published view that the personality of teachers was far more important than that of pedagogy, he still felt able to say to one teacher, "look, you're a nice bloke and the kids like you, but you're not a very good teacher, are you?" (Croall 1983a, p. 328). Other popular teachers were condemned for not being a "community man," for being unwilling to do school repairs, and for lacking emotional contact with the children (ibid.). To his credit, Neill seemed able to recognize his devil within, even if he could not deal with it: "the established Jesus in Summerhill doesn't want any rivals" (cited in Croall 1983a, p. 328).

Neill became worried about the future of the school and saw his public speaking and writing as ways to keep some money coming into the school. However, the mismatch between income and expenditure at Summerhill was destined to mean that the school would remain in financial difficulties for years to come. He also had a horror that the state would close Summerhill. These fears were no doubt flamed by his witness of the treatment of his mentors Homer Lane and Wilhelm Reich. But they probably originated in his childhood, seeing his otherwise unflappable father nearly immobilized through anxiety when the school inspectors called. As it transpired, Summerhill's first two inspections were rather gentle affairs (1949 and 1959). In fact, so supportive was the inspectors' report in 1949 that Neill reproduced it in "The Free Child" (1953). Summerhill, they reported, was "an experiment of profound interest . . . a piece of fascinating and valuable educational research . . . which it would do all educationalists good to see" (p. 171). An inspection in 1959 was similarly supportive, although it raised some serious concerns about the quality of teaching. There were 44 pupils at the time of the inspection, although this dropped to just 24 within 12 months. Neill's explanation for this dramatic change of fortune was that "hardly any parents want freedom for their kids now" (Neill, in Croall 1983b, p. 88). There may have been a more practical concern: Neill was a very old man, and Summerhill was dilapidated and understaffed. There was a growing sense that Summerhill's days were numbered.

In a letter to the *Guardian* newspaper (11 June 1968), Neill denied that he was having a "cold war with the Inspectorate" (Croall 1983a, p. 35). But he accepted that he and they had a fundamental difference:

> An Inspector can inspect learning; you can tell whether the history teacher is doing his job well, but he cannot inspect tolerance or happiness or balance. His job almost makes it take a short view – Willie can't read at 13 – but two of our Willies who couldn't read at 15 are now successful engineers ... as long as education is geared to O and A level exams, schools that do not accept that standard will be odd men out, and Inspectors with conventional views of education will be the wrong men or women to evaluate them ... Summerhill must obey inspectors when they condemn premises. At the moment we are spending a lot on repairing and rebuilding, thanks to many generous friends – but Summerhill will not compromise in its educational philosophy ... (Croall 1983a, p. 36).

As it transpired, it was just as Summerhill looked set for closure that Neill saw its financial future secured. The remarkable success of Neill's next book, "Summerhill: A Radical Approach to Child Rearing," in America in 1960, and later in Britain in 1962, meant that for the first time in its history the school found itself on a relatively secure setting. Neill's books had been on sale in the United States since "The Problem Child" (1926), although sales had been poor. Very slowly, Neill's ideas became popular among some of the better-informed members of America's progressive elite.

For better or worse, Neill was initially known in the United States as a disciple of Reich. The social commentator Paul Goodman was introduced to Reich's ideas through Neill's works, and was a patient student of Reich for a while (Croall 1983a). And the child psychologist and writer Bruno Bettelheim (1970) interpreted Neill's work as an application of Reich's theory in education.

Progressive ideas and practices were more common commonly accepted in the United States than in the United Kingdom, partly due to the local control of education and the subsequent flexibility it offered educators to find an environment for their ideas. Another factor was that the United Kingdom did not have a progressive educational thinker of the stature of John Dewey. Whatever its origin, the situation in the United States in the 1960s was in stark comparison to that following World War II. Then there had been extremely negative reactions to progressive ideas and also to what was perceived to be left-leaning in the United States. This, of course, culminated in Senator Joseph McCarthy's "good scare" from 1950 (Haynes 2000). While Neill's early visits to the United States had caused some degree of controversy, they hardly created a sustained demand for news ideas. But by the early 1960s, the tone of criticism began to change and shift more and more to a liberal than radical left position: "The temper of the time, the inclinations of the young, and the growth of technology have provided a fertile field for [the] development [of Neill's ideas] . . . They look very attractive to a lot of people" (Eisner 1971, pp. 164–5).

"Summerhill" was published on 7 November 1960, in the same week in which J. F. Kennedy won the presidential election. It was not a new book, but rather a collection of extracts from four earlier books: "The Problem Child," "The Problem Parent," "That Dreadful School," and "The Free Child." The selection of material was carried out by the book's publisher, Harold Hart, at an exhausted Neill's request. This was a decision he quickly came to regret. With an eye on mainstream acceptance and sales, Hart exorcized the controversial Reich from the book, and emphasized the significance of the more mainstream Freud on the development of the Summerhill approach, to an extent that was far greater than Neill felt was appropriate. Hart and Neill also battled over the most suitable author of the book's foreword. Neill wanted Henry Miller, but Hart thought him too risky (many of Miller's books were banned in the United States). Hart's alternative, the cultural anthropologist Margaret Mead, refused to be associated with a book by a "Reichian." They eventually settled on the well-known psychoanalyst and writer Erich Fromm. This turned out to be a fortuitous compromise, as Fromm produced a remarkably well-informed essay about Neill's ideas and significance (Fromm 1960).

Sales of "Summerhill" began respectably, and gradually increased until it became one of the best-selling education books ever (by 1917, it had sold 2 million copies; Croall 1983a). With fame came a concern that Neill's ideas were being misunderstood and misapplied. The chief area of confusion, in his mind, was about the concept of freedom.

Word came from the United States that his message was becoming corrupted by some followers, who read him as advocating absolute freedom for children to do as they pleased.

Neill's response was "Freedom not License!" (1966a). This book might charitably be described as hastily produced: it was made up of some of the letters that Neill had received from the United States, along with extracts of his replies. Despite its lack of quality, the book sold well, providing evidence of Neill's growing popularity. An American Summerhill Society emerged, too, with the aim of spreading Neill's word (while its British equivalent had been formed simply to save his school from closure). Neill was ambivalent about some of these developments. He was flattered by the recognition and attention, and he was happy to stimulate ideas and developments, but he did not want the appearance of what nowadays might be called the "Summerhill brand."

The publicity that the book's success brought led to an influx of American students. Neill, an aged and frail man, became a popular media figure, commenting on both education and wider social issues. In the words of one commentator: Neill "was discovered in the 1960s" (Saffange 1994, p. 217). The timing of his book's release in the United States could not have been better, and "Summerhill" quickly became required reading among progressives, anarchists, and libertarians. Its influence spread further when it became an inspiration for many of the leading advocates of the counter-culture, like Paul Goodman's "Compulsory Miseducation" (1962), Herbert Kohl's "36 Children" (1967), and Jonathan Kozol's "Death at an Early Age" (1967). These writers in turn led to Neill Postman's and Charles Weingartner's "Teaching as a Subversive Activity" (1969), Charles Silberman's "Crisis in the Classroom" (1970), and Ivan Illich's "Deschooling Society" (1971). Also, a number of schools appeared that explicitly aligned themselves with the Summerhill idea during the 1960s, and a much larger number of schools acknowledged their debt to Neill. The best known of these schools is probably the First Street School in New York, whose story was told by Dennison in "The Lives of Children" (1969).

By the end of the decade, Neill's Summerhill, which was really little more than a collection of previously published work dating to shortly after World War II, found itself a core text of the 1960s' educational revolution. As one American teacher – trainer observed:

Coming at the end of his life, such success was more a matter of relief than of celebration. Neill was concerned about the future of Summerhill, which had no obvious replacement headteacher. And the influx of new students—many of whom were very young—to the school placed an inevitable strain on relationships within the community. It also put a strain on Neill, who was finding it increasingly difficult to deal with the "breaking out" behavior of the new interns. Teachers and pupils at that time reported frequent breaking of rules, including the most fundamental ones relating to behavior in the Meeting. Neill found himself becoming marginalized as a figure of gentle guidance in his own school.

A visit from local inspectors rekindled Neill's contempt for external intervention, as did a more formal, government inspection in June 1968. The most significant outcome of the local inspectors' visits was the suggestion that its headmaster retires and the school closes. Not surprisingly, staff and pupils responded badly to such suggestions. For his part, Neill was dejected. He wrote to the Anglo-Irish writer James Stern and his wife:

> Everything wrong, not one word of praise ... all premises won't pass the Ministry standard, and it would take a few thousand to put em right. We haven't got em, and it looks as if S'hill after 46 years is to have it ... We all feel as depressed as hell also very angry and disgusted. Two Establishment formal dead men my judges ... To paraphrase Shaw ... He who can does; he who cannot inspects. (in Placzek 1982, p. 69)

For a change, these inspections were not focused on Summerhill, but on independent schools in England in general. Reports of the abuse of children had led to a public outcry, and a demand from the minister concerned that only schools that adhered strictly to proper standards of education and welfare be kept open (Croall 1983a). Nevertheless, defenders of Summerhill were wary of the consequences of a negative report on the school's future, as, by any standards, it was an outlier. So, a letter was published in the *London Times* aiming to garner public support to safeguard the continued existence of Summerhill. Signed by parents and well-known intellectuals, including J. D. Bernal, Robert Morley, and Bertrand Russell, the letter argued for the continued existence of Summerhill on the grounds of its importance as a site of educational innovation:

> Although many of Neill's ideas have been absorbed under the skin of modern educationalists, can we afford to lose so vital a laboratory of ideas as Summerhill? In a world of increasing conformity it is surely to be hoped that regulations should continue to be administered with tolerance and even with latitude." (*The Times* newspaper, 11/06/1968, p. 11)

As it transpired, the inspection was not fatal to Summerhill, although the visitors identified two areas of concern. The first was the state of the buildings in the school. Neill responded constructively to this, partly because it seems to have been unarguable, and a rebuilding program was tentatively launched. The second issue was more of a problem: the quality of the teaching. This has been a recurring theme in the commentary of Summerhill, and reflected Neill's frequently stated opinion that teaching, by which he seems to have meant skills and pedagogy, was a relatively insignificant feature of a positive school experience. Stories abound of Neill's idiosyncratic approach to human resources, including appointments of staff whom he had never met or seen teach, or had no suitable qualifications, and the dismissal of otherwise successful teachers due to personality clashes with Neill.

Meanwhile, Neill's public success seemed to be increasing with every passing year in Britain. He was sought out as a commentator on education and social affairs by both television and news media. In the midst of this celebrity, the publisher Victor Gollancz released the English version of "Summerhill" (1962a), followed by a retitled and slightly re-edited version of his second American title, "Freedom not License!," which was called "Talking of Summerhill" in Britain (1967). According to Croall (1983a), by the end of the decade, "Summerhill" had been translated into Norwegian, Danish, Finnish, Spanish, Portuguese, Hebrew, Italian, French, and German. The consequence of all this was a steady increase in visitors from around the world to the school.

Neill had complained for many years about their interference in the day-to-day running of the school. At one point, hundreds of visitors a week turned up at the school.

One consequence of the inspection was a tightening of focus by Neill on the issue of succession as headteacher of Summerhill. This had been a perennial concern of his, dating at least as far back as World War II, and he had raised the issue with a diverse group of potential candidates. The main criterion for selection in many cases seems to have been simply that you thought they were the right sort of person, and this trumped other possible considerations such as experience or expertise. Perhaps the obvious choice in this regard was his daughter Zoë, but she had married a local farmer, and had begun a family of her own.

The most plausible candidates may have been Neill's closest allies working within the state school sector. R. F. Mackenzie shared Neill's criticisms of the narrow intellectual Scottish curriculum, had introduced a School Council, and tried to do away with the tawse, as Neill had in Gretna (Murphy 1998) in his first position in charge of a school. By a remarkable coincidence, Mackenzie's next appointment was as head of Summerhill Academy in Aberdeen.

In both schools, Mackenzie had experienced significant resistance from some of the staff, especially regarding his views on abolishing the tawse, consulting the pupils, and generally his approach to nonauthoritative dealings with children. This time, he was suspended by the local authority, when disruptions broke out among the staff. For Neill, who remained in contact with Mackenzie throughout the episode, this presented a shocking sense of *déjà vu*:

> Yr letter makes me sad for it told me that Scots education is where I left it over 60 years ago. You are in a hole, laddie. Got to support your family so that you can't tell them all to go to hell so that it means a pioneer, years before this time, has to compromise with all the bloody anti-life buggers ... I was silly enough to think that Aberdeen was advanced enough to appoint a rebel like you. (Croall 1983b, p. 24)

Another state school rebel seems to have actually been offered the role as Neill's successor (Croall 1983a). The Irishman Michael

Duane had been headteacher of the controversial Risinghill School in London, in which he had tried to implement policies in the spirit, if not the letter, of Summerhill (Berg 1968). He was not a follower of Neill so much as an ally, as became clear when his short-lived tenure at Risinghill was abruptly drawn to a close, and the school was shut. Neill wrote a letter to the *Guardian* newspaper about Duane's treatment:

> You describe Michael Duane as my disciple. I do not consider he is. He has been a frequent visitor to Summerhill for some years. He came because he believed in what we believe in – freedom for children. That he learned something from my school is true, but that does not make you a disciple . . . .
>
> No man does something entirely original. He culls from others what he can accept and rejects what you cannot accept. So that no man who has any basic honesty will claim to be a master, and where there is no master there is no disciple.
>
> Duane has done a great job and the Risinghill incident shows that treating children with love and not with the cane is dangerous in this so-called Christian country. The story brings memories of Ibsen's An Enemy of the People, and it isn't much consolation to recall Ibsen's words: "the majority never has right on its side". But Ibsen's other dictum comforts: "the strongest man is he stands alone" (cited in Croall 1983a, p. 18).

On another occasion, Neill wrote, "I had a visit from Duane last night. Bloody hero he is. He has got more publicity for freedom for kids than all my books got" (Croall 1983b, p. 18).

The issue of Neill's replacement largely resolved itself when, following a period of serious ill-health for Neill, his wife Ena took over the running of the school in 1973. Neill's presence in the school had being fading for some years, and toward the end of his life, his daughter recalled:

> Neill was a figure in the background at Summerhill, a strength that we all knew could be relied upon in an emergency or when needed. But he also very much got along with his own life and work while we, the pupils, got along with ours. As his daughter, I can remember

going for long spells of time without seeing much of him at all, except in passing. Many Summerhill kids' main memories of Neill, apart from a few special ones, will be of rushing past him in their daily play and shouting, "Hi, Neill" with a wave before disappearing. One boy wrote home halfway through his first term: "There is a chap here called Neill. I like him." (Readhead 2006, p. 71)

His autobiography "Neill! Neill! Orange Peel!" (named after a Summerhill pupil's playground rhyme) was published in America and Britain in 1972 and 1973, respectively. Most of the manuscript had actually been completed decades earlier. But Harold Hart had taken some time to persuade an extremely reluctant Neill to complete it. The publication of his autobiography signaled a deterioration in Neill's health. Neill wrote a letter to an old friend, Neill Hutton, in July, in which his deterioration and despondency are clear:

I have suddenly grown very old, and think more about painkillers than schools . . . Do I sound pessimistic? I often am these days; seem to be going backwards. Today's papers . . . Suffolk teachers demand to keep the cane. My fan mail shows the other side. It grieves me that I am not fit to answer it now, for I've always did, so bugger old age and its pains and weaknesses, say I. I have an empty shell . . . Not self-pity, just raw fact. (Neill 1983b, p. 244)

The extent of Neill's depression is evident from his letters to friends and colleagues (Croall 1983b). They show him frustrated at his lack of influence, out of the unwillingness of the authorities and the teaching profession to give up many of the practices that he found simply immoral.

Neill died on 21 September 1973, a few days before his 90th birthday, and the start of the new school year at Summerhill.

Summerhill without Neill

It was widely assumed that Neill and Summerhill were so inextricably connected that their deaths would occur at the same time (Selleck 1972).

One commentator wrote: "it is more than doubtful – it is inconceivable – that Summerhill could exist without Neill ... Something cannot be reproduced. It is doubtful that even the original Summerhill will be able long to survive its founder" (Hechinger 1970, pp. 36–7). Another wrote simply that, "The death of A. S. Neill ... marked the end of the saga of Summerhill" (Saffange 1994, p. 217). It was also assumed that the school depended on Neill's personal power for direction and celebrity for sustenance. Others, however, believed that this position overestimated Neill's importance within the school. By the end of his life, and probably by some decades earlier, Summerhill had developed a degree of autonomy from its founder (Danë Goodsman, personal communication).

The extent to which Neill saw himself as inseparable from Summerhill is shown in Child's (1962) collection of essays by independent progressive school leaders (including Bedales, King Alfred's, and Dartington Hall). All of the chapters give an outline of the aims and methods of the specific schools, apart from Neill's account, which is written in the first person, and is as much about him and his philosophy as it is about the school. On the other hand, Neill explicitly separated itself from the fortunes of the school elsewhere: "Summerhill was never a one-man show. If I accept an American invitation to go over for a year to open and run the American Summerhill being set up, I know that the home school will run as smoothly and well as it does now. We are none of this very important, and it has taken me nearly 80 years to realise it" (Child 1962, p. 155).

Ena had been running the school from before her husband's death, and she passed responsibility over to their daughter Zoë in 1985 (Readhead 2006). She had the advantage, of course, of knowing the school intimately, and knowing Neill's vision for it:

> I find myself working in much the same way as him ... The tools Neill gave me through his remarkable school and child-rearing method have been ample preparation for taking up the position I have at Summerhill. It has been an amazingly steep learning curve for me all the way along – but what a wonderful experience and opportunity! As a former pupil of Summerhill, as a parent of four children who have gone through the school, and as a grandparent of two children

at the school, I realise that Summerhill is deep in my bones; it is a great privilege to be principal of the oldest children's democracy in the world." (Readhead 2006, p. 70)

Summerhill was the Neill family business, and Zoë's succession reflected this. But this did not mean that she was unqualified for the position. She had qualified as a riding teacher, and taught in the Lewis Wadhams experimental school in New York (Kamp 1994). So, in many ways, life at Summerhill carried on with minimal disruption.

Disruption, however, was never far away from Summerhill, and even after Neill's death, the school continued to attract infamy. For example, a British Channel 4 film shown in 1993 caused controversy by portraying the school as a Lord of the Flies place. Filmmakers had been given free access to the school, and the result was a shocking portrait. The film showed massage classes, a mock wedding ceremony between a boy and his girlfriend, and a School Meeting was shown during which students voted to abolish bedtimes. One boy was seen killing rabbits; boys were shown making bows and arrows and the editing of the film implied that these were later used for shooting at cats. The film also suggested that many children at Summerhill were homesick, unhappy, and neglected.

Summerhill staff and supporters complained that the program was unbalanced and deliberately provocative, and that the image of the school was the opposite of reality. Nevertheless, the reputation of Summerhill suffered a great deal, especially among potential progressive supporters.

The real threat to the school, however, was the government. Summerhill had been almost continuously under threat of closure by the authorities since Neill first opened his International School in Hellerau. However, Neill's death triggered an unprecedented government interest in his school and its practices, including a gradual increase in the frequency of inspections of Summerhill. The apex of interest in Summerhill, both from the central government and from the media, was reached in the 1990s. During this decade, the school was inspected nine times, making the most inspected British school ever. It later emerged that the government inspection agency had placed Summerhill on a secret list of 61 independent schools marked as "TBW" (To Be Watched) ("Education Bill," UK Parliament. 22 January 2002).

An inspection in May 1990 resulted in a fairly positive outcome, characteristically reported by the UK press in this way: "A co-educational boarding school where staff hug pupils, mixed nude bathing is allowed and lessons are optional is producing well-adjusted, self-confident young people, government inspectors have reported" (*Daily Telegraph* newspaper 12/29/1990). The report itself commented that the quality of classroom teaching was "generally satisfactory" and pupils who attended lessons responded well. Those who took public examinations gained good enough results to continue in University (HMI 1990). As on previous visits, the structural conditions of the school were judged unsatisfactory and Zoë was forced to invest heavily in the equipment of the school (Kühn 2002). They questioned the inclusion in a children's library of books by Proust and Goethe, which "were not really for children" (*Daily Express* newspaper 21.02.2000). A much more positive development from the perspective of the school was that inspectors seemed to have accepted the distinction between freedom and license, which had been such a bone of contention in the past. In addition, although reservations were expressed about the policy of voluntary attendance of lessons, inspectors accepted that Summerhill principles formed a satisfactory basis for sound work. They also praised the climate of relationships, and the attitude and behavior of the pupils.

Visits from inspectors continued throughout the decade, with similar praise and criticism being leveled at the school. Then in 1997, an inspection led to a more critical evaluation of the school. For example, inspectors highlighted the need for the school to pay more attention to young children's literacy and numerous skills, and also to develop better planning and assessment procedures (Newman 2006). Presumably, these demands were met since a follow-up inspection in 1998 acknowledged the success of the school's responses. Yet, government officials continued to pressurize the school, resulting in a highly critical report in 1999.

In hindsight, it is hardly surprising that the first inspections since the election success of Tony Blair's New Labour government were challenging and dismissive of Summerhill. Blair and his combative Secretary of State for Education had launched an unprecedented series of initiatives that transformed the landscape of schools in England (Chitty 2004).

The two prongs of their attack were the somewhat paradoxical pairing of diversification and centralization. In practice, this meant schools like Summerhill were too different for the system to tolerate. Consequently, Blair and Blunkett decided, the school had to close.

The decision to attack Summerhill carried a strong whiff of irony. There was an active movement toward new types of schooling and provision, including some faith schools that seemed to promote values and practices that were quite contrary to those of the democratic liberal mainstream. Yet, Summerhill, a small independent, mostly boarding school with about 90 students at the time, drawn from around the world, was singled out for special attention (Newman 2006; Stronach 2005).

The issue that really drew the ire of ministers and inspectors was also the practice for which the school is probably (in) famous: the right to choose whether to attend lessons or not (Independent School Tribunal 2000, cited by Newman 2006). Some people closely associated with Summerhill question the centrality of the voluntariness of lessons, and point to other practices as more characteristic of the Summerhill approach, such as the School Meeting and the relationships among members of the school (Goodsman 1992; Newman 2006; Readhead 2006). But giving students choice about whether they attended lessons or not caught the public imagination, and seemed to inspire in both government inspectors and ministers a response of incomprehension and rage.

As Newman (2006, p. 60) pointed out, "the question is not why the school was threatened in 1999 but why it had taken so long." Central government concerns about Summerhill as a suitable educational institution dated back to the very beginnings of the school, and the England's draconian inspection regime simply served to offer a new vehicle for investigation. The New Labour government valued freedom and diversity, it seemed, but Summerhill was too free and too different.

That there was a deliberate policy to shut Summerhill is hardly in question. The 1999 inspection resulted in Blunkett issuing the school a notice of complaint, which took issue with the school's policy of noncompulsory lessons. Failure to comply with such a notice within 6 months usually led to closure. However, Summerhill chose to contest the notice in court.

Summerhill's supporters had to learn the new patois of educational improvement, administer satisfaction surveys, gather portfolios of students' work, and bring in external experts to carry out research and evaluation on its effectiveness (Stronach 2005). Even advocates acknowledged the inherent difficulty of the school coming to terms with the new educational landscape. "For Summerhill the nature of evidence of whether it works or not and what it does has always been problematic" (Newman 2006, p. 63). The default response to questions of Summerhill's effectiveness, beyond Neill's homilies about happiness being the only thing that really mattered, had been highly subjective and selective reports of parental and student satisfaction, higher than average examination results, and most commonly of all, listing the career successes of some of the former Summerhillians. There had also been little academic research into the outcomes of a Summerhill schooling. Some critics, however, have pointed to a minority of pupils who found it difficult to adjust to the wider society, remaining dependent on the school and networks of former pupils. According to Punch (1986), these former students had become habituated to live on the margins, and were somehow unmotivated in terms of conventional achievements, and rather than taking an active part in a changing world, opted out into a peripheral, artistic counter-culture.

Perhaps the only serious study in this regard was published in a set of papers by the American educational researcher Emmanuel Bernstein (1967; 1968a; 1968b). Bernstein interviewed 50 former Summerhillians about their lives, careers, and recollections of the Summerhill, and fundamentally about whether they were better or worse able to deal with the demands of the outside world. Not surprisingly, there was a great deal of variation, although only seven interviewees felt they had not benefited from their time at the school. The former students' main criticisms of Summerhill were the underestimation of the importance of academic work and the poorly trained teachers. Bernstein's conclusion was as follows: "Upon completing the five weeks of interviews, my feelings were mainly positive. Almost all the former students were working, raising responsive children, enjoying life" (Bernstein 1968b, p. 70). The inspectors were working within a framework that was quite different, in which aims and objectives and outcomes were integrally connected, in which learning was programmed, and which effectiveness was framed in terms of the relationship between expected and actual results. Perhaps more importantly, there was an assumption that all features of the school experience were made explicit and accountable (Fielding 2001).

The school went to great lengths to meet the expectations of the inspection. However, it could only compromise so much before it risked undermining the distinctive character of the school. For example, Summerhill stressed the value of informal and out-of-the-classroom learning despite the fact that these things were almost totally ignored by the inspectors. The students of the school also argued that they should meet the inspectors, and this proposal was also ignored (Newman 2006; Stronach 2005).

The case of Summerhill verses the Government was heard on Monday 20 March 2000 at the Royal Courts of Justice in London, before a special educational tribunal. By Wednesday, the government's case collapsed, and a settlement was proposed by the government. The weakness of the government's case became apparent very quickly in proceedings, as can be seen in this examination of a senior civil servant by the Summerhill's council:

Question (Rt Hon Geoffrey Robertson QC): Overall, the result of this June 1998 visit is the statute was being complied with, that Summerhill School in July 1998, after eight inspections throughout the last eight/nine years, is providing suitable and efficient instruction. Correct?

Answer (Michael Phipps):
That is correct.

Question:
Why is this school subject to a full report inspection with all the problems of publicity and the like only eight months later?

Answer:
Correspondence from the school following the June 1998 visit threw doubt on its commitment to implement the 1997 plan. (cited by Newman 2006, p. 61)

The demands that Summerhill refused, and which resulted in the "notice of complaint" were: compulsory lessons or private lessons; continuous assessment; and separate toilets for staff and students, and males and females. These areas related to principles of such centrality within the Summerhill philosophy that to remove them would rob the school of its character. Clearly, the Tribunal agreed.

The judges retired and allowed the Summerhill community to have a meeting in the courtroom to decide whether they would settle or not. The meeting was chaired and recorded by the children in the usual Summerhill manner (Vaughan 2006). The nature of the settlement was notably broader than could have been decided on the judge's authority alone. The tribunal only had the power to annul the notice of complaint, whereas the settlement made provisions for Summerhill to be inspected using unique criteria in future, to take account of its special educational philosophy.

Somehow, Neill foresaw this predicament in his 30 years before:

The Ministry has very much let me alone, and will do so until I die. What will happen then I cannot guess. Some Minister may say: 'We tolerated that school until the old man died, but we cannot go on allowing a school in which children can play all day without learning lessons.' (Neill 1972, p. 195)

Intermission: Hylda Sims (1993)
Life at Summerhill

(The writer Hylda Sims was a pupil at Summerhill in the 1940s. This account of her time there was published in the *Friends of Summerhill Trust* Journal. It is reproduced with permission of the Summerhill School).

Summerhill was the most important five years of my life, as close to the bone as who your mother and father were, having a round face and being a girl. The 22 schools I attended before being sent to Summerhill leave only fragments in my memory. One was a primary school in Norwich with a teacher called Miss Tench who shouted a lot. We had to sit quietly in our desks and she held up a pin in front of the class and said she wanted to hear it drop. When the air raid siren wailed, she marched us brusquely across the asphalt and by the time it had risen to a shriek we were sitting in silence again along the dank walls of a concrete bunker, though I don't think she still had the pin. After a very long time a shrill, high note sounded and she marched us back again. It was scripture by then so she told us about God in a loud voice then we had to drink your milk. After that we got ten minutes peace because it was playtime.

Maybe this sort of thing gave me my permanent fear of enclosed spaces, my dislike of bossy people and my suspicion about God's agents on earth and milk. But at Summerhill I created my view of myself and the world and it has been my yardstick.

I have been in to 22 schools because my father was an itinerant market trader and we moved around the country living in a caravan which he built over our heads. When the war came this rambling life had to stop and my parents settled in Norwich. They were communists and they took words like freedom and equality literally. They wanted me to go to a school where people didn't say "no". They felt Summerhill would be a free and equal "yes" school. It had been evacuated to North

Wales at that time and they saw it as a safe haven from both Hitler and Miss Tench. It was.

Summerhill had a waiting list, but my parents lent our redundant caravan to the school, so they could find bed space for three more pupils. My father drove up to Llan Ffestiniog in the big square Citroen with the caravan dragging and swaying behind as we climbed the steep Welsh hills. It was a perfect summer day. Butterflies, dragonflies and sheep what everywhere and clumps of scarlet rhododendrons overhung the winding roads.

The house belonged to a Lord Newborough and was built halfway down the valley facing three mountain peaks—Molwyn, Molwyn Fach and Molwyn Bach. There was a long paved area at the front and two sets of steps grandly leading down to terraced lawns. In the middle of one of these was a disused and empty swimming pool and, overhanging up from the top terrace to the lower, a big tree with a rope swing fixed to its fork. To the left of the house was a craggy wooded land and the pieces of climbable rock that jutted out from among the trees had glittering bits of quartz on their services. You walked up a steep path behind the house to get to the village. The property there was bounded by a gate with a large piece of slate hanging from it so that it clamped behind you.

It was a great relief to see the back of my parents, having paid the usual lip service to all their anxious advice, and to get on with the important business of exploring the territory and getting to know the other kids. Quite quickly I got used to the idea that, unlike everywhere else I clean, the adults didn't stop you doing this, and though they were quite friendly and even make jokes, they mostly minded their own business and let us mind ours. Pretty soon we found out who our favourite adults were and liked to sit around in their rooms in the evenings talking and drinking cocoa.

The biggest problem I had in the first term was with modesty. This word was used as Summerhill only in the sense of being shy of being seen without your clothes on. People said "she's modest," and laughed not unkindly but somewhat mockingly when you got dressed and undressed in bed.

The first time I saw a little boy take all his clothes off and stand nonchalantly putting his pyjamas on I rushed off giggling to shock someone with the story. The response was puzzled "so what?" I had great difficulty taking a bath because the bathrooms, being the warmest and most intimate spaces in the house, were social meeting places. A boy called Michael would watch any approach I made to the bathroom and rush in after me trying to get on with my bath. He was blonde and elegant and I was half love with him and this made it worse. Perhaps the cynical reaction on the part of the other kids cured me. By my second term I was holding court in the bath and laughing with the rest to see the latest arrivals struggling to get in and out of their clothes underneath towels and blankets and going without baths for weeks.

I didn't notice Neill for a long time, and was surprised to learn that he was the old man I had often seen patiently raking leaves at the side of the house. Neill sometimes asked kids to have PL's with him. These "private" or "psychology" lessons were therapy sessions which he gave to kids who he felt needed them. I had heard that he asked stupid questions like "do you envy your brothers penis?" or "do you think you are really a princess who was left on your parents doorstep as a baby?" My friend Winnie had a PL every week and seemed to enjoy them. I felt a bit jealous but Winnie said you had only to ask and he would give you one. So I asked. I went to Neill's room for my PL one Friday morning. Neill was sitting comfortably in his big armchair and motioned me to another. He said nothing. Neither did I. I waited. He waited too. Nothing happened. After a while he lit his pipe, put the matches on the arm of his chair, picked up the newspaper from in a nearby table, opened it out and disappeared behind it. I set waiting and watching. He carried on reading. I became increasingly impatient.

"Aren't you going to ask me some questions?"

"Nope."

He turned on to the next page and I could hear the easy sucking ways of his pipe. A thin cloud of smoke floated above the times. On impulse I grabbed his matches, lit one and set fire to the corner of his newspaper. Without haste he lowered it to the floor and placed is large square toe over the flame, reducing that part of the paper to blackened ash. "Good," he said, "I didn't think you had the guts to do that. Wish you had chosen the other corner though – I hadn't quite finished that crossword."

We thought Neill had a rather feeble sense of humor. He made foolish proposals in the meeting sometimes which we normally voted down. One meeting he said he thought we were all tired of running the school democratically, and so he was going to try having a dictatorship like in Germany. So a triumvirate of dictators was selected by him from among the older boys to be in charge. We very soon got fed up with them going to the front of the dinner queue, declaring early bedtimes everybody but themselves and ordering us about. They couldn't think of much else to do. We called a special meeting and voted them out of office. They stepped down without putting up a fight. They too had had enough.

After this a pupil who was interested in politics suggested in the meeting that we should run things like they did in parliament, with the government and an opposition. We had an election and my side won. I became a member of the cabinet as Minister of Social Affairs and had to organize things to do in the evenings. After a while we got fed up with parliamentary government and reverted to our usual open, one person one vote system.

The Saturday self-government, meeting with its majority voting system, it's termly elected secretary and its rotating chairperson survives at Summerhill with very few changes today as if it is the natural way for children to run things. A constant topic in meetings was bedtimes—when they should be and how they should be enforced. Sometimes we abandoned bedtimes altogether but this never worked and the younger ones particularly would become dazed and pale with tiredness after two or three days. A big boy of gentle but firm disposition called Bunny Leff took on the task of getting us to bed and was so successful at it that he became the sole bedtime officer for many terms. He would go round ringing the dinner bell and shouting "8 o'clock bedtimes" and so on. For some reason was stopped whatever we were doing and took ourselves meekly off to bed. This was probably the only time in the history of Summerhill when bedtimes weren't a problem.

I was quite clever despite, or because of, my many previous schools and was put in a class of about eight other kids who are mostly a bit older than me. We had lessons in the morning and I usually went to them unless I had something better to do. Neill taught us maths and sometimes English. He had on the staff a number of European refugees and they taught us French and German. For the first few weeks I made a fool of myself by forgetting where I was and behaving like we used to do in other schools. A question would be asked and I've suddenly issued my arm up as if I've been bitten by a snake and start bouncing up and down in my seat shouting "Miss, Miss!" or "Sir, Sir!" I'd forgotten in my anxiety to be first with the answer to the teacher called Nina or Robin and nobody was going to pat you on the head and give you a silver star after knowing where Timbuktu was. I soon learned that the only time you put your hand up at Summerhill was when you wanted to say something in the Saturday night meeting. This was held each week to decide the rules of the school and what to do about those who broke them. You also raised your hand to register your vote, and everybody's vote counted for one.

In the afternoons we would go to the art room, sit around talking in our rooms, go exploring in the hills and wooded valleys near the school or go up to the village. The art room had a tortoises stove in the middle of it and it was a great place to congregate on cold days. In the evening is there would be dancing or games in the lounge or Neill would do spontaneous acting-sort of drama improvisation workshops.

Crazes went by seasons. In summer we organized vast games of prisoners in the grounds, sometimes by moonlight, in which the whole school took part. We made all sorts of strange swings in the front of the house from bits of junk—old bedframes, chairs, and bits of rope. We lay in empty swimming pools sunbathing and watching small green lizards darting over its hot flaky concrete sides. On really hot evenings we held meetings there and then slept on the grounds wrapped in our bedsheets. Sometimes groups of us would trek up Molwyn and camp overnight by the lake just below the summit. In winter we made huge long ice slides down the hill beside the school and went tobogganing.

We used to have crazes of making things. The first year I was there people made sandals. Someone made by cutting foot-shaped pieces of wood out in the workshop, sawing off the toe and joining it together again with a hinge and then tacking bits of scrap leather on the tops to put your foot through. In Ulla's sewing class we made rope sandals by coiling pieces of rope, sewing the coils together on the insides to form the sole and sewing on fabric tops. In a climate like Wales the wooden ones were better, for every time it rained the rope ones became floppy and heavy and gathered crusts of mud.

Table tennis was a constant craze and I got quite good. In summer we tramped off to a sloping field about a mile from the school with Corky our science teacher and played hockey. Both hockey and football were played without much sense of competition and games included all ages, both sexes and staff and pupils. We went swimming in a natural pool in one of the fast flowing rivers nearby. You could stand on a big flat rock directly under another big flat rock and the water would cascades down in front of you like liquid diamonds covering you with a fine cold spray.

Kids who'd been at Summerhill before the war used to pine for Leiston where you could cycle. They remembered Leiston as having constant sun and endless space. Neill hated Wales with its excess of rain and its puritan chapel-going culture, but I loved it. In Llan there were three fish and chip shops and you could get scallops—flat rings of potato fried in batter—and fizzy lemonades into which they put shots of bright pink raspberry flavoring for an extra ha'penny. In Blaenau you could get set teas in the front parlours of respectable Welsh widows and then go and watch the Marx Brothers or Rita Haworth. You could go on trips to the exotic gardens of Port Merion and then run across a huge expanse of warm wavy sand to a friendly sea. The war was distant and nobody worried if there were chinks of light round the black curtains.

When we got back to Leiston we made blackout shirts out of these curtains in Ulla's class and decorated them round the bottom with colored rick rack braid. But Leiston in general was a big disappointment to me. The army had lived in the house in our absence and everything was painted a dingy shade of khaki. The village was drab, only two inferior chip shops and not a mountain to be seen in all that doll Suffolk countryside. We went bathing at Sizewell close to a small power station. There were large areas of dune land ringed off with barbed wire because of unexploded mines, and sticking out from the menacing grey sea were huge girders known as dragons teeth which had been planted there against the threat of invasion.

However I was getting older and taking part in a lots of things. With two other kids I wrote a serial "radio" play, which we performed every Thursday evening behind a sheet in the theater and in which I had a big part. A few very good teachers who had been connected with the school before the war reappeared. Leslie Morton, a famous Marxist historian, taught us history, and his wife Vivienne taught us English. With then we did a production of MacBeth. Winnie and I both auditioned for the part of Lady Macbeth, and I didn't really mind when she got the part and I had to be her understudy and the first witch. I got a boy friend, Rusty, one of the best looking and most talented boys in the school.

And then the next term I was elected to the end of term committee. The end of term committee was elected by the meeting just after half term. Its purpose was to collect the money and make all the arrangements for the end of term dance which was the big event of every term and took place on the last Saturday. First there would be plays written and performed by the kids and staff in the theater in the early evening and then the lounge which had been decorated by the end of term committee would open for the dance. The EOTC would choose a theme which was kept a secret and the lounge was closed to all but the EOTC while it was being decorated, and so when you entered the lounge after walking over from the theater you would find it had been magically transformed to, for instance, Aladdin's Cave or a desert island stuck up in the corner of the lounge was the gram box and each end of term we would add to our collection of records. This was the responsibility of the EOTC and the gram committee. We were very keen on Jazz and did our own Summerhill version of ballroom dancing to Fats Waller, Duke Ellington, Nelly Lutcher and Louis Armstrong's Hot Seven. Neill thought that a liking for jazz was evidence of a father complex so the grand committee would let him have one of his syrupy swing records every so often, when he'd get up and dance with one of the kids, doing an eccentric slow quickstep with his big feet turned in, stooped over his little partner holding her arm out in the traditional pump handle. Half way through the dance there'd be a floorshow, sometimes a ballet choreographed by the older girls, and after that refreshments—sausage rolls, cakes and tarts which had been made by the EOTC the night before. In the dance itself there'd be competitions—elimination dances, musical chairs, statues and Neill's competition during which he'd ask questions, often humorous, and if you didn't know the answer you had to get off the floor. There would be prizes for all the competitions and the EOTC went to Ipswich on the train to get those and the balloons and the new records.

To do everything properly—the prizes, the records, the decorations, the refreshments—we needed a lot of money, so we would spend the run-up to end of term organizing all sorts of fund raising experiments— jumble sales, raffles, a collection from the staff, visitors and parents, and we'd make things in the workshop. There were always quite a lot of people on the EOTC, maybe about twelve, and there was a policy of including little kids, older kids and staff. The art teacher and the good painters, of which there were many, were always involved.

Before the lounge was open we'd polish the floor. This meant putting a thick layer of polish on, wrapping your feet up in old rags and skating over it until all the polish was absorbed and it was shiny.

We older girls didn't come into the lounge until at least half an hour after the dance had started. The early bit was for kids and visitors who didn't know any better. We liked to make our entrance down the front stairs when things had got started, wearing the dazzling creations we'd been making all term in Ulla's.

End of term was sure happiness and even if you'd just split up with a boy friend it was a good opportunity to find another. The only problem was that you all had to go home the next day, and home was never as much fun as school.

At the end of the dance, the people who were leaving that term would go into the middle and we'd link arms round them and seeing Auld Lang Syne. Then we would hug and kiss the leavers and cry a bit.

Neill has said that the "absence of fear is the best thing that can happen to a child". Of course there are always things and people to fear, even at Summerhill, and sometimes for no definable reason. I was afraid of the dark and trees falling on me. However not to be ruled by fear is a great boom and rare in schools. When he speaks of abolishing "the chasm between old and young", Neill pinpoints the important difference between Summerhill and other places.

I remember that when I was at home my mothers adult friends would glance at you and say "she's grown, hasn't she."

The more perspicacious ones would address you directly, but in a specially modulated voice – "Haven't you grown!"

My toes would curl with embarrassment at these sort of remarks even at a very young age so I would blush, look down or hide behind my mother. This would be a signal for them to deliver the final insult: "Isn't she shy!" If you didn't hide but you gave some verbal response they would laugh even though you had said nothing funny, as if the voice of this talking doll was a joke in itself.

At school people like Miss Tench had their own version of what was good for you which really coincided with your own.

Adults at Summerhill were not like this. They spoke to you as one human being to another, didn't laugh unless they thought the joke was funny and always listened to the content of what you said. They didn't think what you ought to be doing was any different from what you were doing. They were neither God nor the Devil so we didn't have to respect, propitiate, challenge or destroy then. Released from unhealthy preoccupation with what adults were thinking and doing about me, I absorbed myself with intense enjoyment in the day to day living of my life.

Summerhill may seem odd to most people because they have such different memories of school. Summerhill seems normal and sensible to me, and I wonder why all schools are not run on much the same lines.

Chapter 3

Key Themes of A. S. Neill's Work

Schools of thought

A fundamental presumption of traditional approaches to schooling is that the features of schools that have been present for generations are generally sound. Their soundness has been demonstrated by their ability to stand the test of time. If schools are unsatisfactory, therefore, it is because they have misapplied these proven methods, or because they have succumbed to the fads and fashions that bedevil education (Cox and Dyson 1969). Progressive education or "new" education, as it was often called in Britain, is defined primarily in terms of a rejection of this presumption and defies precise definition beyond a condemnation of traditional discipline and learning by rote. It rejects the assertion that traditional methods have, in fact, succeeded over time. As was seen in the infighting among members of the New Education Fellowship, the reasons for this dissatisfaction with traditional methods can vary widely. And it might be argued that the main thing most progressives have in common is a shared enemy.

The ongoing, dynamic tension between traditional and progressive approaches to schooling is one of the defining themes of the history of Western education (Bailey et al. 2010; Bantock 1980; 1984). It is also the source of its most heated debates (Barrow 1978; Darling 1994; Entwistle 1970; Ravitch 2000). These debates rarely result in abridgsment, let alone consensus, because their foci are not relatively superficial matters of teaching methods, but deeply felt articles of faith about human nature and values. Methods do not operate autonomously; they are expressions of educational aims, which, in turn, reflect values and beliefs. So, standard discussions about methodological effectiveness are always somewhat unsatisfactory because the criteria for effectiveness are derived from values and aims that are not articulated. So, different approaches usually follow parallel lives, interrupted only by occasional hostile exchanges.

An interesting exemplar of such hostilities is a book published in 1970, in which a range of well-known writers were gathered to discuss Neill and Summerhill. The school had existed for 50 years, and had been the target of countless commentaries. The sheer quantity of attention was due to the fact that, even by the standards of progressive schools, Summerhill offered a radical departure from traditional practices. It was about issues that extended further than a single school and headteacher; the discussion was not just about Summerhill; it was also about alternatives to education, writ large. The editor of "Summerhill: For and Against," Harold Hart, was Neill's US publisher, so it might be conjectured that he had ulterior motives for encouraging a strong exchange. And the book did certainly contain an extremely diverse range of views. It is presented as a confrontation between two camps: the traditionalists and the progressives. However, even in the very narrow terms of this debate, it is obvious that such a strict distinction operates ineffectively. Some apparently traditional educators spoke encouragingly about Summerhill, while some so-called radicals condemned Neill and his ideas. While the book was clearly intended to represent a battle between two educational tribes, the eventual product reveals groups only in the loosest sense.

The polarization between traditional and progressive education is so widespread that it might be supposed to have some validity, but as Darling (1988) has persuasively argued, it is both unhelpful and inaccurate:

> It legitimizes a confrontation style of educational debates in which abuse of the other side is common, and the re-examination and refinement of one's own views is not. The opposition is rarely given credit for having a case which is even prima facie respectable, either intellectually or morally, and this is coupled with a refusal to admit even minor difficulties or weaknesses in one's own position.
>
> It further suggests that while there is little or no common ground between the opposing sides, Each side speaks with a single voice. The extent of the differences of opinion within each group is not fully appreciated by its members because (a) the more energy

devoted to attacking the opposition, the less attention is spent on observing one's own side; and (b) the defense of one's own group is facilitated by a degree of self-deception about the unity of the groups views.

The polarisation effect obscures the possibility that one may, without inconsistency, side with the traditionalists in some circumstances and the progressives in others. (p. 158)

Darling's final point is especially resonant with regard to Neill. He is, of course, routinely cited as a leading representative of the progressive education movement (Barrow 1978; Carr 1984; Darling 1988; Spring 2006), yet Summerhill was criticized by school inspectors (presumably the very embodiment of traditionalism and conservativism) for using teaching methods that were judged to be overly traditional (Goodsman 1992; Hemmings 1972). And Neill himself maintained only the most superficial sense of collegiality with the progressives throughout his career, many of whom he regarded as no better than the traditionalists (Hemmings 1972).

Progressive critics of progressivism have tended to be marginalized within debates. During the middle part of the twentieth century, people like Neill and Dora Russell were labeled extremists, even by other radicals like Beatrice Ensor and Adolphe Ferrière. However, by the 1960s and 1970s, the influence of more radical educational thinking was such that it was difficult to leave it at the extremes. In the United States, in particular, writers like Illich (1973) and Holt (1969) were far better known to the general public and teachers than middle-off-the-road progressives. The cause of the radical discontent with standard progressivism was not one of degree. While progressives rejected traditional authoritarian approaches to education, and wished to replace it with a softer, more restricted authority, the radicals rejected both positions (Darling 1988). And while the lines of attack from the radical educational thinkers were many and varied, one dominated: authority. Traditionalists and progressives simply took it for granted that schools are essentially paternalistic institutions based on the belief that some people (adults) know best what is good for children. The curriculum is the manifestation of this authority, and it constitutes what those in authority believe children need (ibid.). Presented this way, it is difficult not to agree with Darling that Neill's philosophy of education probably fits best with radical theorists.

Neill's views echoed those of another influential writer on alternatives in education, John Holt (1969, p. 75), who wrote about "would-be progressives" who,

> thought or at least talked and wrote as if they thought, that there were good ways and bad ways to go coerce children (the bad ones mean, harsh, cool, the good ones gentle, persuasive, subtle, kindly), and that if they avoided the bad and start to the goods they would do no harm.

Like Holt, Neill felt no sense of association with "would-be progressives," because he saw the assumption of the need for authority, and feared that liberalizing authority would mean that it would be less likely to be objected to. Gentle coercion is more difficult to recognize, and therefore more likely to slip by defenses than harsh coercion. And this is why Neill "would rather see a child educated by a drill sergeant than by a higher-life person" (cited in Hemmings 1972, p. 37).

Disagreements about the core elements of education, such as teachers and teaching, schools, and curricula, are much better understood with reference to this difference than to surface distinctions between traditionalists and progresses. However, this revised classification of educational thought that is made explicit by Darling (1988), and is held implicitly by commentators such as Lister (1974), Gribble (1998), and Meighan and Harber (2007), is limited because it is really a description of differences, rather than the causes of differences.

Neill's vision

An interesting approach to understanding the origins of philosophical differences—in education, politics, morality, and numerous other domains—is offered by the economist Thomas Sowell in his essay "A Conflict of Visions – Ideological Origins of Political Struggles" (2002). In observing arguments for and against a wide variety of positions, Sowell writes that he noticed that in many cases participants seemed to be arguing not so much against each other, but past each other. In other words, each person was arguing not against the others' position but what they perceived those positions to be, which was often far different from the actual positions held. Sowell concluded that underlying and prior to formalized theories, paradigms, worldviews, or any rationally articulated models were what he called "visions," which are similar to Joseph Schumpeter's concept of "pre-analytic cognitive acts" (1954, p. 41).

Educational philosophy has tended to focus most seriously on questions of values, rather than visions (Bailey et al. 2010). But Sowell argues that values are more likely to derive from visions than visions from them. This is not to deny the importance of values, of course, but simply to identify causation. It is only derivatively that visions involve clashes of moral principles or practices. This is why people with the same moral values can reach quite different political and moral conclusions. According to Sowell, visions provide metaphysical foundations on which formal theories are built. They are often highly subjective, "more like a hunch or a "gut feeling" than ... an exercise in logic or factual verification" (Sowell 2002, p. 16), but they can be highly influential, with a "sense of causation" (ibid.). Visions also have a sense of meaning that forces some order on the streams of data bombarding the observer. Perhaps more usefully, Sowell further defined a vision as, "what we sense or feel before we have constructed any systematic reasoning that could be called a theory, much less deduced any specific consequences as hypotheses to be tested against evidence. A vision is our sense of how the world works" (ibid., p. 4). In other words, visions are fundamental premises. They are often implicit, and provide the consistency behind beliefs and actions: "At the core of every moral code there is a picture of human nature, a map of the universe, and a version of history. To human nature (of the sort conceived), in a universe (of the kind imagined), after a history (so understood), the rules of the code apply" (Lippmann 1965, p. 80).

The focus of Sowell's analysis of visions is human nature, and the possibilities of human reason and power to act purposefully to achieve desired ends. While recognizing that there is a myriad of potential visions, Sowell groups them into two broad categories: the "constrained vision" and the "unconstrained vision." These differ fundamentally about the capacities and limitations of humans, and frame them in radically different ways. The moral and psychological natures of humans are seen so differently that concepts like freedom, knowledge, and society necessarily differ as well. The constrained vision is associated with the thought of Adam Smith, Thomas Hobbes, Edmund Burke, Thomas Malthus, Alexis de Tocqueville, Friedrich Hayek, Milton Friedman, and authors of the Federalist Papers. It looks at human beings as basically unalterable in their nature. So, Adam Smith believed that "moral or socially beneficial behaviour could be evoked from man only by incentives . . ." (p. 23), and Thomas Arnold justified corporal punishment in terms of "the naturally inferior state of boyhood" (cited in Stanley 1845, p. 118). A representative summary of the constrained vision is Hobbes' claim that political institutions were all that prevented a life that would be "solitary, poore, nasty, brutish, and short" (1651/1996, p. 89). Behind such comments is a presumption that, rather than wasting effort in a futile attempt to make people better than nature has made them, society can accomplish more by acknowledging the limits within which people function: "In the unconstrained vision, human nature is itself a variable and in fact the central variable to be changed" (Sowell 2002, p. 87). In this case, it is accepted that people can be selfish and stupid, but there is an indelible assertion that, given the right contexts, they will grow and develop. The unconstrained vision was held by thinkers like William Godwin, Jean-Jacques Rousseau, Voltaire, Baron D'Holbach, Thomas Paine, Marquis de Condorcet, Robert Owen, George Bernard Shaw, Thorstein Veblen, and J. K. Galbraith. Sowell did not discuss education or psychology in his analysis, but if he did, he may well have listed A. S. Neill, Homer Lane, and Wilhelm Reich as members of this tradition. Reich is, perhaps, particularly interesting in this group since the fundamental difference between his vision and that of the Freudian school is that Reich believed that the Unconscious was not evil (Neill 1953, p. 64), whereas "Freud believe[d] in original sin" (Neill 1920, p. 24).

A paradigm example of the constrained vision is the Calvinism of Neill's youth. It taught that humanity is totally depraved, and that every person born comes with a corrupted heart, morals, and will. Therefore, people's natural actions and affections are immensely sinful (Muir 1929). This insistence of total depravity does not mean that all people are as evil as they could be. They still can make choices, but no matter how good they may be, they are never going to be in favor with God. On the other hand, it seems quite clear that Neill, Lane, and Reich were following unconstrained visions. In many respects, Neill's view was very similar to that of the anarchist Godwin: both shared an aspiration of the long-term development of a sense of social duty, believing that the benefits of immediately effective incentives like punishments or rewards were illusory and halted development. Godwin wrote that "the hope of reward [and] the fear of punishment [were] wrong in themselves [and] inimical to the improvement of the mind" (Godwin 1969, p. 171). Believing that moral instruction created a tension between the child's instinctive drives and social conformity, wrote, "I believe that it is moral instruction that makes the child bad. I find that when I smash the moral instruction a bad boy has received he automatically becomes a good boy" (1960a, p. 221). In his ontology, moral instruction was one of a number of adult practices that expressed disapproval of the child in his or her entirety, including instincts and interests. To moralize is to impose alien expectations on children who are perfectly fine already. This is what Neill and Lane meant when they said that they are "on the side of the child" (Neill 1915, p. 117; 1972a, p. 184; Lane 1928): they saw themselves standing with the child, avoiding the temptation to interfere with his or her interests, and giving freedom to be his or herself.

Godwin believed that humans are "perfectible," continually improvable. They are capable of justice and virtue and not just isolated individuals but all people. For this reason, rewarding existing behavior was antithetical to the goal. Neill thought that children were already perfect. He followed Homer Lane in his faith that "Human nature is innately good and the unconscious processes are in no way immoral" (1928, p. 130). His explanation for the self-evident issue of misbehavior was framed in a way that merely reinforced his argument:

> To ask a little child to be unselfish is wrong. Every child is an egoist . . . . when he has an apple his one wish is to eat that apple. And the chief result of mothers encouraging him to share it with his little brother is to make him hate the little brother. Altruism comes later, comes naturally if the child is not taught to be unselfish.

By suppressing the child's selfishness the mother is fixing that selfishness. An unfulfilled wish lives on in the unconscious. The child who was taught to be unselfish will remain selfish through life. Moral instruction thus defeats its own purpose. (Neill 1960a, pp. 250–1)

Those with the constrained vision generally do not look to any special causes of crime or other antisocial behavior. People commit crimes because they are people; because they put their own interests or egos above the interests or feelings of others. Therefore, social contrivances are necessary to prevent antisocial behaviour. According to the constrained view, natural incentives to commit antisocial acts are so commonplace that counterincentives must be created through such potent forces as moral instruction and punishment. This is because each new generation of children is, in effect, "an invasion of civilisation by little barbarians who must be civilised before it is too late" (Sowell 1987, p. 150). Growing up to be a decent, productive person depends on practices at home and at school that engender moral values, self-discipline, and consideration of others. Problems occur when this process does not "take."

Those with an unconstrained vision see the process of healthy development in exactly the opposite way. Moral values develop as a result of getting out of children's way. The unrestrained vision tends to lead to an emphasis on internal disposition rather than external incentive. So, social forces are seen as the cause, not the prevention of antisocial behavior. This is the driving force behind Neill's responses to what at other schools would be called "misbehaviour." Since the child is born with a satisfactory nature already, Neill is able to assert that it is misguided to try to shape his character. He goes so far as to say that "there is no need whatsoever to teach children how to behave" (1960a, p. 224). Just as Homer Lane had encouraged his boys to smash up plates and furniture, Neill let some of his children commit petty offenses like stealing and smashing windows. As he writes in "The Problem Child," his reasoning was based on his reading of the needs of the individual child:

If I should be painting a door, and Robert came along and threw mud on my fresh paint, I would swear at him heartily, because he has been one of us for a long time and what I say to him does not matter. But suppose Robert had just come from a hateful school and his mud-slinging was an attempt to get his own back against authority. I should join in his mud-slinging because his salvation is more important than a door. (Neill 1926, p. 27)

Those with an unconstrained vision tend to attribute antisocial behavior to some special cause. Godwin said: "it is impossible that a man would perpetrate a crime, in the moment when he sees it in all its enormity" (1969, p. 276). The post-Freudian world was more inclined to look toward the etiology of behavior. For example,

The theory of rehabilitation is based on the belief that healthy, rational people will not injure others, that they will understand that the individual and his society are best served by conduct that does not inflict injury, that a just society has the ability to provide health and purpose and opportunity for all its citizens. Rehabilitated, an individual will not have the capacity – cannot bring himself – to injure another or take or destroy property. (Clark 1970, p. 220)

It is not surprising, therefore, that unconstrained thinkers often turn toward a therapeutic approach. Writers like Carl Rogers (1969), not to mention Reich and Lane, saw no difficulties in transposing their psychology to the sphere of education, and Rogers might well have been speaking on behalf of Neill when he wrote that "the only learning which significantly influences behaviour is self-discovered, self-appropriated learning" (p. 153). It is for this reason that Lawton (1977, p. 78) declared that Neill maintained "that the best thing teachers could do was to leave children alone to develop naturally."

Neill's unconstrained vision meant that he had confidence that children will develop into reasonable, considerate, well adjusted, ethical adults. This expectation is unaffected by the recognition that children are often self-centered. Accompanying this optimistic view of children's natural endowment is a secondary sets of theories related to their psychology. For example, Neill followed Freud and Homer Lane in believing that at certain stages children develop a desire to be well-thought-of by others which drives them toward socially acceptable forms of behavior (1960a). He wrote, "When we look at an infant we know that there is no wittedness in him any more than there is wickedness in a cabbage or a young tiger" (1926, p. 17). Neill followed Homer Lane in believing that every child "brings with him a life force" (ibid.), which expresses itself as a will to live, which drives us to eat, to explore, to gratify our desires. On some occasions, Neill called this life force the "will of God"; attempts to stifle or even direct the life force, therefore, are inherently immoral as they are really seeking to corrupt the will of God (ibid.).

Neill's was not quite the "Froebelian dream of the child" as sweet and innocent (Nathan Isaacs, cited in Dearden 1968, p. 34). Post-Freudian progressive thinking had been indelibly marked by talk of the unconscious, base instincts, and sexuality: "If Neill sees children as innocent, it is the innocence of animals rather than the innocence of cherubs" (Darling 1988, p. 50). Young children operate at the level of instinct, he thought, and were energetically impelled by drives and instincts to gratify their interests (Neill 1960a). So, he did not view self-centeredness as a flaw in human nature, but as a natural characteristic of the early stages of life that will be outgrown with time and freedom. In the meantime, however, it ought to be accepted, neither fought nor resisted. At the same time, then had a horror of the "spoiled" child (Neill 1960a; Carr 1985). Recognition of children's egotistical state, plus an advocacy of a noninterference on the part of the adult, did not equate with license or justification for allowing children to do as they want. Confidence in children and in the way they will develop underlie Neill's views on education.

Many of Neill's ideas resemble those of Jean-Jacques Rousseau, who believed, as Neill, that people are born good, and that society and its institutions corrupt people and make them miserable and cruel (Darling 1988; Müller 2009). Neill's "complete belief in the child as a good, not evil, being . . . in the goodness of the child has never wavered; it rather has become a final faith. My view is that a child is innately wise and realistic. If left to himself without adult suggestion of any kind, he will develop as far as he is capable of developing" (Neill 1960a, p. 4). Neill's view of human nature—particularly child nature—nature reads like a paraphrase of Rousseau. Not surprisingly, many people have associated Neill's thinking with that of the Romanticism of Rousseau

(Beck and Earl 2003; Krogh and Slentz 2001; Müller 2009); others have highlighted the similarities in their work, especially with regard to their views of human nature (Darling 1984, 1988; Miller 2007; Suissa 2010). According to Cleverley and Phillips (1986), Neill was "the most notable figure in the Rousseauean tradition" (p. 38), and Flanagan (2006) even claimed "It might be said that the revolution in child liberty initiated by Rousseau in the eighteenth century culminated in twentieth-century England at Summerhill School" (p. 174). For his part, Neill himself claimed never to have read Rousseau's treatise on education, "Emile," until decades after he established Summerhill (1972a):

> I have often been called a follower of Rousseau, but I did not read Emile until fifty years after I opened Summerhill. I felt very humble to discover that what a man wrote in theory two hundred years ago I had been practising in ignorance of his ideas. Also I was somewhat disappointed. Emile was free but only in the set environment prescribed by his tutor" (Neill 1972a, p. 264).

Perhaps the similarities in philosophies of the two men stemmed from their biographies. Both grew up in, and rejected, harsh Calvinist environments with unyielding emphases on self-restraint, self-denial, guilt, fear, and the authority of elders and God (Müller 2009). Both sought alternatives to their childhood realities, and in doing so, both explored visions of human nature associated with values like freedom, self-regulation, and honesty.

A consequence of Neill's unconstrained vision is that he disclaims personal credit for the improvements in the young people: "It is not I who cured the [delinquents]. It is the environment ... of Summerhill [which] gives out trust, security, sympathy, lack of blame, absence of judgement" (Neill 1960a, p. 284). "It took me years ... to learn that it is freedom that was helping Summerhill problem children, not therapy" (ibid., 294). The only time that Neill tended to interfere with the experience of his children was in the case of "problem" children who came late to the school. These children received "Private Lessons," or "PLs." These were Neill's quasi-psychoanalytic sessions which he believed sped up the process of re-education: "At Summerhill it is love that cures; it is approval and the freedom to be true to oneself" (ibid., p. 52).

Generally speaking, though, the translation of Neill's unconstrained vision into practice can be summarized by a set of principles, such as: allow children freedom to grow emotionally; give children power over their own lives; give children the time to develop naturally; and create a happier childhood by removing fear and coercion by adults (Vaughan 2006, p. viii). Or, to précis still further, "leave your child alone" (Neill 1962a, p. 315).

The philosopher of education Robin Barrow called Neill's view the "optimistic thesis." According to this, there is no problem of moral upbringing for us to worry about; there is no need to us to determine what is good and steer children toward it, because children will have, of their own accord, adopted morally acceptable values and patterns of behavior (Barrow 1978). According to Barrow, Neill's vision raises a number of questions. First, how can he or anyone else be certain that a child is born good? Indeed, it is not clear what it means since it is not clear what is involved in being born good, and what kind of evidence would be appropriate to determine the matter one way or the other. Barrow goes on to say that there are contradictions in Neill's view. For example, why does he say that the child is born good, and then that given the right conditions he will learn what is right? More seriously, if people are all good, it is logically impossible that evil should ever have a resident in the world, for evil arises out of corruption of others. However, Barrow's comments miss the mark, because Neill was not offering a thesis in which corruption is caused only by other people. His Freudian insights allow Neill to depart from Rousseau's narrow focus on the corrupting influence of society, and include repression and other psychological problems that can arise autonomously or spontaneously or due to human ignorance or well-meaning mistakes.

Barrow is correct to judge that Neill's theory of children's innate goodness is no more than a "hunch" (ibid.). The central point of Thomas Sowell's analysis was that most "theories" and "philosophies" are built on a foundation of visions that are precognitive acts. As Abercrombie (1969, p. 47) observed, "All of us have undergone from birth an 'apprenticeship in seeing'." By the time we are adults we are no longer aware of the judgments and assumptions we make about human nature. Consequently, when we observe children, it is, in part, from within our vision of human nature. And strongly held visions—like Neill's obviously was—can be extremely resistant to contrary criticism and refutation (Bates Ames 1970). It might be said that all educational engagement is vision-laden. So, Neill's vision incorporated the assumption that children have much good, and this led him to see children in certain ways, to ask certain questions about their education and development that may not have occurred to another observer who adopted a different vision such as the doctrine of original sin (Cleverley and Phillips 1986). While some teachers would see "naughty" children as bad, Neill focused on the factors that might have interfered with the child's natural impulse, or that might have spoiled that child. Conversely, children that might have been seen as normal or unexceptional or even well behaved were often seen by Neill as sick or unhappy: "The moulded, conditioned, disciplined, repressed child – the unfree child, his name is Legion, lives in every corner of the world . . . He sits at a dull desk at a dull school; and later, he sits at a dollar desk in an office or on a factory bench. It is docile, prone to obey authority, fearful of criticism, and almost fanatical in his desire to be normal, conventional and correct" (Neill 1960a, p. 95). Despite their providence, such visions are hugely influential in determining the character of the more formal aspects of one's worldview.

The consequences of different visions when translated into practice can be quite stark. Carr (1984) makes a case that the differences between the practical implications of the work of Neill and the analytical philosopher R. S. Peters (1966) are not as great as might first appear. Carr makes the valid point when he says that both wished to develop qualities of self-determination and self-regulation. Neill (following Lane) presumes that self-control requires the prior development of certain qualities of attachments to other people, and, on occasion, even Peters seems to accept this point too, especially during his early psychological writing (Carr 1984). However, Peters and other traditionalists assumed a different "order of logical priority and psychological dependency" (Carr 1984, p. 52). In other words, while Neill locates relationships before the development of moral rules, Peter's theory organizes them in the reverse way. Carr may have underestimated the differences between the constrained vision thinkers like Hobbes and Peters and the unconstrained vision of Neill and Homer Lane. Nevertheless, he makes an important point when he says that the practical differences between thinkers like Neill and the traditionalists can be much less than first appears. In particular, both wished to develop qualities of self-determination and self-regulation. But their visions lead them to adopt quite different approaches. Neill (following Lane) presumes that self-control requires the prior development of certain qualities of attachments to other people (even Peters seems to accept this point too on occasion; 1962). Peters (1966, p. 196) captures the essence of the debate:

> Little ... Is yet known about the conditions which favour the development of such autonomy. Do children in fact learn to behave autonomously by being brought up from the earliest years in a very permissive atmosphere without a proper framework of order? This seems highly improbable both on general grounds and on the basis of the slender empirical evidence that there is about such matters ... Autonomy implies the ability and determination to regulate one's life by rules which one has accepted for oneself – presumably because the reasons for them are both apparent and convincing.

Peters argues that rational self-regulation and autonomy are built on a foundation of prerational training, which he calls the "paradox of moral education" (1981, p. 51).

Neill (and Lane) escaped this paradox in his denial of the necessity of prerational training. They argue, in its place, that the relatively free development of personal relationships and honesty and trust were most important in the early stages, and that early constraints on behavior undermine the whole moral education enterprise. Neill's unconstrained vision is that the natural instinctive responses of the child are good and kind, and that, given the right environment, love, respect, and trust toward others will develop as a matter of course. If, however, the child grows up in the wrong environment, warped by psychological pressure or abuse, he will express hostility, resentment, and mistrust. Carr observed that "whereas for Lane and Neill, the fostering of virtues of attachment via the visioning of optimum conditions for their emergence is the first priority since they are predisposed to the development of qualities of self-control and discipline, for Peters it is, in a sense, the other way around" (Carr 1984). The constrained view of Peters' morality equates, to a large extent, with a respect for moral rules and principles. Once these qualities have been internalized, healthy relationships will follow.

Neill (and Lane) can be seen as offering a solution to the problem identified by Peters (Carr 1984). In fact, their explicit reference to Freud can be seen as an attempt to supply precisely the theoretical base that Peters demands. And his theory of removing causes of repression and stress from children's lives can be interpreted as removing impediments to the development of rational autonomy. They saw the mechanism identified by Freud's concept of repression as in large part the key to many of the emotional and behavioral disorders of their problem children. Neill and Lane do not accept the Piagetian stage-like view of moral development that Peters takes for granted (Peters 1966, p. 5). They also denied the inevitably of the paradox of moral education, or the presumption that rational moral development requires prerational training (in the form of obedience or submission to social rules).

Carr (1984) argues that Neill and Lane's approaches to the problem of moral development were significantly influenced by the fact that their early work was with delinquent or "problem" children. While techniques to instill a degree of self-control and discipline in well-balanced and psychologically healthy children might work effectively, they are less likely to be effective with children with severe hatred, distrust, and resentment. But, this is not a persuasive argument, as precisely the opposite argument could be applied. Neill and Lane both turned to the new psychology to identify insights on the treatment of their young people. They focused on the psychoanalytic concept of repression as a key to understanding the source of the emotional and behavioral disorders. And, in addition, they concluded that the heavy-handed interference in the instinctive life of the child, or any attempts to impose some kind of moral order on the child's basic nature, would lead to resistance or to an irrational fixation upon objects of desire (Carr 1984). However, it could be argued, using essentially the same psychological theory, that precisely the opposite conclusion ought to be drawn. It could be suggested that "problem" children require more, not less structure and external control, to compensate for their lack of positive early experiences, and that so-called healthy normal children have a degree of emerging self-regulation that would allow them to benefit from a greater degree of freedom. So, Neill and Peters do seem to have approached fundamental issues of education and values with different presumptions, and these different starting positions are neither evidence-based nor rationally derived. They are prerational visions.

The notion of visions helps explain an otherwise perplexing aspect of Neill: his attitude to religion. Depending on which of Neill's books or articles is read first, readers might assume he was either a deeply religious man or a zealous atheist. His daughter, Zoë Readhead, thought that the matter was a simple one:

> I think it would be incorrect to attribute any religious beliefs to Neill. He would have, frankly, turned in his grave at the very suggestion!
>
> "His belief in the goodness of children (and mankind) came mainly from his observations. The reason he mentioned it so often is because he was writing to a world in which religion was the standard, particularly when it came to schools and children.
>
> "My father was not a religious man. In fact he was anti-religious. If he referenced God in his writing regarding children's innate goodness it would be aimed at those who talked of "original sin" and used that as a means to keep children under control – for their 'own good'." (personal communication 17/6/1010)

Zoë Readhead's view is supported by Neill himself on a number of occasions. He wrote to the playwright Arthur Miller:

> you puzzle me when you speak of God . . . God the word doesn't mean a thing to me, meaning that I can't visualise or fantasy any Power that is external to me. Like Reich, I can see no purpose in life. I guess that the godly argue that God slew millions in two world wars and 4 million Jews in order to chasten his creations." (Croall 1983b, p. 358)

And he told the poet Robert Graves that he scraped his razor on the Bible: "Thank God I am an atheist!" (ibid., p. 214). From certain perspectives, Neill's rejection of religion was total, and he noted that "religion as I remember it . . . is nothing I wish to be identified with"

(Neill 1960a, p. 132), and an ex-pupil recalls that "he was prejudiced, for some good personal reasons, against religious education and he never considered ways in which it could be taught effectively at his school" (Lamb, cited in Potter, undated, unpaged).

Yet, Neill showed respect for the teachings of Jesus throughout his work. In a *New Era* article in 1920, he advices his reader to "read and reread the life of Jesus Christ" (1920, p. 131). He argued there that Christianity, like freedom, had never been given a fair trial. His (and also Lane's) work was littered with references to Jesus and his teaching, such as this comment from "That Dreadful School": "We do not consciously follow Christ's teachings, but from a broad point of view Summerhill is about the only school in England that treats children in a way that Christ would have approved of" (1937, p. 121). It was with a sense of irony that Neill often said, "I am a very religious person; what man brought up in Calvinist Scotland could fail to be?" But it does seem to be the case that his upbringing instilled in him a Christian sensitivity. On two occasions Neill wished to become a parson. These feelings were to color his whole vision of the world and his educational project. They were already present in his first book when, commenting on Nietzsche's ideas, he notes: "If pity and kindness are wrong, then wrong is right" (1916, p. 108). Neill dreamt of a world governed by love, a love that would establish universal harmony, a world reflecting the message of Christ, the "original" message, that which was perverted by the evangelists (ibid., p. 75). In this sense, he thought that Summerhill was the only truly Christian school in England, precisely because it did not promote religion, and, before he had learned about Stalin's crimes, Soviet Russia was the only really Christian country, because—in the spirit of Jesus—it had abolished the churches (Neill 1960a).

Here, we have the resolution of the apparent contradiction in Neill's thinking. His vision led him to reject manifestations of religion that sought to repress people with guilt and hate, and it led him to embrace the teachings of Jesus, which he felt compatible with his unconstrained vision because he thought it offered a way toward freedom. Later, when he met Homer Lane and Wilhelm Reich, he found the secular religion of psychoanalysis (Fromm 1959): "I think that the foundation of true justice is self-analysis . . . in my Utopia, self-examination will be the only examination that will matter" (Neill 1960a, pp. 145–6).

Homer Lane said that each person is only constrained to love. Those who hate are merely expressing love in a negative way. Neill found in this the gospel which he had sought and the experience of the Little Commonwealth was a "Christ-like experiment to encourage me" (1916, p. 53; cf. Saffange 1985).

For all of its controversy, Summerhill was established and infused with a highly moral character, and Carr (1984; cf. 2002) is correct to describe the book "Summerhill" as a treatise on moral education. This is the irony of the book: although it is fundamentally about the moral development of young people, Neill repeatedly claims that moral instruction of young children is dangerous or dangerous or invidious, and also that Summerhill is largely characterized in terms of its freedom from any such moral education. Hameline wrote that Neill, "far from being immoral, was engaged in a constant pastoral enterprise" (1985, p. 72; author's translation). The bounds of Neill's sense of morality were set by his unconstrained vision.

Happiness and interest

For Neill, the aim of education is to find happiness, which means being interested in life (Fromm 1960). Childhood, he believed, was the unique critical period in human development during which time children develop their innate characters and interests, and their dispositions to be happy. The commitment to happiness is clearly an expression of Neill's unconstrained vision: happiness grows from a sense of personal freedom, and deprivation of this sense of freedom during childhood, and the consequent unhappiness experienced by the repressed child, is responsible for many of the psychological disorders of adulthood. Consequently, Neill often wrote about happiness in negative terms, and he is much clearer about the sources of unhappiness than of happiness. There may have been another reason for his negative framing of happiness. For him, happiness is the natural state of childhood. It is not an accomplishment to be achieved. So, like other "givens," happiness is most apparent when it is obstructed, repressed, or denied.

In the style of so many radical reformers, Neill lay the blame for unhappiness squarely at the door of society. He thought that the society of his day was "sick and unhappy" (1960, p. 102). The metaphor of sickness is significant since Neill understood traditional moralism, with its reliance on enforcement through reward and punishment, as a form of repression. Society fears life, and in particular, it fears emotions as they are relatively unpredictable. A fear of children and their emotional life is the source of repressive authority at home and school (Neill 1972a), and results in the reproduction of generations who grow up just as their parents did: unhappy cowards (ibid.). Bad schooling is an especially potent cause of children's unhappiness because it represses (in the case of traditional schools) or manipulates (in the case of the progressives) their interests. They compel obedience, and they ignore the natural needs and desires of children. So-called progressive schools can be worse. Children will only achieve happiness if they are free, because happiness is usually caused by inner hostility created in the child by external repression. This hostility cannot be expressed toward parents, teachers, and other authority figures, and so is turned inward and becomes self-hate. Self-hate needs expression, and this expression often takes the form of antisocial behavior. To some extent, this conception shows the influence of Freudian theory, but it would be more accurate to say that Neill's view of happiness and unhappiness took its shape most clearly from Homer Lane. Like Lane, Neill concluded that the "problem children" produced by this mechanism required, more than anything else, the s of repression. The difficulty is that schools, parents, and society are incapable of addressing the real needs of these children and helping them achieve happiness because they are the cause of their unhappiness. Neill saw Summerhill as a solution to this predicament.

Nowhere, he believed, was society's antihappiness more apparent than in its attitudes toward sex. If a child is taught to think of his or her natural sexual interest as something which should not be indulged, he will come to see these natural inclinations as bad, and the resulting self-hatred will be generalized as hatred of others. In typical Freudian terms, he thought that censoring children when they discuss or engage in forms of sex play (such as masturbation) prevents the acceptance of sexuality in maturity. Ironically, this repression can lead to promiscuity (ibid., p. 110) and unhappy marriages (ibid., p. 199). At the same time, unreleased sexual energy becomes translated into anxiety and hate (ibid., p. 191).

Despite the fact that the majority of Neill's writing on happiness is devoted to its absence, he does have some positive contributions to make on the subject. He conceives of happiness primarily as a subjective state of mind: "if the word happiness means anything, it means and inner feeling of well-being, a sense of balance, a feeling of being contented with life" (1960, p. 308). How is happiness to be achieved? According to Neill, the primary driving force behind individual happiness is interest: "I hold that the aim of life is to find happiness, which means to find interest" (ibid., p. 37). Only in an environment of complete freedom can this aim be achieved, as it is only through freedom that the child is able to realize his or her true interests. These interests are personal to the child, and "completely spontaneous" (ibid., 149). When they are achieved, Neill believed, the child will be capable of finding happiness and fulfillment in life.

"The doctrine of interest" (Saffange 1985) was a key concept of the educational theories of the new educationists. According to Neill's contemporary, Adolphe Ferrière (1922, p. 229), it was "the lever which moves mountains ... the keystone of the Active School." Neill probably picked up an awareness of the importance of interest at this time. In a chapter in a book on the New Education Fellowship, he wrote that "interest is the only criterion" (1921/1922, p. 229). However, as Saffange (1985) noted, Neill's use of the concept of interest was rather less complex than that of philosophically minded thinkers like Ferrière: "When a boy makes a snowball, he is interested ... I don't care what a child is doing in the way of creation, whether he is making tables, porridge or sketches ... or snowballs ... there is more true education in making a snowball than in listening to an hour's lecture on grammar" (1921a, pp. 13–14).

As elsewhere, Neill's confidence was bolstered by the insights of the new psychology in which he immersed himself (Saffange 1994). He interpreted Freud's theories as supporting his commitment to following children's interests, and argued that interest was the expression of the life force (or libido) (1923; 1926). "A Dominie in Doubt" gives an equation that Neill would follow for the rest of his career: "The aim of education is to allow emotional release so that there will be no bottling up and no future neurosis, and this release comes through interest" (1920, pp. 114–15). Consequently, "The whole idea of my school is release; it is the living out of an interest" (1926, p. 111), and the job of the teacher is "to find out where a child's interest lies and to help him to live it out ... my pupils never go to a lesson, it takes such faith and patience to realize that they are doing the right thing" (1945, p. 145).

The power of interest to produce effective learning was presented by Neill as an argument against parental and teacher authority, compulsory attendance at lessons, and an overemphasis on teaching methods. Given the central importance of interest, then, it is quite surprising how weak was his analysis. He believed that interest grew naturally, and his interpretation of this carried with it a strong dose of fatalism:

> If left to himself without adult suggestion of any kind [a child] will develop as far as he is capable of developing. Logically, Summerhill is a place in which people who have the innate ability and wish to be scholars will be scholars; all those who are only fit to sweep the streets will sweep the streets. (1960, p. 20)

However, Neill's own life story provides numerous instances that falsify his claim, such as his belated embrace of mathematics and Greek, thanks to the pedagogic skills and warm personalities of Aeneas Gunn Gordon and Ben Thomson. And, of course, it is surely unlikely that his life's work just happened to be in precisely the same area as that of his father.

Neill's individualism led him to significantly underestimate the importance of the social setting in which all human beings live. He believed that it was both pointless and immoral to force a child to learn something that did not stem from the child. Genuine learning, he thought, required a desire to learn springing from interest. Interest is a necessary condition of true learning, and "true interest" is "completely spontaneous" (Neill 1960, p. 149). The strict differentiation of "true" and other interests was an important part of Neill's pedagogy, and justified such things as voluntary attendance of lessons and a disdain for inspiring teaching, may have been ultimately impossible to maintain because human beings do not live in social and cultural isolation. It is difficult to know what Neill's phrase "true interests" really means, and he never explores it. It implies, though, a child following his or her own subjective interests, independent of anyone else. It also implies that interest arises from within the child. Such a view, of course, completely ignores the self-evident social nature

of childhood and learning (Darling 1988). From the perspective of
the child, the distinction between true interests and other interests is
meaningless and indistinguishable.

It is almost inevitable that children in a small boarding school like
Summerhill will feel a pull to conform with some practices, and a tendency
to identify with older children, teachers, and groups. Maurice Punch's
fieldwork at Summerhill revealed precisely this phenomenon, although
the peculiar character of Summerhill meant that social influence was
less hierarchical than would be expected in a traditional school:

> I felt that the ideal of "non-interference" by staff was often compro-
> mised by the staff's manipulation of the student society. But, I turn,
> the pupils could subvert the free offered to them with collective
> behaviour, and by powerfully enforced group norms and sanctions,
> that were the antithesis of the school's most cherished values. (Punch
> 1986, pp. 61–2)

And, of course, the structure of the school enforces certain messages and
values and priorities itself, as Neill himself concedes:

> . . . we can be accused of molding character by negation. We give
> them art and science, and self government and playtime, lessons
> and cinema because we feel that these things are important, but
> because we consider religion unimportant, we withhold it . . . We
> do therefore select and choose according to our own make up . . .
> Frankly I cannot see how we can do otherwise . . . (Neill 1945,
> pp. 115–16)

As Darling (1988, p. 59) observes, "Interests are often infectious," and
this is especially the case during childhood. Neill himself recognizes this
when he allows the "schoolboy craze" (1960a, p. 34) as a source of interest.
But this allowance undermines Neill's case as: if he is willing to allow all
interests and acquired by social contagion—where it is presumably not
possible to separate true and acquired interests—it is difficult to see why
he would exclude interests elicited by stimulating teaching.

Another way of looking at this issue is by co-opting the concept of
"adapted preferences" from the development studies of the philosopher

Martha Nussbaum (2000) and the economist Amartya Sen (1998). They demonstrated that desires and interests are highly malleable, and mediated by identities, norms, and institutions. Nussbaum developed this point when she argued that women in particular often find their options restricted by notions of obligation and legitimacy, which affect the decisions they feel that they are able to make. Thus, women's perceptions of themselves are largely constituted by the circumstances before them, and, as Annas (1993) put it, in a society where women have fewer options, they settle for less. The point is often made about the conceptual limitation of negative freedom (i.e., freedom from interference) (Berlin 1969): thus, one finds oneself freer, other things being equal, by wanting to do nothing. Insofar as one wants to do nothing, one may encounter fewer obstacles in the pursuit of one's goals. The process of adaptive preference is not necessarily or even typically a conscious act, as norms and expectations become internalized. The fortunate few become adapted to their wealth of opportunities; the rest adapt their expectations and desires to the lower level of life they are accustomed to. How can they demand fundamental elements of well-being if they are unaware that they exist? (Nussbaum 2000). Essentially, this is a twist on Marx's conception of ideology as false consciousness. Relying on personal preference will, in contexts like these, simply reinforce dominant structures and stand in opposition to radical change, both personal and institutional (Bailey 2009).

Neill occasionally recognized this problem:

> ... We can be accused of moulding character by negation. We give them arts and science, self-government and playtime, lessons and cinema because we feel that these things are important, but because we consider religion unimportant we withhold it ... We do therefore select and choose according to our own make-up ... Frankly I cannot see how we can do otherwise ..." (Neill 1945, pp. 115–16)

He fails to see that the inevitably adaptive effect of social and institutional pressures on children undermines his distinction between true and false interests, and, in doing so, significantly weakens his case against external influence and stimulation.

Freedom and authority

Neill's overriding concern is with children's happiness. A necessary condition for the development of happiness is the removal of repression, and one of the major forms of repression in school and society is adult authority. Authority is essentially a form of repression, and he argued that adults should not direct children or try to shape them; they should not impose rules or sets of expectations toward which children would feel obliged to aspire. These strictures are partly because of the inherent damage of repression, and partly because of the suspect motives of those who wish to impose authority. Neill argued that the motives of those who impose authority are suspect. Adults and teachers, he believed, usually exercise power for a sense of feeling powerful, or to live vicariously through the children.

While it is obviously the case that there are certain individuals who behave in this way, it seems very odd to ban all exercises of influence of the children in this way. Most adult interference in children's lives are, if not always wise or well-informed, at least well-intentioned. For Neill, these forms of authority are even worse precisely because they do not appear to be acts of authority. Repression is most insidious when it is invisible.

It is clear that Neill's unconstrained vision dictates that children's lives should be characterized by freedom rather than authority:

> How can happiness be bestowed? My own answer is: Abolish authority. Let the child be himself. Don't push him around. Don't teach him. Don't lecture him. Don't elevate him, Don't force him to do anything. (Neill 1960a, p. 297)

By freedom, he did not mean an absolute withdrawal of adult responsibility, nor succumbing to every childish fancy. Everyone has to recognize that there are limits to how far one can do what one wants, and for that reason there is no such thing as complete or absolute freedom (ibid.). Neill goes to some lengths to make it clear that he is not advocating adults giving up all responsibility for the care of children. He is advocating, in his own words, "freedom not license." He had no hesitation in stopping children from doing potentially dangerous acts. This creates one the interesting idiosyncrasies of Neill's writing: on the one hand, he is explicit in his advocacy of children's freedom; on the other, he is damning of the phenomenon of the spoiled child, especially where his spoiling is the result of a deliberate policy based upon the failure of the parents to understand the difference between freedom and license.

The distinction between freedom and license is an important one, and is often misunderstood by critics of the Summerhill philosophy: "It is this distinction between freedom and license that many parents cannot grasp. In the disciplined home, the children have no rights. In the spoiled home, they have all the rights. The proper home is one in which children and adults have equal rights" (Neill 1962, p. 112). Neill was insistent that a belief in children's freedom and in noninterference in their affairs is not the same as a neglect of their safety and welfare (Carr 1984). Children must be safeguarded from harm but there are obvious straightforward ways of accomplishing this that do not constitute any unreasonable violation of their self-regulation: "Only a fool in charge of young children would allow unbarred high bedroom windows or an unprotected nursery fire" (Neill 1953, p. 36). Despite some of his rhetorical flourishes, Neill did not really believe that a child should be entirely self-regulating. Once an adult has made himself responsible for providing and maintaining a particular kind of environment for growing children (even if it is relatively free), he has already begun to interfere with the development of the child.

According to critics like Barrow (1978), such exceptions to the principle of self-regulation make Neill's theory obviously inadequate and blatantly contradictory. And what is really an issue is the degree to which only areas in which the child should be left to do what it feels like doing rather than be subject to the deliberate restraints of other children or adults. But this criticism is a little unfair as it ignores the freedom/licence distinction completely. In particular, it overlooks the fact that Neill recognizes that children's freedom is only possible with certain conditions because everybody's freedom is so limited. There is, he says, "no such thing as complete freedom" (1960a, p. 309). So, he does not advocate freedom without qualification, and he does not believe that every child's fleeting wish needs to be granted. Neill distinguishes between a "disciplined" environment, in which parents or teachers have all the rights, and children have none, a "spoiled" home or school, where children have all the rights, and the adults have none, and, finally, there is a proper, "free" home, where adults and children have equal rights (1962, p. 105). In other words, Neill argued that both groups are equally entitled to have their rights respected, and everyone is entitled to do as they please so long as their actions do not harm someone else or obstruct someone's freedom. So, he felt perfectly justified in forbidding dangerous activities at the school, not because they would hurt other people, but because it would be dangerous for the child.

In addition to the general social limits placed on anyone living within a close-knit community was a particular institution that was distinctively Summerhillian, self-government. Indeed, the case could be made that self-government is the most fundamental feature of Summerhill life, despite the fact that it has been largely ignored by media commentators and government inspectors in favor of less central issues like voluntary attendance and informal staff-student relationships. But it is self-government that is at the core of the Summerhill experience.

Neill's introduction to the concept was, of course, from Homer Lane. He was an immediate convert:

> The school that has no self-government should not be called a progressive school. It is a compromise school. You cannot have progression unless children feel completely free to govern their own social life where there is a boss, freedom is not there, and this applies more to the benevolent boss than to the disciplinarian. (1937, pp. 45–6)

The ease with which Neill, who was at the time a young, inexperienced, and rather ambivalent teacher, embraced the idea of self-government is noteworthy. The only example he had seen was the Little Commonwealth that, by all accounts, was a rather chaotic affair (Wills 1964). But Neill recognized in it a way to reconcile a tension that lay at the heart of his worldview: between individualism and social order.

Neill, himself, was a resolute individualist: "He was the kind of fellow who would paint his bicycle blue when everyone else's was black" (Hemmings 1972, p. 3). He sought to make his pupils into people who stood against the force of the crowd while acknowledging their social duty. He warned his students at Gretna: "The one thing that will save the people is individualism ... your country needs you ... to set it right" (1916, pp. 101 and 120). Education, if it is to be worthy of its name, needs to teach children to live their own lives with honesty while living actively within their community. Self-government, it seems, showed a vehicle for reconciling the demands of the individual and the group in a way that was respectful of both.

There are other reasons why self-government might be valuable in a context like Summerhill. Neill thought that the general meeting, in particular, was vitally important: "more important than all the textbooks in the world" (Neill, in Lamb 1992b, p. 23). He believed that the experience of governing one's self and others was "the most valuable asset in education and life" (Neill 1932, p. 112). Skidelsky (1969) argued that these sorts of experiences are therapeutic, as it can lead to the release of tensions through discussions. He also suggested that it can help expose problems such as bullying in a relatively neutral way. Therefore, terms like "anti-authoritarian" or "permissive," which have often been used by commentators to describe Summerhill, do not appear to capture the essence of Summerhill, as authority was not simply abolished at the school but replaced with perhaps more appropriate and even more powerful means of creating socially responsible and intelligent people (Müller 2009). Neill was aware that communal authority is likely to give rise to less resentment than that of teacher authority, and consequently teachers are released from the demands of disciplining unacceptable behavior, freeing them to build closer relationships with the children. And self-government offers children an experience of genuine democratic citizenship, in which they learn about the importance of rules, and to distinguish between necessary and unnecessary rules. Danë Goodsman made this point, and highlighted the central importance of the communal meeting in the effective running of the school:

Because the meeting actually controlled all behaviour and suddenly the meeting was gone so that you had nothing and nobody – who

would protect you. Because as a kid in Summerhill I didn't have
a sense that adults were there looking after me, that there was a
hierarchy or something. I had a sense that this thing – the meeting
looked after me. (Interview 18/7/11).

The practical consequences of Neill's dictum that "Freedom means
doing what you like, so long as you don't interfere with the freedom of
others" (1960a, p. 44) are much more complex than might first appear.
The weekly general meeting, with an elected Chairperson, is attended
by almost the whole school. Neill's description (cited in Vaughan 2006,
p. 9) was that the General School Meeting was the venue where "all
school rules were voted by the entire school, each pupil and each staff
member having one vote." Although Gribble's (1998, p. 20) description
of Summerhill as "a society of children, run by and for children" may
be more rhetorical than factual, children are always in a huge majority
in any meeting. Through this mechanism, the Summerhill community
makes its rules, deals with disputes, and decides on punishments. By
Neill's reckoning, "no culprit at Summerhill ever shows any signs of
defiance or hatred of the authority of his community" (1962, p. 21) since
he has played a part in creating and sustaining the system of justice
that has dealt with him. Goodsman (1992), an ex-pupil of Summerhill,
offers a fascinating reflective insight into what this experience of self-
government meant for a young member of the school:

> Without delving too deeply into notions of "free will" versus
> socialisation, or putting too simplistic a world view, I would like to
> make the claim that Summerhill provides an environment where
> children are enabled to be "self-actualising," to understand that what
> they do will not only affect themselves, but others. Through the
> democratic process of the meeting, children can actually see issues
> through and be active participants in, or inventors of, their culture.
>
>   As an ex-pupil, I cannot stress enough the very real sense that I had
> as a child that if I wanted to change something it was in my power
> to do so, coupled with the understanding that I was responsible for
> myself – no one else could or would be. As a product of Summerhill,
> I find that many of the views of childhood that were part of an
> understanding that I grew up with are not mirrored elsewhere in

society. Several issues regarding the problems of childhood that are raised by the mainstream, have little or no resonance for me. One such, is the disenfranchisement of the "adolescent." My own experience led me to believe my teen years would be and indeed were, an increasingly social and socially aware time. Subsequently, from my teaching experience in the mainstream, I learned that adolescence is seen as a particularly problematic stage – a stage where young people often display their most anti-social natures. As a Summerhillian I can only conclude that this anti-social stage is not a result of hormonal changes, but something relating to the position that society in general puts such young people into." (Goodsman 1992, p. 229)

In addition to voting equity, all members of the community were seen to share equal rights in initiating proposals for new policies to be voted upon. For example, a 6-year old's vote holds the same weight as that of a 17-year old's vote, or Neill's. According to Appleton (2000), who worked as a houseparent at Summerhill for 9 years:

You are then able to challenge the validity of any law, and propose it is dropped or replaced by a more relevant one. Likewise you may want to draw up a new law to cover something you think needs to be defined more clearly. There is usually some discussion, and then further proposals may be taken. These are then voted on and whichever one is passed becomes law until someone chooses to challenge it. So the school laws are forever in a state of evolution, reflecting the needs of the community at any given time. (p. 104)

This process can produce more than 200 rules that govern the Summerhill community (Vaughan 2006).

Neill reinforced the power of the meeting and the relative irrelevance of adults in day-to-day decision-making by making deliberately provocative proposals. Hylda Sims recalled him once suggesting that the school give up democracy and become a dictatorship like Germany (1993):

So a triumvirate of dictators was selected by him from among the older boys to be in charge. We very soon got fed up with them going to the front of the dinner queue, declaring early bedtimes everybody but themselves and ordering us about. They couldn't think of much else to do. We called a special meeting and voted them out of office. They stepped down without putting up a fight. They too had had enough.

Goodsman (personal communication 18/7/11) reported similar occasions, some of which seemed designed to undermine Neill's own authority:

I mean Neill's thing and he used to do it with his little experiments. He used to propose completely outrageous things in meetings and he actually did do it . . . And we'd all say, "Oh, for god's sake, Neill." And vote against him. I don't think as a kid I saw that he was making a point. I just thought it was Neill just being a fool, you know.

She interpreted his actions as sending a message to the adults as well as the children in the meeting:

what I think he was constantly doing, not reminding us because our relationship with him was very different, but reminding his staff, you know, this is powerful. These kids will not just listen to me and willy nilly put their hands up. They listen to me and think is that rubbish or not rubbish. (ibid.)

According to Piper and Stronach (2008, p. 131), the culture of self-government produced a distinctive citizenship which in turn was the "generator of identity. It was dynamic and self-formative, in that participants choose what to take an interest in, and in choosing learned something of their own desires, responsibilities and identity." They compared this Summerhill identity with a tribe, and the headteacher, agreed, "I think it's like a tribe, but it's more than that, it's just a life area. It's an area where everything happens and it's definitely not a school . . ." (Zoë Readhead, cited in ibid.).

The world of Neill's free child is not one of the unbridled self-expression of all of his desires and interests, as is commonly portrayed in both the academic literature and the media (e.g., Rafferty 1972;

Chamberlain 1989; cf. Neustatter 2011). Such interests have to be negotiated in a common interest with one's community.: "The result is self-discipline" (Neill 1960a, p. 44). Summerhill pupils are not entirely free from constraints, and while they enjoy great scope for play and choice in matters of curriculum, they are also compelled by numerous rules, too, and those who break the rules may well be punished (Gribble 1998). However, there is a difference that makes all the difference. Rules in Summerhill are made by members of the school community, who also decide the punishments. Insider and outsider accounts agree that conflicts between children and teachers are extremely rare (Goodsman 1992; Gribble 1998; Neill 1962; Stronach and Piper 2008). Children see staff generally as their friends, and this relationship removes many disciplinary difficulties. The problems that inevitably arise time to time in a small, closed community, are dealt with by the community, and not an individual.

In fact, matters were not quite so simple. Neill claimed that "When there is a boss, freedom is not there, and this applies more to the benevolent boss than the disciplinarian" (1937, p. 31). However, it is misleading for Neill to claim that there was not a boss at Summerhill, or that the boss was the school community. As Goodsman makes it clear, of course there was a boss behind everything. It was Neill's school; he and his family have owned it since its founding. Neill was the guiding force behind the school. Although he rarely manipulated meetings, he did occasionally do so. For example, when it took too long for one meeting to reach a decision, Neill unilaterally abolished it. On another occasion he declared himself dictator, prompting the children eventually to rebel. Croall's (1983a) interpretation of these events is that they give evidence of Neill's genius to do the right thing at the right time. There is another interpretation, of course, and that was that Neill was the leader of the Summerhill community, and he could not help but structure freedom in his own terms. This seems an entirely plausible and defensible position, as Neill was preparing the young people in his charge to live a life of freedom by teaching them the necessary skills through experience.

There were other ways in which members of Summerhill's community were directed by Neill. For example, after explaining that at Summerhill "afternoons are completely free for everyone," Neill casually added that "tea is served at four" (1960a, p. 12). This might seem to be a trivial example of an inconsistency in Neill's philosophy of noninterference, but it does make the point that Neill could be blind to his own influence, as well as the influence of the institution of Summerhill. For someone in Britain during Neill's era, afternoon tea was simply accepted as a sign of civility, and so it is only proper that it takes place at Summerhill. However, it is very difficult to believe that taking tea at four is a daily coincidental confluence of individual drives and desires.

Another problem arises once the real world of Summerhill impinges upon the philosophy of Neill. He claimed that children were free to do as they wanted at Summerhill. But, in fact, there were countless activities that his pupils would not be able to do, whether it is due to the idiosyncrasies of Neill's employment policy, the relative poverty of the school, or simply the boundaries set by real life. If a child wanted to be a tennis player, an astronaut, or a cowboy, what does he do? In practice, he goes to mathematics lessons or woodwork, as they are available to him. These activities are not what he wants to do, but are the best or the most readily accessible options available under the circumstances (Waks 1976). Being free to do what one wants does not, in practice, guarantee that you will be able to do what you want, for being given the freedom to do what you want is not just a matter of noninterference. Two other conditions are necessary for the child's "drives" to be met: certain material or environmental conditions of the action and a certain degree of ability or skill in the action (Waks 1976).

Learning and teaching

According to Sowell's (2002) analysis, many holders of an unconstrained vision presume that human nature is malleable and changeable. Consequently, they often construct detailed programs and pedagogies to ensure that this potentiality is realized. Perhaps the classic statement of this approach is that of the psychologist, B. F. Skinner, who claimed that babies come into the world with no preconceived notions about the world, are then shaped by their environment, and are slowly conditioned through various schedules of reinforcement (Lieberman 2000). Skinner's attributed maxim, "Give me a child and I'll shape him into anything," is an explicit statement of the unconstrained vision. Neill's reflections led him to precisely the opposite conclusion: "Allow the children freedom to be themselves" (1962, p. 4). His philosophy of nonintervention meant that Summerhill became characterized as the "do-as-yer-like school" (Neustatter 2011). He believed that the child is "innately wise and realistic . . . Left to himself without adults suggestion of any kind, he will develop as far as he is capable of developing" (1960a, p. 4). Interference by parents or teachers is not only unnecessary, but also harmful as it enforces uniformity of behavior and represses the child's natural drive to live his own life. Children acting to satisfy the expectations of adults dull their understanding of their own desires. So, the adult needs to learn "to wait and watch a child make little or no progress," confident that so long as the child is not "molested or damaged [he will] succeed in life" (1960a, p. 29). Neill believed that noninterference in the development of the child was the source of Summerhill's success.

Neill's was a psychological conception of freedom. Initially, this was based upon his interpretation of the psychoanalytic framework of Freud, and Homer Lane's rather loose reinterpretation of it. But this was soon replaced by the work of Reich, who prompted Neill to think in terms of drives and inner forces. These forces "motivate life" (1960a, p. xxiii), and are either expressed, which causes happiness, or are repressed, which causes neuroses and unhappiness. Repression, usually caused by adult interference, can result in boredom or aggression. Some children, Neill thought, had become so repressed by external pressures that their life force had become blocked. In such cases, he initially believed that therapy was needed in the form of "Private Lessons" (a label chosen because he was not a qualified therapist). These sessions involved relaxed conversations with individual children and, initially, some Freudian analysis. Later, under the influence of Reich, he would offer pupils body massage. With time, however, he concluded that the freedom was preferable to therapy, and that leaving the child to do as he wanted was usually enough. The freedom of Summerhill resulted in children being less bored and more capable of self-expression, after a period of working through their problems in their own time in the course of the natural activities.

It is clear that Neill saw emotional support as one of his most important roles at Summerhill. In fact his entry in "Who's Who" described him as a "child psychologist," rather than a teacher (1972). This identity was not new: in "Dominie Abroad" he wrote, "it has come to me as something of a sudden shock that I am no longer interested in teaching. Teaching English bores me stiff. All my interest is in psychology" (1923, p. 196); and he began his Preface to "Problem Child" (1926, p. 1) with the words, "Since I left teaching and took up child psychology . . .".

Was Neill anti-intellectual? This has been a recurring theme in commentary on his work and philosophy (Hechinger 1970; Ornstein 1977). Neill's public stance on the academic side of schooling was simple and clear: the emotions matter more than the intellect because if you educate the emotions, the intellect takes care of itself. On occasion, his tendency toward rhetoric led him to make even stronger statements, such as "Academic learning has little in it of intrinsic value" (1948, p. 24). However, such sentiments seem to be due more to Neill's desire to shock the reader, rather than a genuine statement of belief. His more typical position was that the individual's decision whether or not to follow an academic path lies entirely with the student, and that decision can only honestly be made once that individual has satisfied certain emotional requirements. Neill's resistance to an overemphasis on the intellect was provoked, or at least informed, in part by his reading of the new psychology coming into the country from Europe. He thought that people like Freud and Jung, not to mention Homer Lane, had demonstrated that children must be allowed to live out their inherent need to play and not be saddled with the duty, discipline, work, and ambition of adulthood too soon. He believed that there is an innate and organic unfolding of needs, capacities, and impulses in the development during childhood, and what is suitable to one stage may not be suitable to another; it is only possible to get to the later phases in a healthy way by going through the earlier ones. It is the neglect or suppression of this growth pattern that makes schools the hate-filled places they are, and which renders all their obsession with learning and knowledge so pointless (Friedman 1974).

In response to friendly questioning about his approach to children's freedom by the philosopher C. E. M. Joad, Neill reflected: "His is an intellectual approach, while mine is an emotional one. Thus he cannot grasp the difference between freedom and license because he presumably is occupied with philosophical ideas about both. He thinks about children; I live with them ..." (Croall 1983a, p. 202). And one of the teachers at Summerhill told Croall (1983a, p. 331), "there was an anti-intellectual atmosphere to an extreme degree, from the Neills, some of the staff and pupils." The psychoanalyst Erich Fromm, in his Foreword to the American version of "Summerhill," was probably correct when he claimed that Neill "underestimates the importance, the pleasure and the authenticity of an intellectual in favour of an artistic and emotional grasp of the world" (1960, p. xv). Neill's attitude toward the intellect seems to be framed within an understanding of it as cold and primarily about memory and repetition, which seems to have be derived from his childhood and early teaching experiences.

His private beliefs seem to have been more ambivalent. Croall (1983a, p. 331) wrote about Neill's "pretend dislike of learning," and many of the Summerhill staff interviewed by him provide clues to Neill's personal love of learning and scholarship. By all accounts, he was delighted to be conferred Honorary degrees (a Master of Education and two honorary doctorates) from British universities, even if his outward response was predictably ironic. For example, when the University of Newcastle awarded him an Honorary Doctorate in 1966, Neill said, "I had a glorious time in Newcastle ... only my halo did not fit very well" (cited in Croall 1983a, p. 207). He used his autobiography to offer a more balanced view:

I have often criticized universities and schools because they develop the intellect to the neglect of the emotions. Summerhill attempts the opposite. Nevertheless, Summerhill fails in those instances when a child grasps freedom emotionally without the intellectual capacity to amalgamate head and heart. (Neill 1972a, p. 231)

And again:

Is education to mean better scientists, engineers, doctors, instead of more balanced, happier, more tolerant human beings? A good education would mean both. (Neill 1972a, p. 484)

However, he also acknowledged that there are priorities: "If the emotions are committed to be really free, the intellect will look after itself" (1960a, p. 99), and "I hold that education should concern itself with the emotions and leave the intellect to look after itself" (Neill 1972a, p. 485). Stressing the academic side of school too forcefully and too early is unhelpful and potentially harmful, he thought, and the wise teacher needs to hold back from pushing this aspect until the student is ready to study "of their own accord" (1960a, p. 108). Neill responded to potential critics by claiming that those pupils who did decide to study for examinations (such as for university) worked through the syllabus much quicker than those in ordinary schools (ibid., 113). He failed to mention inspectors' claims that this is not true, and that academically ambitious pupils were severely handicapped by their lack of preparatory work in early years (Darling 1988).

So, Neill prioritized the emotions before the intellect because he felt that was the route to the proper development of both. He was critical of traditional schooling because it developed the intellect at the neglect of the emotions. While some of Neill's comments suggest an aim of the equal development of both emotions and the intellect—"Is education to mean better scientists, engineers, doctors, instead of more balanced, happier, more tolerant human beings? A good education would mean both" (1972a, p. 484)—there is a much stronger sense of inequality: "emotion is of infinitely more moment than intellect" (ibid., p. 474); "Is it possible that I am overdoing the imagination business? Shall I produce men and women with more imagination than intellect? No, I do not think there is a danger. The nation suffers from lack of imagination; few of us can imagine a better state of society, a fuller life" (ibid., p. 376).

Whether or not Neill was actively anti-intellectual, there is little doubt that he was keen to put the traditional emphasis on the development of the intellect through reading and study in its place: "Parents are slow in realising how unimportant the learning side of school is. Only pedants can claim that learning from books is education. Books are the least important apparatus in a school . . . All that any child needs is the 3Rs: the rest should be tallness and clay and sports and theatres and paints . . . and freedom" (Neill 1937, p. 29). Later he wrote, "We have art and hand work teachers but cannot afford a dance or a music teacher, to me of much more important than a maths or history teacher" (Neill 1973, p. 154). It is probably not a coincidence that Neill's lists of worthwhile activities reflect very closely his own interests, which he occasionally acknowledged himself. For example, in a letter to Bertrand Russell, he wrote, "I find myself supplying environments according to my own interests" (cited in Croall 1983b, p. 31). Croall's interviews with old Summerhillians suggest that Neill sometimes found it difficult to acknowledge that children's interests were different from those of his own. On occasion, he would snatch books away from those sitting and reading.

In some respects, Neill seems to have held a rather crude, innatist view of intelligence—some have it and others do not. The claim that children are naturally good and ought to be given freedom to regulate their own lives can be reframed as a fatalist credo. There would seem to be some truth in this interpretation as Neill did take it for granted that children's futures are written in the stars: ". . . Summerhill is a place in which people who have the innate ability and wish to be scholars will be scholars; whilst those who are only fit to sweep the streets will sweep the streets" (Neill 1962a, p. 20). Neill's use of the phrase "only fit to sweep the streets" rather undermines his proclaimed indifference to career success. This comment shows that the lesson Neill took away from his unconstrained vision was that children's development should not be forced; you cannot make a silk purse out of a sow's ear. To try to do either of these would be, at the least, pointless, and could be harmful to children's development and happiness. So, teachers and schools are very limited in what they can do. They cannot stretch or accelerate; they are restricted to providing a supportive and happy environment in which natural growth can take place. Once this setting is established, the best thing a teacher can do is to step back and shut up.

The clearest instance of this principle in practice is, perhaps, the most (in)famous feature of the Summerhill approach: voluntary attendance at lessons. No student was ever compelled to go to lessons, although most do, and those individuals who attend lessons only sporadically are liable to being condemned by their classmates for holding them back (Neill 1937). The place of lessons at Summerhill was explained by the former Summerhillian Danë Goodsman (1992, p. 225), as follows:

> Lessons were not considered the centre of school life but became one of many resources available in a process of "self education". They were of value because they were available to be chosen or

not, and for Summerhillians, it was this act of choosing that was educational. Through choosing, the children are enabled to learn about the responsibilities involved in making their own decisions. Voluntarism . . . embodies a type of "choice" boundary. Decisions to attend or not to attend lessons created consequences and it is this notion of actions and consequences that made these choices "authentic". Education was seen as an emancipatory process, enabling individuals to be autonomous beings. (Goodsman 1992, p. 225)

With a philosophy in which interest determines relevance, lesson attendance was seen as an expression of readiness. Zoë Readhead, the most recent headteacher of Summerhill, claimed: "If you choose to go to class, you are usually ready to learn and don't need the work to be sugar-coated to make it palatable" (cited in Vaughan 2006, p. 100). And another Summerhillian, Joshua Popenoe (1970, p. 28), wrote: "All lessons are optional. The idea is that if a child is allowed to play as long as [he] likes, when [he] finally decides [he] wants to learn something, the motivation is entirely [his] own." Goodsman is no doubt correct that voluntary lesson attendance showed how freedom created responsibility. Recognizing and responding to the needs and interests of others would almost inevitably teach important lessons about the recognition of the limits on freedom in a social setting like a school: "Part of the effect of non compulsory teaching in Summerhill is the equality between teachers and students; staff are seen firstly as individuals and secondly as teachers. Further reported side-effects of this equality was in the view that staff learn from pupils how to teach" (Goodsman 1992, p. 226).

There are serious negative consequences of this approach to voluntariness, too. It is possible, of course, that some will fall in love with a particular subject area based on their personal drive to learn. But surely such individuals are unusual, as for every child with an interest in history or mathematics, there will probably be many more intrigued by dinosaurs, computer games, or the Nazis. More significantly, it is very difficult to see how anyone can develop an interest in a subject to which they have never been introduced. Without some sort of structured curriculum, delivered by a competent teacher, it is difficult to imagine how children will be in a position to make an informed judgment about their passions and interests because their introduction is based on happenstance and luck, or fad and fashion. This is essentially Rosemary Chamberlin's point (1989, p. 107) when she writes:

> I have argued that our justification for compelling children to attend school (all receive an equivalent of education elsewhere) is that there are certain things I need to know in order to survive in our society, to become part of the community and play their part of it, and to be able to make reasons choices as individuals. If this is the case then clearly it would be inconsistent to allow children complete academic or personal freedom when they are at school if this meant that they did not learn all that had been thought important enough to justify their compulsory attendance.

Chamberlin interprets Neill's resistance to compulsory lessons in terms of an idiosyncratic belief that the purpose of education and the nature of the childhood centered on happiness, which in turn meant pleasure or hedonistic satisfaction, but this is not accurate. It would, of course, be ridiculous to justify voluntary attendance at lessons because it makes children discontented or grouchy. But that is not what Neill was suggesting. His focus was on the realization of interests, and voluntary attendance is his attempt to respect the role of interests in determining people's happiness.

Recall that a founding principle of Neill's vision was that "a child is innately wise and realistic. If left to himself without adult suggestion of any kind he will develop as far as he is capable of developing" (1960a, p. 20). Neill's equation of happiness with freedom only makes sense with the addition of another clause, namely that every child does actually possess this innate wisdom. Herein lies Neill's difficulty, as it leaves little room for many of the characteristics that make humans human, such as error, prejudice, and ignorance. The degree of wisdom attributed by Neill to children is beyond that normally found in geniuses, and this is magnified by the fact that he does not seem to allow for the influence of social support in decision-making.

Even at a fairly rudimentary level, the difficulty of leaving children to follow their innate wisdom becomes apparent. There is an assumption in Neill's work that individuals realize their potential simply by being offered freedom and choice. But "while innate scholarly ability is essential for the development of scholars, it is not realistic to expect to wish to be a scholar to be present in every academically gifted child. Surely the sampling of the delights and possibilities of scholarship . . . is part of the process" (Hechinger 1970, p. 41). The academic universe is full of subjects that, on first blush, seem dull or impenetrable, but later become intensely exciting. How would one of Neill's students know? How would they learn? We do not know what we do not know. In practice, his educational prescription in this specific context seems to amount to little more than caprice or luck. If a child is fortunate enough to stumble accidentally across a book or a television program on a complicated or opaque subject, he might become intrigued enough to want to find out more. If this is does not happen, there is a danger that such knowledge remains lost to them forever. And the problem becomes exacerbated if the social background of the children is acknowledged. So, a child in an intellectual, books-laden family environment is far more likely to stumble across ideas and disciplines that provoke further study than a child who is not fortunate enough to live in such an environment. The cumulative advantage of the former stems from luck, irrespective of ability and interest (Bailey 2007).

The school has conventionally been framed as a correction to the shortfalls or idiosyncrasies of home life. Neill's unconstrained vision, though, left little room for the school to affect learning. He did not seem to care very much about what the children and the teachers did in the classroom: "I never visit lessons and have no interest in how children learn" (1937, p. 24). A teacher during the postwar period, Lucy Francis, reported that Neill would rarely visit classes, and when he did he had little concern for what the children or teachers were doing; he just wanted to make sure that the children were in the classroom because they wanted to be there (Walmsley 1969). He even used his authority in the school to protect the children from what he perceived interference from adults, such as by charismatic teaching. He said that he "was all for teachers who make their subjects interesting, who can make them live" (Lamb 1992, p. 104), but he also doubted that lessons were worth the effort (ibid.). Consequently, teaching quality was ultimately an ad hoc matter. For example, Stewart (1968) cites one Summerhill teacher who taught at different times biology, history, geography, mathematics, general science, and Latin. He, himself, had not studied some of the subjects before, let alone taught them. This range of subjects, combined with the age and ability ranges at Summerhill, means that consistently high-quality teaching would be impossible, no matter how committed the teachers might have been. Neill followed Lane in rejecting "all teaching not specifically requested by the children themselves, and . . . when such teaching is requested, pedagogic method is of no great importance" (Waks 1976, p. 195). There are no special Summerhill methods because "we do not consider that teaching in itself matters very much . . . Whether a school has or has not special method school teaching long division is of no significance, for long division is of no importance except to those who want to learn it. And the child who wants to learn it will learn it no matter how it is taught" (Neill 1960a, p. 5).

An example of Neill's approach to teaching is given by an American visitor to Summerhill (Snitzer 1968, p. 13):

> All right, this is our first algebra class, so I'll begin by saying that in algebra we deal with letters instead of numbers. Is that clear? For example (writing on blackboard):
>
> $$a + a = 2a$$
> $$b + b = 2b$$
> $$3a + 6a = 9a$$
>
> (Snitzer 1968, p. 13)

The lesson continues in this style which, apart from the informal nature of the interaction between teacher and pupil, is highly traditional.

CLANCY: Oh, hell, I can't get this stuff at all.
Neill, are we going to have algebra all week?
NEILL: Yes, we are.
CLANCY: Well, I'll see you next week then. (He gets up and leaves.)
NEILL: All right, one more before the bell . . . Roy, last night I taught Biscuit (his dog) to count apples, and he counts better than you.
ROY: What the hell's the joke, Neill'?
NEILL: Okay, okay, there's the bell. Get out of here, all of you."
(Snitzer 1968, p. 83)

is account is revealing at a number of levels. At the level of simple teaching methods, the approach is simply awful: Neill's explanation of algebra was incoherent; he made no effort to engage the students or to show the practical relevance of algebra; and he dealt with individual difficulties by resorting to insults. Nor did he ask about the learners' prior knowledge or experience or interest in algebra (and it is a fair assumption that many of the learners will have experienced algebra, as they often came from other schools).

Neill might have replied that the authority within the classroom is relatively trivial in comparison with the pupils' freedom not to turn up in the first place. Teachers offer lessons, he might have said, and the students decide to take them or leave them. But this is only persuasive if we discount the fact that these lessons take place in a social context that dictates that the outcomes of these lessons do really matter, for example, in terms of exam success. The teachers at Summerhill are not volunteers offering to teach their skills to the local children from a sense of civic obligation; they were professionals working (albeit unconventionally) in a culture of qualifications.

Neill seems to have had an indifference to the outside world. His lessons were presented as take-them-or-leave-them. However, absolving himself of responsibility for his pupils' learning, for all of its other possible virtues, risked losing those children who needed the lessons most. He implicitly accepted this point when he reported with engaging frankness that "freedom works best with clever children" (1960a, p. 112).

Neill would probably have been unmoved by this sort of criticism. His was primarily a psychological, not sociological conception of education. Specifically, he was concerned with dealing therapeutically with the various pathologies with which other schools infected their young people. He felt that freedom—real freedom—was the only way that children could find their passions and interests. Those who found it hardest to achieve in Summerhill were, in Neill's view, those who had already been damaged by "spoon-fed" education. An example of this was Winnifred, who came to Summerhill when she was 13:

She set herself out to have a good time, and she had – for a few weeks. Then I noticed that she was bored. "Teach me something", she said to me one day: "I'm bored stiff". "Right ho!" I said cheerfully, "what do you want to learn?"

"I don't know", she said.

"And I don't either", said I, and left her.

Months passed. Then she came to me again.

"I am going to pass the London Matric." [An examination at the end of formal schooling] She said, "and I want lessons from you."

Every morning she worked with me and other teachers – Worked well. She confessed that these subjects did not interest her much, but the aim did interest her. (Neill 1926, pp. 108–9)

There is a popular misconception that Neill advocated nonauthoritarian teaching methods that reflected his other alternative dispositions. Swartz (1984), for example, refers to Neill as a "Socratic educational theorist" (p. 71), which he equated primarily with the rejection of teacher authority. According to Swartz, Summerhill showed the Socratic approach in action. But this was simply not the case. Goodsman highlighted the irony of Summerhill's approach to teaching:

Paradoxically, the fact that lessons are 'free' had not resulted in innovative classroom practice. Lessons took a traditional 'teacher led', 'chalk and talk' form. Another factor which created conservative practice was the fact that, as Summerhill has no classroom discipline problems, teaching staff did not need to change or adapt practice to maintain interest or order. Nor did they belong to networks of professional development. However there was an understanding from both staff and pupils that Summerhill offered alternatives to the mainstream, and the main difference lay in the interaction between pupils and teachers as opposed to the structure or form of the lessons. (Goodsman 1992, p. 225)

Neill's real target in his attack seems to be the hidden persuasion that he saw as an inherent part of so-called brilliant teaching. According to this view, the brilliant teacher diminishes the child's autonomy by his continuous exercise of the powers of persuasion (Hemmings 1972). But surely, his insistent maintenance of the unconstrained vision and its expression in the doctrine of interest seems to restrict, rather than protect children's autonomy. There are whole areas of exciting and worthwhile experiences that would remain forever alien to children if their curriculum was based solely on their own interests. Few children, one would imagine, would choose to learn grammar, or mathematics, or a second language, unless their interest had been provoked by a teacher or a parent in some way. This stimulus is not an assault on the children's autonomy. In fact, it could be said to facilitate further autonomy on the part of the child.

Was Neill a Fox or a Hedgehog?

Isaiah Berlin once drew on a Greek folk tale for the metaphor of the Fox and the Hedgehog: "The Fox knows many things, but the Hedgehog know one big thing" (Archolochus, cited in Berlin 1978, p. 26). Hedgehogs have just one response to a threat: they roll themselves into a ball, presenting spikes to predators. Foxes, by contrast, have no single response to challenges, as they "know many little things" (ibid.). According to Berlin, the Fox—Hedgehog distinction is a useful way of categorizing thinkers. Are they Foxes? Does their work contain sub-themes and mutually inconsistent lines of argument? Or are they Hedgehogs, whose works center upon a single dominant argument or position from which all else is extrapolated? Do they find comfort in certainty, like Hedgehogs, or do they adapt and learn, like Fox?

Philip E. Tetlock (2005), a political psychologist, drew on this distinction in his exploration of the judgment of experts. The Hedgehog cognitive style focuses on closure, or a sense of finality, in order to feel happy. Decision-making is informed by unambiguous models and data. Verdicts are binary, decisive, and repeatable. Hedgehog thinkers tend to rely on formulae or precedents, and are resistant to challenges to their models. They relate everything to a single central vision in terms of which all that they say makes sense. Compare this mindset with the Fox cognitive style. Foxes are cautious of a commitment to any one way of seeing the issue, and to consider different perspectives. They tolerate dissonance within a model, and are open to a range of ideas without seeking to fit them into, or exclude them from, any one all-embracing inner vision. According to Tetlock's analysis, Hedgehogs tend to flourish and excel in environments in which uncertainty and ambiguity have been excluded (ibid.), whereas Foxes use a style which works best where neither the interpretation of the operating environment nor the correct nature of, or balance among, targets is clear.

Almost all of those who have sought to analyze Neill as a philosopher of education have implicitly taken him to be a Fox. A standard, and not overtly critical interpretation of Neill's thinking, is offered by Hobson (2001, p. 5):

> (Neill) lacks a systematic, considered philosophy of education, especially a coherent theory of knowledge. His ideas are based primarily on his own experiences and observations, supplemented with some study of psychological (especially psychoanalytic) theory. Certainly one's own experiences are an important part of any educational theory but they need to be supplemented by some more systematic philosophical position such as the nature of knowledge, learning, morality, human nature, society etc. . . . . He also tends to oversimplify complex philosophical issues such as the crucial distinction between freedom and licence, where he thinks it sufficient to merely distinguish the two conceptually and give some random examples of acts he calls either freedom or licence.

Potter (undated) carried out the useful task of showing Hobson's judgment to four experts on Neill and Summerhill: two former Summerhillians (Danë Goodsman and Albert Lamb) and two friends of Summerhill (David Gribble and Bryn Purdy). Only Goodsman took serious issue with Hobson's view. However, Gribble, Lamb, and Purdy seemed to accept the charge, but viewed it as irrelevant. For example, Lamb wrote, "Neill never claimed to have a systematic, considered philosophy of education. He would probably have questioned whether such a thing were possible or of any value. Educational theory, as applied to young people, always presupposes some form of compulsion, some way in which Adults Know Best and should continue to have the right to impose their program on children" (unpaged).

Neill himself often wrote in support of this interpretation of his approach. In his autobiography, he wrote: "I am a doer. I often act by instinct and rationalize afterwards" (Neill cited in Philpot 1985/6, p. 148). Whether or not such comments should be taken at face value is unclear. Neill certainly maintained a lifelong disdain for "mere theory" and the academics who produced them.

The preceding chapters have argued that contrary to this "standard view," Neill did have a systematic and largely consistent philosophy of education. Indeed, some of the weaker or at least idiosyncratic aspects of his work—such as his views of teaching and learning—can be traced to his willful refusal to abandon his unconstrained vision of children's natures. This commitment acted like a unifying thread that ran through his work. While it is certainly the case that some of Neill's writing lacked a strong sense of coherence, it is not the case that there was no higher intention. On the contrary, Neill's vision of education and the Summerhill "experiment" are best understood as attempts to enact a vision of education, and this vision can be characterized as centering upon one overriding concept: children's innate goodness and wisdom.

Chapter 4

The Reception and Relevance of A. S. Neill's Work

Reception

Neill was a thinker and writer drawn to radical positions. Summerhill School remains noteworthy in part because of the relative extremity of its philosophy and practices. Reactions to the man and the school tend to reflect the Manichaeism of the object of commentary. And they reflect the visions of education and human nature of the commentators themselves.

Judgments of the importance and influence of A. S. Neill are probably best described as mixed. On the one hand, advocates place Neill alongside the likes of Jean-Jacques Rousseau and John Dewey as an educational innovator. For example, UNESCO lists him as one of the world's 100 most important educationists, the United Kingdom's *Times Education Supplement* placed him as one of the 12 most important educationists in the United Kingdom in the last millennium (Newman 2006), while the educational writer Herbart Kohl called "A. S. Neill ... one of the greatest democratic educators of the last century" (2005, p. viii). At the height of his popularity, Neill seemed set to become the "Doctor Spock" of the 1970s (Rossman 1970; Eisner 1971). Albert Lamb, a former Summerhill pupil and teacher, described Summerhill as "the grandparent of all free schools" (1992b, p. 1). The academic Jane Morse (1996, p. 13) called Summerhill "the paradigm for freeschoolers."

For supporters, the very existence of a school like Summerhill is a source of inspiration and validation (Lange De Souza 2000). Edith Mannin (1930) captured this spirit when she wrote:

People have come from the other side of the world to meet to Neill and learn of his methods. He is literally unique. And the community he has built up around him, courageously, after years of struggle and set-back, and always refusing to compromise with his principles, even when it meant financial loss and a heart-breaking starting all over again, is, I think, the happiest place in the world. My admiration for A. S. Neill is unbounded. He is one of the very few people in this queer world doing something of real value. He is the pioneer of the New Education, with all the true pioneer's unflinching courage. (p. 222)

As Saffange (1994, p. 227) noted, for some, "Summerhill was, and will long remain, a mythical place where, at one time, a world of love and harmony came into being." The school might fairly be described as the manifestation of Rousseauian vision of education that even Rousseau himself was unable to describe. Bryn Purdy (cited in Potter, undated) asked: "May we not claim, however, that A. S. Neill was the Greatest, if not the most complete, Educator of the Twentieth Century?"

The centripetal force of such a vision for some is matched by a centrifugal rejection for others. Rafferty (1970, p. 24), an unapologetic defender of traditional schooling, claimed that "Summerhill degrades true learning. It is a caricature of education." For him, and for others in Hart's (1970) debate on Neill's work, Summerhill is so radically different from the standard conception that it is barely recognizable as a school at all (Barrow 1978). Raffety, who was in charge of the Californian school system at the time of writing, saw in real threat of "the breakdown of our Western code of morality implicit in the spread of Neill's hedonism to the majority of the next generation" (Rafferty 1970, p. 20). He also drew attention to images of "sex perverts" (p. 15), "frolic in the park, a daisy-picking foray, or an experiment in free love" (p. 17), concluding: "What the unkempt and sometimes terrifying generation of tomorrow quite obviously needs are more inhibitions, not fewer" (p. 18). Neill, for his part, claimed to live too far away from a library to borrow and did not like to buy books. So, he relied on the ideas and thinkers of his youth, half a century old. This fact helps explain Danica Deutsch's dismissal of the book Summerhill as "outdated radicalism" (1962, p. 194). Even those who were inclined to agree with Neill's criticisms of traditional schooling pulled away from supporting his positive philosophy and its translation into voluntary attendance at lessons and equity in decision-making (Noddings 2003). Others, like the writer Paul Francis, were anxious that "Folk heroes like Neill ... have a dangerously enthusiastic following in teacher training institutions" (1975, p. 49).

Neill had few disciples in the sense of followers who carried on his ideals and writing. To the obvious exception of his daughter Zoë, who currently runs Summerhill, we might add other former Summerhillians like Goodsman (1992), Purdy (1997), Newman (2006), alongside educators who fell under Neill's influence as they searched for alternative approaches to schooling, such as John Aitkenhead, R. F. MacKenzie (1970), and Michael Duane (1971). Advocates of the Summerhill ideal, however, generally lack the uncritical, evangelical zeal that is something of a characteristic of supporters of other alternative educational thinkers, such as Steiner and Montessori. In fact, he went to some lengths to discourage discipleship, as was seen in the United States where he actively sought to stop people using the Summerhill name and associating themselves with his work.

Historians of education have generally taken Neill's significance for granted, although the precise nature of that significance is sometimes somewhat vague. Often, he is cited as a (presumably recognizable) representative of a certain tradition of educational thinking, although whether that tradition is a "progressive" one (e.g., Skidelsky 1969; Selleck 1972) or something more radical (e.g., Spring 1975; Suissa 2010) remains an open question. Child (1962), a former Principal of Dartington Hall School, felt comfortable to place Summerhill alongside such stalwarts of English progressivism as Bedales, King Alfred, and his own school, while Gray (2009) identified the publication of "Summerhill" as a pivotal inspiration for the radical education reforms espoused by the likes of Herbert Kohl, Jonathan Kozol, Neill Postman, Charles Weingartner, and Ivan Illich.

David Gribble's recent study "Real Education" (1998) discovered democratic schools offering varieties of freedom in countries ranging from Japan to Ecuador and from New Zealand to India, and these were found in a number of different settings intended for children of all ages and from many backgrounds. These were schools around the world that had been founded because of Neill's inspiration or which had borrowed or adopted many of his ideas for their philosophy. However, Ray Hemmings, in his 1972 book "Fifty Years of Freedom," was already finding that many of Neill's ideas had been misunderstood or were being diluted in the process of their adoption by other schools. Hemmings discovered that although Neill had had some influence on state schools, particularly in such matters as the development of friendlier relations between teachers and pupils, other things advocated by him, such as sexual liberalism and voluntary attendance of lessons, were much more frightening for the mainstream education system. The establishment of some school councils was also a pale shadow of the self-government envisioned by Neill. Most schools were still run by adults, and children were merely allowed a modicum of democracy or freedom by benevolent adults in charge.

There were two high-tides in Summerhill's fame and influence. The first was during the 1920s and 1930s. The second was during the 1960s and 1970s. Both of these coincided with periods of dramatic social change: the former when the liberal elite were searching for new ways to think and educate; the latter during the high tide of counter culture. Neill, himself, would have practiced his ideas regardless of the wider social milieu; however, their reception was certainly significantly influenced by the spirit of the ages.

It was in the 1920s that Neill became well known among teachers and readers of educational literature, and by the 1930s he had become an "educational celebrity" (Limond 1999 p. 86). In fact, he was probably Britain's first educational celebrity. The *Teacher* magazine described Neill as "the most popular writer on education today" (cited by Darling 1988, p. 41). Annabel Williams-Ellis, reviewing the five "Dominie" books for the *New Statesman* in 1924, wrote that they "are having a very distinct effect upon education both in the 'crank' and in the primary school. Nearly all the more alive and up-to-date teachers in Britain have read and argued about his notions" (cited in Croall 1983a, p. 153).

At this time, he was known as a charismatic and dogged spokesmen for the new psychology of psychoanalysis. His books, which were written in an unusually informal and accessible style, spoke of many of the themes that were occupying the minds of liberally minded readers, such as the tension between discipline and authority, and between the intellect and the emotions. They also sought alternatives to the traditional, didactic style of moral instruction that by the late 1930s had so obviously failed.

The publication of "Summerhill" in 1960 in the United States marked the birth of an American cult. The book quickly became a best-seller when it was published, and made the school a center of avant-garde, progressive education and made Neill a reluctant leader in a heated educational controversy. He came to "symbolize a decade of nonconformist fervour" (Saffrange 1994, p. 217). Summerhill-type schools started appearing across the country, and the "Summerhill Society" was established to give these new schools a sense of community.

While Summerhill School became a symbol of hope for many, the book "Summerhill" had a much greater impact. It was that rarest of things: a radical text that was easy to read and even funny! This was a departure from the standard, self-righteously angry progressive fare, and meant that individuals were able to discover Neill's ideas for themselves. Van Petten Henderson's (1957, p. 250) account Deweyan progressive surely applies with equal force to most movements:

> It is doubtful whether many teachers really understood (the Progressive Education Association's) Philosophical foundations. Certainly, few had studied Dewey's philosophy against any background of other philosophies ... To some extent the movement was popular because it constituted a revolt against the boring formalism of the traditional school.

Of course, Neill's writing generated a similar contempt with traditional schooling, but it was also able to communicate a set of relatively simple ideas and practices in a way that Dewey could not.

Radical educational critics embraced the book as evidence that their ideas were workable in practice. Writers like Kozol and Goodman envisioned free schools as creating idyllic enclaves, protected from the corrupting effects of wider society (Gartner et al. 1973; Goodman 1970; Mitchell 2007). Summerhill was otherworldly and Neill idiosyncratic enough to mean requirements: "for New Left students on our course campuses, Neill has become symbol as well as mentor" (Keohane 1970, p. 401).

A well-known example (at the time) was the "Children's Community School" (Kozol 1972). Following Summerhill, children were allowed to do what they liked when they liked, on the premise that both teaching and learning were most successful when most spontaneous. The mission was to treat the children with love and understanding, in hopes that violent thoughts would not consume the child's personality. There were no classes or grades and the children were allowed to come and go as they pleased. They wandered from room to room, free to choose from among sand tables, clay, blocks, and books. A child was taught to read or write only if he or she expressed a desire to learn. William Ayers, who later became a leading educational philosopher, was the driving force behind the school. Inspired by Neill's books, Ayer believed that children (who were as young as 3 and 4 years old) would ask someone to teach them to read as soon as they wanted to read. Unfortunately, that time never seemed to arrive (Powers 1971).

The school soon began running into problems. Ayers blamed the school's difficulties on harassment from local officials. He and some other teachers were central members of a self-described communist revolutionary group that conducted a campaign of bombing public buildings during the 1960s and 1970s, in response to US involvement in the Vietnam War. In fact, the school failed because parents were taking out their children due to fears that the libertarian environment meant that their children could not read, and were being turned into racists.

The extent of Neill's influence in America cannot neatly be measured by the sale of the books, or the number of schools that claimed an ancestry from Summerhill or have admitted to have been influenced by Neill. What is clear is that Neill's ideas and practices, which had been with him for 40 years, reflected the spirit of the age in 1960s' America, which made his ideas seem modern and relevant to a younger generation seeking new values. Herb Snitzer (1983, p. 56) claimed that "Neill influenced thousands of teachers." According to George Dennison, part of Neill's (and Reich's) appeal can be traced to his form of argument:

Such men allied themselves with forces and powers they believed existed in nature. The everyday phenomenon that led them to their beliefs affected other people too, and look so much like influence that it's hard to know where ideology ends and human nature begins. I think that Neill has being extremely influential even in schools that don't remotely resemble Summerhill. I don't mean that you find many teachers adapting his attitude in toto, but that you find important modifications all down the line, in schools and out, that can be traced to Neill and other libertarians. (Cited by Croall 1983a, pp. 262–3)

As Dennison recognized, it is difficult to point to many specific instances of "Summerhillian" educational innovations in schools. Aside from Summerhill itself, the most evident expressions of Neill's influence are the late-twentieth-century advocates of democratic education, deschooling, and homeschooling, like John Taylor Gatto (1992), John Holt (Meighan 2007), supporters of the International Democratic Education Network, and members of Alternative Education Resource Organization. Many of these have picked up Neill's ideas and adapted them for their contexts, providing energetic and radical critiques of the compulsion-based schooling that is still prevalent in almost all countries. And the central principles each of these thinkers and teachers has picked up from Neill relate to authority. As Neill reflected in his autobiography:

I do not want to be remembered as a great educator, for I am not. If I am to be remembered at all, I hope it will be because I tried to break down the gulf between young and old, tried to abolish fear in schools, tried to persuade teachers to be honest with themselves and drop the protective armour they have worn for generations as a separation from their pupils. (1972a, p. 20)

The extent to which the remarkable changes to standard practices of schooling that have taken place from the publication of Neill's first book in 1915 to the present day can be attributed to Neill's influence is obviously impossible to calculate. At the least, though, it might be suggested that Summerhill was an important part of a movement that has been transformatory. According to Paulo David, Secretary of the UN Committee on the Rights of the Child,

The convention of the Rights of the Child makes particular reference to children's rights to participate in decisions affecting them and Summerhill, through its very approach to education, embodies this right in a way that surpasses expectation.

Modern teachers have become sensitized to children's needs to the point where their relevance to their practice is often simply taken for granted. Teachers are cautious in their criticism of children and their efforts. They are aware that some types of information will be beyond some children's grasp at specific times, and efforts are made to represent information in ways that are accessible to the widest possible audience. Perhaps most significantly, there is a widespread reaction against the old-fashioned assumptions of schooling that placed the curriculum at the heart of the enterprise, and tried to fit children to it (Darling 1988). There can be little doubt that the characters of almost all schools in the developed world today are incomparably more nurturing, supportive and civilized places than they were when Neill was a child and a teacher.

Would these changes have taken place without Neill and Summerhill? Yes, they probably would. There were, after all, a number of other progressive educational thinkers, such as Homer Lane, Dora Russell, and the New Education Fellowship before World War II, and John Holt, Ivan Illich, and the radical educationists of the 1960s and 1970s. And it is worthwhile being reminded that what in hindsight became identified as the "child-centred" tradition in education stretched back from John Dewey and Maria Montessori to Froebel, Pestalozzi, and Jean-Jacques Rousseau (Cleverley and Phillips 1987; Darling 1988, 1994; Entwistle 1970).

Relevance

Neill and Summerhill were significant in the evolution of progressive approaches to schooling, both in the United Kingdom and around the world. The standard progressive response to Neill's work goes something like this: his ideas were exciting and provocative, but Neill took them too far, and they would not work in the real world. This line of criticism fails on a number of counts. First, it is patently false that these ideas could not work in practice, because they did. Unlike almost any other high-profile progressive writer, Neill actually established and ran a school. Second, while Summerhill cannot be considered a template to be replicated by other schools, it can be considered as a type of experiment to be studied.

Indeed, Neill and a number of commentators have used precisely this language (e.g., Neill 1953, Croall 1983a; Carr 2002; Child 1962). Even by the time of the publication of "Summerhill" in the 1960s, Neill was still able to write: "We set out to let children alone so that we might discover what they were like ... The pioneer school of the future must pursue this way if it is to contribute to child knowledge, and, more important, to child happiness" (1960, pp. 108–9). This is the perspective of an experimental school.

Darling suggests that the popular description of Summerhill as an experimental school is not accurate. He points out accurately that Neill's approach to schooling came from a strong personal conviction. Summerhill was not a setting for studying children in the natural settings; "this policy was followed because it was thought to be beneficial the children to be treated like this" (Darling 1988, p. 47). Neill is not the observer, let alone the dispassionate scientist. His stance is not that of the researcher; it is that of the advocate.

Neill certainly did not assume the role of a researcher or scientist. However, perhaps Darling's conception of an experiment is too restrictive. Neill was neither dispassionate nor objective in his approach to innovation. But then, as was being discovered by philosophers of science at about the same time as Summerhill was developing, no enquiry is ever like that (Phillips 1987). Science's objectivity does not come from some idealized position of impartiality, but from intersubjective testing and criticizing (Bailey 2000). And pace Darling (1988), there does seem a sense throughout Neill's writings that he sought to "try out" ideas and practices to discover how they worked, especially during Neill-the-teacher's formative years. If this is accepted, Summerhill may well be the longest running educational experiment there has ever been.

The nomenclature of Summerhill as an experimental school is not incompatible with a second label: demonstration school. This was a label with which Neill was more comfortable, even from the earliest days of Summerhill:

> Visitors come to see my 'experiment'. But there is no experiment. There is only a demonstration. In an experiment one tries to see what will happen; in a demonstration one knows what will happen. (Neill 1928, p. 70)

It is certainly true that Neill did not set up a school as a setting for study. Summerhill was established in its form because Neill believed that it was in the interests of the children that it was that way. His practices, such as voluntary attendance at lessons and self-government, were not primarily hypotheses he was testing, but things he had worked out for himself or were adapted from people he admired like Homer Lane.

It has been argued that Neill's philosophy and practice were inspired by an unconstrained vision of human nature. Part of his impatience with most so-called education was that he felt it failed to follow the logical consequences of their guiding presumptions, and of the unconstrained vision. So, they ended up using the language of freedom, while ultimately falling back into practices of repression. For his part, Neill thought that he was taking child-centered ideas and practices to their logical conclusions. His critics, and even some friends, argued that he had taken them to the point where if they were any more radical they would become incompatible with any kind of schooling (Darling 1988, p. 72). His vision is an extreme; the end of a continuum. This makes enough great academic interest. But what makes it even more interesting is that, almost unknown among progressive theorists, Neill puts his ideas into practice. This does not mean, of course, that the lessons learned at Summerhill are necessarily transferable to all schools. Many progressive educational initiatives were developed in the private sector where the context of residential schooling, in rural locations with small classes and shared ideals between parents and teachers, meant that the progressive pedagogical practices were often hardly transferable to the world of universal compulsory schooling (Cunningham 2001).

Neill himself came to recognize this issue. During the first half of his career, he expressed a hope that a socialist state would create a national system of boarding schools that would be similar to Summerhill: "Naturally, I want to specify that such a school will be a free school, with self-government and self-determination of the individual child, that is, I visualize a nation of Summerhills" (Neill 1944, pp. 19–32). Neill dreamt of spreading the free school idea through the world; he even wrote to Henry Ford to suggest the production of school caravans to carry Summerhill's message to other countries (Spring 2006). Gradually, though, he had a change of heart, and abandoned his grand ambitions of social change through schools like Summerhill: "I have to compromise . . . realising that my primary job is not the rest formation of society, but the bringing of happiness to some few children" (Neill 1960, p. 35).

Darling (1988) seems to doubt the literal meaning of Neill's abandonment of a wider responsibility for Summerhill. Instead, he suggested, Neill was really just acknowledging that social reform does not necessarily mean changing society; it can begin by changing individuals: "Given Neill's views, this is not an irresponsible flight from political involvement, (as some have seen it), but hard-headed realism" (Darling 1988, p. 45). Neill sought to walk a difficult balance between idealism and realism throughout his career. He was aware that unfiltered messages from the likes of Homer, and especially Reich, could result in the closure of Summerhill, and the end of his message. He was also aware that the existence of Summerhill also rested on the fact that many of the elements of the unconstrained vision were seen through to what Neill thought to be their logical conclusions.

Much of Neill's writing, and that of the Summerhillians who followed him, present the school as a heroic challenge to traditional schools. Most social groups seek to perpetuate their existence and identity over time through a combination of rational, bureaucratic structures and "dynamic conservatism" (ibid., p. 312) that fights to stay the same. Some groups, however, set out deliberately to combat the innate tendency to "dynamic conservatism" and form "anti-institutions" (ibid.). Schools and teachers are usually the paradigm cases of functionaries of the state (Flanagan 2006, p. 4). They transmit beliefs and values, and are generally restricted in the range of aims and methods they are allowed to employ.

According to Durkheim (1956, p. 81), it is taken for granted that the state must, "see to it that nowhere our children left ignorant of [the necessary principles and values], that everywhere they should we spoken of with the respect which is tuned them." So, children need to be intellectually initiated into society by means of the frame work of conceptual structures through which they can comprehend the world. Jeffcoate (1979) distinguished this "transmissionist" approach to schooling—because it was concerned primarily with the transmission of relatively established knowledge and values—from the "transformationalist" approach—that maintains that schools are fundamentally concerned with the transformation of community values. Neill himself was not sufficiently interested in curriculum issues to worry about such matters. And for that reason, perhaps, his lack of interest resulted in a fundamental inconsistency within some of his practices. Nevertheless, there is little doubt that he sought to undermine many of the assumptions that he thought repressed and sickened society.

Dissent and conflict framed Neill's philosophy, and Summerhill is the "archetypal alternative school" (Darling 1994, p. 244). Indeed, he often positioned Summerhill as what Maurice Punch (1974a) called an "anti-institution." An anti-institution is a social group that deliberately sets out to combat a tendency toward conservatism, while most social groups try to perpetuate their existence and identity over time through a combination of rational, bureaucratic structures and "dynamic conservatism" (ibid., p. 312) that fights to stay the same. Summerhill, especially when combined with Neill's extreme individualism, could be counted as a paradigm case of an anti-institution, and combat what was seen as the deadening hand of tradition and conservatism. Indeed, Punch's (1974b) account captures certain elements of the spirit of Summerhill very well:

> It is an attempt to live perpetually on the margin, resisting the encroachment of formalisation. It is the attempt to retain the spontaneous, immediate, ephemeral joys of 'communitas' against the fate of 'declining into the norm-governed, institutionalised, abstract nature of law and social structure." (p. 312)

Goodsman, a Summerhillian, captures the essence of this when she writes, "Summerhillians found mainstream education wanting. Nevertheless, the mainstream was culturally important as the 'other' against which the school defined itself" (Goodsman 1992, p. 225). Likewise, Stewart (1968, p. 292), a critical friend, wrote, "In most senses Summerhill opposes the society in which it is set and the values on which it is based" (Stewart 1968, p. 292).

Neill was fond of quoting a sentiment from one of his favorite authors, Ibsen, that "the strongest man is he who stands alone" (Croall 1983a, p. xii). This was a position in which he often found himself, even within the company of the Progressive school movement. While he developed friendships with a small number of other educators, such as Bertrand Russell and Curry of Dartington Hall, these are the exceptions, and only serve to underline his isolation from the "moulders," "moralisers," and "highlifers," Perhaps it is not a coincidence that his closest friendships were with Homer Lane and Wilhelm Reich, both antiestablishment figures, subject to criminal convictions, and both died shortly after their sentence. Neill recognized this himself; to Reich he wrote: "We both at to think of the world is gegen [against] us" (In Croall 1983b, p. 320). Neill was undoubtedly more realistic and politically aware then either Lane and Reich. Both of them were all-or-nothing at thinkers. As a school teacher, Neill recognized that he needed to compromise on some issues like sex, or the future of the school would be undermined. But Neill retained an imprint of Lane and Reich's approach throughout his life, and especially in his rhetorical writing. He also followed them in defining himself and his work primarily in contrast to the mainstream.

Implicit within his worldview was a recognition that consensus can mean conformity, which can result in a suffocating "political correctness." In systems like education, therefore, dissenters' insights can be useful, even vital. The legal scholar Cass Sunstein (2005) has argued that it is in society's best interest to discourage conformity and rigidity, and to promote opinions and ideas. And the vehicles for this are dissent and dissenters: "The general lesson is clear. Organisation and nations are far more likely to prosper if they welcome dissent and promote openness. Well-functioning societies benefit from a wide range of views ..." (pp. 210–11). Yet, even in democracies that pride themselves on their tolerance of difference, social (and sometimes political, economic, and legal) pressures always exert a pull toward conformity, and the pressure placed on dissenters to conform can be great.

This may prove to be the greatest legacy of Summerhill: "Through the continued functioning of Summerhill, a new generation of educators is reminded that radical ideas can be made to work" (Darling 1994, p. 251). Only a small number of radical educational thinkers have tried to put their ideas into practice, and even fewer have succeeded. Most alternative schools have been rather short-lived affairs, torn apart by internal conflicts or beleaguered by government hostility. But Neill always positioned himself as an outsider, repeatedly condemned the progressives of his youth as much as the traditionalists, and continued to defy classification. In fact, even the way Summerhill conducted its battles with government inspectors in the 1990s was distinctive. Instead of adopting what might have initially seemed to be the most plausible defense available to them, by "addressing the broader social implications of the threat by a centralist government to an alternative school and broadening support for their campaign by engaging with other groups (such as struggling comprehensive schools in deprived areas, frustrated teachers and parents) who felt their autonomy and rights to make educational choices similarly threatened – the school community chose to focus their campaign on the particular validity of Neill's educational philosophy and their rights to defend this philosophy against that of the mainstream educational establishment" (Suissa 2010, pp. 96–7).

The education authorities have never accepted Summerhill. When they went back on their decision to close the school, some, as Hemmings (1972, p. 241) noted, interpreted this not so much as a mark of recognition as a kind of tolerance of "a mere relic." Others, however, were able to find inspiration by the fact that a school with Summerhill's aims was able to exist at all. For all of its flaws and inconsistencies, the school represents the practical realization of the unconstrained vision, and its translation into an approach to schooling based on trust, freedom, and democracy. Neill, himself, was aware of both the limitations and necessity of his school: "The future of Summerhill itself may be of little import. But the future of the Summerhill idea is of the greatest importance to humanity. New generations must be given the chance to grow in freedom. The bestowal of freedom is the bestowal of love" (1962, p. 92).

Chapter 5

Conclusion

Whether or not Neill thought of Summerhill as an experiment, it can certainly be seen this way from the point of view of the wider education system. There is an essential tension between conformity and dissent within any social system. Schooling and other social structures embody a set of values, assumptions, and core practices that give it shape and character through time. In most cases, conformity is a sensible course of action, as lacking sufficient knowledge ourselves, we tend to rely on tradition and the judgment of others to provide relatively reliable decisions on our behalf. There are times, however, when following the crowd is problematic. An intolerant conformity deprives the public of potentially valuable information. Innovations and other departures from the norm test aspects of the system, and potentially introduce new knowledge into it. These views reflect the inherently conservative nature of most social systems: they seek to ensure their continued existence.

Cass Sunstein (2005) highlights an irony at the heart of this situation. Conformists are often respected for protecting social interests by staying with the majority. In contrast, dissenters tend to be characterized as extreme individualists or egoists who put themselves and their views ahead of the group. But, Sunstein argues, the opposite is often the case, as it is the dissenters who benefit the group, and the conformists who only protect their own interests: "conformists are free-riders, benefitting from the actions of others without adding anything of their own ... By contrast, dissenters often confer benefits to others, offering information and ideas from which the community gains a great deal" (p. 12).

John Stuart Mill is the philosopher possibly most associated with the defense of dissent in society. "On Liberty" contains his justification of the freedom of the individual in opposition to the claims of the state to impose control. In this essay, Mill also warns of a second danger to liberty, which democracies are prone to, namely, the tyranny of the majority:

> Like other tyrannies, the tyranny of the majority was at first, and is still vulgarly, held in dread, chiefly as operating through the acts of the public authorities. But reflecting persons perceived that when society is itself the tyrant — society collectively over the separate individuals who compose it — its means of tyrannizing are not restricted to the acts which it may do by the hands of its political functionaries. Society can and does execute its own mandates ... Protection, therefore, against the tyranny of the magistrate is not enough; there needs protection also against the tyranny of the prevailing opinion and feeling, against the tendency of society to impose, by other means than civil penalties, its own ideas and practices as rules of conduct on those who dissent from them; to fetter the development and, if possible, prevent the formation of any individuality not in harmony with its ways, and compel all characters to fashion themselves upon the model of its own. (Mill 1859, p. 13)

Of course, social cohesion is an important quality of any group, and dissent is not always worthwhile. But dissent can often provide a corrective to action, if it is allowed to be expressed. Numerous empirical studies have highlighted the dangers of insulated forms of "groupthink" in terms of narrow and inflexible decision-making, and an increased risk of failure (e.g., Tetlock et al. 1992).

Openness to new ideas, including those from outside the group, is an important element of effective decision-making. In settings like education, where the empirical basis of much of the conventional practice is limited, and in which even core questions of aims and purpose are contested, tolerance of diversity would seem somewhat essential.

Neill's ideas have attracted a great deal of attention since he first started presenting them early in the twentieth century. Typically, discussion has tended toward extremes. For example, contributors to the collection "Summerhill: For and Against" (Hart 1970) offered almost incommensurable interpretations, with one writer saying that he would rather send his children to a brothel than to Summerhill, while another called it a "holy place" (ibid., pp. 17 and 28). Today, Neill and Summerhill are not as directly influential as they once were. There are very few schools that seek to replicate the Summerhill effect. Neill's books, while still read, have nothing of the influence they once had, are rarely taught within universities, and when they are discussed, they are generally viewed as historical oddities.

There is another way in which a thinker or his school might influence practice, and that is by nudging the development of ideas in one way or another. In this respect, it seems almost unarguable that Neill and Summerhill are of enormous significance. Modern-day education systems are never the result of rational planning and implementation alone. The footprint of history is indelibly marked on them. While Neill would almost certainly not recognize today's education methods as "Summerhillian," he would have to acknowledge that the general tone of state schooling is significantly different from that even 50 years earlier, and that a form of progressivism is simply taken for granted by teachers in almost all schools. And such a dramatic change is due, in no small part, to the actions of thinkers like Neill. According to Purdy (1997), a former teacher at Summerhill, it is difficult to identify any direct impact on the attitude of the state system of education toward the self-determination of children from Neill's work. But, he claims, Neill had a marked effect on the wider social environment of schooling. Importantly, Neill was not simply one member of a school of thought. He stood alone, and articulated a vision of schooling that was viewed by many to be extreme and unrealistic. The fact that he was able to realize his vision could be said to have offered a degree of confidence to those for whom the mild liberalism of the new education movement was simply not enough.

For a "thinker," Neill had a surprising aversion to theory. Although a prolific writer, what he wrote was often no more than outbursts of enthusiasm, vehement assertions, anecdotes, and indignant reactions, but also, it must be admitted, it consisted of oversimplified arguments. He neither troubled to present his ideas in a logical sequence nor to ascertain if they corresponded to reality. Bates Ames (1970, p. 75) wrote that "Neill constructs a theory of how a child thinks, and what he things the child needs, and even when that theory is refuted by all the objective evidence, he still insists on treating children as if they were as he imagined them to be." Actually, Neill was driven by his intuitive vision of the children as innately good and wise. So, unlike his contemporaries, Nell never approached educational problems in terms of needs but in terms of rights. Even when he borrowed the term of "self-regulation" from Reich, it was to say that it meant "the right of a baby to live freely without outside authority in things psychic and somatic" (1953, p. 42). This explains why his books and articles were often misunderstood and distorted. Later in life, he was still surprised to have written for years without having succeeded in clarifying his core beliefs and actions.

In some respects, Neill's educational project was really complete by 1914, before he had met Lane or Reich, and before he had read a single educational book: "These bairns ... have done what they liked ... I know that I have brought out all their innate goodness" (1915, pp. 151–2). From this perspective, his subsequent books and articles are simply variations on this theme, and his interactions were all used to confirm that theme. And aversion to "theory" meant that, in practice, many of these assumptions were never put under the light of reflection of criticism. He did not adequately distinguish between abstract theory in the academic sense and practical theory that is a necessary feature of all action. So, in many central ways, Neill remained enslaved by traditional models or theories. Nowhere is this more obvious and then in his views on the curriculum. He simply did not see it as an issue requiring serious thought. He was enslaved by a narrow and traditional view of knowledge because he had no conception of any alternative view. Indeed, it never occurred to him that this was something on which they could be an alternative view. And therein lay his problem: "Those who shun theory become the prisoners of theory" (Darling 1988, p. 82).

Radical schools have an inherently valuable function to offer alternatives to state-funded schools. Alternative forms of schooling have a long history of being used as experimental laboratories for field-testing and validating innovative educational ideas and practices. Ideas that have merit in these alternative settings have the potential for use in the wider educational environment. These types of schools have been instrumental in developing new curricula and different learning models, with examples including education for disruptive students, open education, and behavior modification. Other such models include the Montessori system, kindergarten movement, and Steiner-Wardorf schools, Outward Board, and others. Elements from each of these have leaked into the mainstream. Indeed, the whole enterprise of radical schooling can be considered a strategy for school reform, whether it is within or outside of the system. These schools have introduced new concepts and expectations, as well as new ways of thinking about learning, curriculum, and teaching.

Neill's philosophy and practices were an expression of a vision of human nature as unconstrained, characterized by an intuitive sense that children are good and kind, and that, given the right environment, love, respect, and trust toward others will naturally develop. Many others have held a similar vision, but it is difficult to think of another who has so doggedly sought to follow through the implications so wholeheartedly. His notions of freedom and democracy, still considered controversial, have nonetheless influenced others. It is as if the extreme character of Neill's views has shifted the center of gravity of educational debate. He was one of a small group of radical educational thinkers whose persistence, charisma, and dogmatism forced a sea change on teachers and schools

> Neill more than anyone else has swung teachers' opinion ... from its old reliance on authority and the cane to hesitant recognition that a child's first need is love, and with love respect for the free growth of his personality; free that is from the arbitrary compulsion of elders, and disciplined instead by social experience. Today's friendliness between pupil and teacher is probably the greatest difference between the classrooms of 1963 and those of 1923. This change owes much to Neill. (Pedley 1963, p. 174)

Summerhill, on the other hand, remains a pedagogical site of "radical democratic practice" (Dolby 2003, p. 264), and it was once suggested by government inspectors that Summerhill constituted a "piece of fascinating educational research" (Ministry of Education 1949). Will Neill join that small group of educational pioneers, such as Froebel, Dewey, and Steiner, whose legacy continues for a long time after their death? Time will tell. However, Summerhill has remained the most consistent and the most extreme of the radical schools. Whether or not it ought to be considered an experimental school is not really the issue; its doggedness, not to mention its longevity, provides a unique resource for those interested in educational thinking.

References

Abercrombie, J. (1969), *The Anatomy of Judgement*. Harmondsworth: Penguin.

Allender, D. and Allender, J. (2006), How Did Our Early Education Determine Who We Are as Teachers? Proceedings of the Sixth International Conference on Self-Study of Teacher Education Practices. Herstmonceux Castle, England.

Anderson, R. D. (1995), *Education and the Scottish People 1750–1918*. Oxford: Clarendon Press.

Appleton, M. (2000), *A Free Range Childhood: Self Regulation at Summerhill School*. Brandon, VT: Foundation for Educational Renewal.

Arthur, M. (2003), *Forgotten Voices of the Great War*. London: Ebury Press.

Auden, W. H. (1933), *Poems* (second edition). London: Faber and Faber.

Ayers, W. (2003), *On the Side of the Child: Summerhill Revisited*. New York: Teachers College Press.

Badley, J. H. (1923), *Head Master, Bedales: A Pioneer School*. London: Methuen.

Bailey, R. P. (2000), *Education in the Open Society: Karl Popper and Schooling*. Aldershot: Ashgate.

Bailey, R. P. (2007), Talent Development and the Luck Problem. *Sport, Ethics and Philosophy* 1(3): 367–77.

Bailey, R. P., Carr, D., Barrow, R. and McCarthy, C. (2010), *Handbook of the Philosophy of Education*. London: Sage.

Baker, E. F. (1967), *Man in the Trap: The Causes of Blocked Sexual Energy*. New York: Avon Books.

Bantock, G. H. (1980), *Studies in the History of Educational Theory. Volumes 1: Artifice and Nature, 1350–1765*. London, George Allen and Unwin.

— (1984), *Studies in the History of Educational Theory. Volume 2: The Minds and the Masses 1760–1980*. London, George Allen and Unwin.

Barnard, H. C. (1961), *A Short History of English Education, 1760–1944*. London: Hodder and Stoughton.

Barrow, R. (1978), *Radical Education: A Critique of Freeschooling and Deschooling*. New York: John Wiley and Sons.

Bates-Ames, L. (1970), In H. Hart (ed.), *Summerhill, For and Against*. New York: Hart Publishing.

Bazeley, E. T. (1928), *Homer Lane and the Little Commonwealth*. London: Unwin and Allen.

Beck, J. and Earl, M. (2003), *Key Issues in Secondary Education*. London: Continuum.

Berg, L. (1968), *Risinghill: Death of a Comprehensive School*. Harmonsdworth: Penguin.

Berlin, I. (1969), *Two Concepts of Liberty. In Four Essays on Liberty*. Oxford: Oxford University Press.

—(1978), *Russian Thinkers* (ed. H. Hardy and A. Kelly). Harmondsworth: Penguin.

—(1991), *The Crooked Timbre of Humanity*. London: Fontana.

Bernstein, E. (1967), Summerhill: After 50 years the First Follow-up. *The New Era* 48(2): 30.

—(1968a), Summerhill: A Follow-up Study of its Students. *Journal of Humanistic Psychology* 8: 123–36.

—(1968b), What does a Summerhill Old School Tie look like? *Psychology Today*, October: 38–41: 70.

Bettelheim, B. (1970), In H. Hart (ed.) *Summerhill: For and Against*. New York: Hart Publishing.

Blavatsky, H. P. (1893), *The Key to Theosophy*: Being a Clear Exposition, in the Form of Question and Answer, of the Ethics, Science, and Philosophy for the Study of which the Theosophical Society has been Founded. London: Theosophical Publishing Company.

Boadella, D. (1983), *Wilhelm Reich: Leben und Werk des Mannes, der in der Sexualitt das Problem der modernen Gesellschaft erkannte und der Psychologie neue Wege wies* [Wilhelm Reich: life and work of the man who saw the problem of sexuality in modern society and whose psychology showed new ways]. Munich, Germany: Scherz.

Boyd, W. and Rawson, W. (1965), *The Story of the New Education*. London: Heinemann Educational Books.

Brehony, K. J. (1997), A Dedicated Spiritual Movement: Theosophists and Education 1875–1939. Faiths and Education, XIX International Standing Conference for the History of Education at National University of Ireland Maynooth. 3rd–6th September, 1997.

—(2004), A New Education for a New Era: The Contribution of the Conferences of the New Education Fellowship to the Disciplinary Field of Education, 1921–1938. *Paedagogica Historica* 40(5 and 6): 733–55.

Brown, G. D. (1901), The House with the Green Shutters. London: John MacQueen.

Campbell, B. F. (1980), *Ancient Wisdom Revived*. Berkeley, CA: University of California Press.

Carleton, J. (1991), Self-regulation Part I: Its roots in Reich and Neill. *Journal of Orgonomy* 25(1): 68–81.

Carr, D. (1982), Education and the Promotion of Human Freedom. *Educational Philosophy and Theory* 14: 37–49.

—(1984), Moral Philosophy and Psychology in Progressive and Traditional Educational Thought. *Journal of Philosophy of Education* 18(1): 41–53.

—(1985), The Free Child and the Spoiled Child: Anatomy of a Progressive Distinction. *Journal of Philosophy of Education* 19: 55–63.

—(1988), Knowledge and Curriculum: Four Dogmas of Child-centred Education. *Journal of Philosophy of Education* 22: 151–62.

Carr, D. (2002). Moral education and the perils of developmentalism. Journal of Moral Education, 31(1), 5–19.

Chamberlin, R. (1989), *Free Children and Democratic Schools: A Philosophical Study of Liberty and Education.* New York: Falmer.

Child, H. A. T. (ed.) (1962), *The Independent Progressive School.* London: Hutchinson.

Chitty C. (2004), *Education Policy in Britain.* Basingstoke: Palgrave Macmillan.

Clark, R. (1970), *Crime in America.* New York: Simon and Schuster.

Cleverley, J. and Phillips D. C. (1986), *Visions of Childhood: Influential Models from Locke to Spock.* New York: Teachers College Press.

—(1987), *Visions of Childhood: Influential Models from Locke to Spock.* Sydney: Allen and Unwin.

Cohen, B. (1981), *Education and the Individual.* London: Unwin.

Collini, S. (ed.) (1993), *Arnold: Culture and Anarchy and Other Writings.* Cambridge: Cambridge University Press.

Coué, E. (1922), Self-mastery through Conscious Autosuggestion. New York: American Library Service.

Cox, C. and Dyson, A. (eds) (1969), *Black Paper 2: The Crisis in Education.* London: Critical Quarterly Society.

Croall, J. (1983a), *Neill of Summerhill: The Permanent Rebel.* London: Routledge and Kegan Paul.

Croall, J. (ed.) (1983b), *All the Best, Neill: Letters from Summerhill.* London: André Deutsch.

Cunningham, P. (2001), Innovators, Networks and Structures: Towards a Prosopography of Progressivism. *History of Education* 30(5): 433–51.

Darling, J. (1984), A. S. Neill on Knowledge and Learning. *British Journal of Educational Studies* 32: 158–71.

—(1986), Child-Centred, Gender-Centred: A Criticism of Progressive Curriculum Theory from Rousseau to Plowden. *Oxford Review of Education* 12(1): 31–40.

—(1988), Child-centred Education and the recent Philosophical Critique. Unpublished Doctoral Thesis, University of Aberdeen.

—(1994), *Child-Centred Education and its Critics.* London: Paul Chapman.

De Mendelssohn, P. (1954), *Marianne: der Roman eines Films und der Film eines Romans* [Marianne: the novel of a film and the film of a novel]. Munich: Kindler.

—(1993), *Hellerau: mein unverlierbares Europa* [Hellerau: my captive Europe]. Dresden, Germany: Dresden-Hellerau Verlag.

Dennison, G. (1969), *The Lives of Children.* New York: Random House.

Dolby, N. (2003), Popular culture and democratic practice. Harvard Educational Review, 73(3), 258–84.

Deutsch, D. (1962), Outdated Radicalism. *Journal of Individual Psychology* 18: 194–6.

Duane, M. (1971), Neill and Summerhill. Unpublished manuscript. Available from http://www.risinghill.co.uk/NeillandSummerhill.htm (accessed 16 July 2011).

Durkheim, É. (1956), *Education and Sociology* (trans. S. D. Fox). Glencoe, IL: Free Press.

Eisner, E. (1971), The Metaphor and the Measure: Controversies in Educational Practice. *Contemporary Psychology* 16(3): 164–6.

Ensor, B. (1920a), Note. *Education for a New Era* 1(1): 67, 113.

— (1920b), The Outlook Tower. *The New Era* 2: 125–7, 155–8.

— (1921), The Outlook Tower. *The New Era* 2: 155–8.

Entwistle, H. (1970), *Child-Centred Education*. London: Methuen.

Ferrière, A. (1922), *L'École Active* [The Active School]. Geneva, Switzerland: Editions Forums.

Fielding, M. (2001), OFSTED, Inspection and the Betrayal of Democracy. *Journal of Philosophy of Education* 35(4): 695–709.

Flanagan, F. M. (2006), *The Greatest Educators . . . Ever!* London: Continuum.

Francis, P. (1975), *Beyond Control: A Study of Discipline in the Comprehensive School*. London: George Allen and Unwin.

Freedman, D. M. and Marshall, J. D. (2011), A. S. Neill (1883–1973): Early Life and Career, Significance to Education. http://education.stateuniversity.com/pages/2292/Neill-S-1883–1973.html (accessed 4 July 2011).

Friedman, N. (1974), Education and the Transformation of the Self: An Essay on Neill! Neill! Orange Peel!. *The School Review* 82(3): 495–514.

Fromm, E. (1959), *Psychoanalysis and Religion*. New Haven, CT: Yale University Press.

— (1960), Foreword. In A. S. Neill (ed.) Summerhill. New York: Hart Publishing.

— (1970), In H. Hart (ed.) Summerhill, For and Against. New York: Hart Publishing.

Gartner, A., Green, C. and Riessman, F. (eds) (1973), *After Deschooling, What?* New York: Harper and Row.

Gatto, J. T. (1992), *Dumbing Us Down: The Hidden Curriculum of Compulsory Schooling*. Philadelphia, PA: New Society Publishers.

Geheeb, P. (2009), Allocution de Paul Geheeb à ses collaborateurs et élèves à la reprise du travail éducatif à Versoix le 17 avril 1934 [Remarks by Paul Geheeb to employees and students at the resumption of educational work in Versoix 17 April 1934]. In H. Näf, Une école humaine. L'École d'Humanité vue de l'intérieur [A human school. The School of Humanity from the inside]. Berne, Switzerland: Zytglogge.

Godwin, W. (1969), *Enquiry Concerning Political Justice–Volume 1*. Toronto, Canada: University of Toronto Press.

Goodman, P. (1962), *Compulsory Mis-Education*. New York: Vintage.

—(1970), In H. Hart (ed.) Summerhill, For and Against. New York: Hart Publishing.

Goodsman, D. (1992), Summerhill: Theory and Practice. Unpublished Doctoral Thesis, UK: University of East Anglia.

Gorham, D. (2005), Dora and Bertrand Russell and Beacon Hill School. *Russell: The Journal of Bertrand Russell Studies* 23: 39–76.

Gray, T. (2009), Fun City: Kenneth Koch among Schoolchildren. Texas Studies in Literature & Language, 51(2), 223–62.

Gribble, D. (1998), *Real Education: Varieties of Freedom*. Bristol: Libertarian Education.

Hameline, D. (1985), *Preface. Libres regards sur Summerhill: L'oeuvre pédagogique de A. S. Neill* [Fresh Eyes on Summerhill: the educational work of A. S. Neill]. Berne, Switzerland: Peter Lang.

Hart, H. (1975), *The Dominie Books of A. S. Neill*. New York: Hart Publishing.

—(ed.) (1970), *Summerhill: For and Against*. New York: Hart Publishing.

Haynes J. E. (2000), *Red Scare or Red Menace? American Communism and Anti-Communism in the Cold War*. Chicago, IL: Ivan R. Dee.

Hechinger, F. (1970), In H. Hart (ed.) Summerhill, For and Against. New York: Hart Publishing.

Heelas, P. (1996), *The New Age Movement: Religion, Culture and Society in the Age of Postmodernity*. Cambridge, MA: Blackwell Publishing.

Hemmings, R. (1972), *Fifty Years of Freedom: A Study of the Development of the Ideas of Alexander Sutherland Neill*. London: Allen and Unwin.

Hendrie, W. F. (1997), *The Dominie: A Profile of the Scottish Headmaster*. Edinburgh: John Donald.

Her Majesty's Inspectorate (HMI) (1990), Summerhill School, Leiston, Suffolk: 12–16 May 1990. A report by HMI. London: Department of Education and Science.

Hobbes, T. (1651/1996), *Leviathan* (Ed. R. Tuck). Cambridge: Cambridge University Press.

Hobson, P. (2001), A. S. Neill. In J. A. Palmer (ed.), *Fifty Modern Thinkers on Education: From Piaget to the Present*. London: Routledge.

Holmes, E. (1911), *Is and What Might Be*. London: Constable and Co.

Holmes, H. (ed.) (2000), *Scottish Life and Society Volume 11: Institutions of Scotland: Education*. East Linton: Tuckwell Press.

Holt, J. (1969), *How Children Fail*. Harmondsworth: Penguin.

—(1973), *Freedom and Beyond*. Harmondsworth: Penguin.

Hopkins, R. L. (1976), Freedom and Education: The Philosophy of Summerhill. *Educational Theory* 26: 188–213.

Illich, I. (1973), *Deschooling Society*. Harmondsworth: Penguin.

Isherwood, C. (1977), *Lions and Shadows*. New York: New Directions Publishing.

Jeffcoate, R. (1979), *Positive Image: Towards a Multiracial Curriculum*. London: Writers and Readers Publishing Cooperative.

Jenkins, C. (2000), New Education and Its Emancipatory Interests, 1920–1950. *History of Education* 29(2): 139–51.

Kafka, F. (1977), *Letters to Friends, Family, and Editors* (trans. R. and C. Winston). New York: Schocken Books.

Kamp, J.-M. (1994), Kinderrepubliken. Geschichte, Praxis und Theorie radikaler Selbstregierung in Kinder- und Jugendheimen [Children's Republics. The history, theory and practice of radical self-government in children's and youth centers]. Unpublished Doctoral Thesis, Germany: University of Essen.

Kamp, M. (1998), *Die Pädagogik A. S. Neills* [A. S. Neill's Pedgagogy]. Hagen, Germany: Fernuniversität-Gesemthochschule.

Keohane, M. (1970), A. S. Neill: Latter-Day Dewey? *The Elementary School Journal* 70(8): 401–10.

Kohl, H. (1967), *36 Children*. New York: New American Library.

— (2005), Series Foreword. In W. Ayers (ed.), *On the Side of the Child: Summerhill Revisited*. New York: Teachers College Press.

Kornegger, P. (2009), *Living with Spirit: Journey of a Flower Child*. Indianapolis, IN: Dog Ear Publishing.

Kozol, J. (1967), *Death at an Early Age*. Boston, MA: Houghton Mifflin.

— (1972), *Free Schools*. Boston, MA: Houghton Mifflin.

Krogh, S. L. and Slentz, K. L. (2001), *The Early Childhood Curriculum*. Mahwah, NJ: Press Incorporated.

Kühn, A. (2002), A. S. Neill und Summerhill: Eine Rezeptions- und Wirkungsanalyse [A. S. Neill and Summerhill: an analysis of reception and effects]. Unpublished Doctoral Thesis, Tübingen, Germany: Eberhard-Karls University.

Kühn, A. D. (1995), *Alexander S. Neill*. Hamburg, Germany: Reinbek.

Lamb, A. (1992a), The Experience of Summerhill. *SKOLE: The Journal of Alternative Education* 8(1): 1–14.

— (1992b), *The New Summerhill*. London: Penguin.

Lane, H. (1928), *Talks to Parents and Teachers*. London: Allen and Unwin.

Lange de Souza, D. (2000), Holistic Education: Learning from their Experiences of Three Holistic Teachers. Unpublished Doctoral Thesis, Cambridge, MA: Harvard University.

Lawson, M. (1981), The New Education Fellowship: the formative years. *Journal of Educational Administrative and History* 13(9/0): 24–8.

Lawson, M. and Petersen, R. (1972), *Progressive Education: An Introduction*. Sydney, Australia: Angus and Robertson.

Lawton, D. (1977). Education and social justice. London, Sage Publications.

LeShan, E. (1970), In H. Hart (ed.) Summerhill, For and Against. New York: Hart Publishing.

Leue, M. (1989), Whaddya Mean, Free. *SKOLE: The Journal of Alternative Education* 5(1): 60–66.

Lieberman, D. A. (2000), *Learning: Behavior and Cognition*. Belmont, CA: Wadsworth/Thompson Learning.

Limond, D. (1999), '[A]ll our Scotch education is in vain': The construction of Scottish national identity in and by the early Dominie books of A. S. Neill. *History of Education* 28: 297–312.

Lippmann, W. (1965), *Public Opinion*. New York: Free Press.

Lister, I. (ed.) (1974), *Deschooling: A Reader*. Cambridge: Cambridge University Press.

Lucas, H. (2011), *After Summerhill: What Happened to the Pupils of Britain's Most Radical School?* Bristol: Pomegranate Books.

Lucas, H. and Lamb, A. (2000), Neill's Diamonds. An oral history of Summerhill School. Unpublished manuscript.

Mack, E. C. (1971), *Public Schools and British Opinion Since 1860*. Westport, CT: Greenwood.

Mackenzie, R. F. (1970), *State School*. Harmondsworth: Penguin.

Macleod, D. (2001), Scottish Calvinism: A Dark, Repressive Force? *Scottish Bulletin of Evangelical Theology* 19(2): 226–56.

MacMunn, N. (1921), *The Child's Path to Freedom*. London: G. Bell and Sons.

Mannin, E. (1930), *Confessions and Impressions*. Harmondsworth: Penguin.

Mannoni, M. (1970), *Preface. In Libres enfants de Summerhill* [Free Children in Summerhill]. Paris, France: Maspero.

Matthias, W. (1980), An A. S. Neill/Summerhill Chronology. *Contemporary Education* 52(1): 50–4.

Mauco, G. (1971), *La paternité* [Paternity]. Paris, France: Éditions Universitaires.

Meads, G. H. (1934), *Mind, Self and Society*. Chicago, IL: University of Chicago Press.

Meighan, R. (2007), *John Holt*. London: Continuum.

Meighan, R. and Harber, C. (2007), *A Sociology of Educating*. London: Continuum.

Meyers, A. (2001), Examining Alternative Education over the past Thirty Years. *Health Sciences* 109: 76–81.

Mill, J. S. (1859), *On Liberty*. London: John W. Parker and Son.

Miller, J. P. (2007), *The Holistic Curriculum*. Toronto: Canada: University of Toronto.

Ministry of Education (1949), Report by His Majesty's Inspectors on the Summerhill School, Leiston, Suffolk East, Inspected on 20th and 21st June, 1949.

Mitchell, E. (2007), Educational Antidisestablishmentarianism. PHILICA. COM Article number 7.

Montagu, A. (1970), In H. Hart (ed.) *Summerhill, For and Against.* New York: Hart Publishing.

Morse, J. (1996), The Ends of Education. *Educational Change*, Spring, 1–26.

Mowat, C. L. (1955), *Britain between the Wars, 1918–1940.* London: Methuen.

Muir, E. (1929), *John Knox: Portrait of a Calvinist.* London: Lowe and Brydone.

— (1993), *An Autobiography.* Edinburgh: Canongate.

Muir, W. (1968), *Belonging.* London: Hogarth Press.

Mulkay, M. (1985), *The Word and the World.* London: Allen and Unwin.

Müller, S. (2009), Freedom and Authority in Alexander S. Neill's and Jean Jacques Rousseau's Philosophy of Education. Unpublished Doctoral Thesis, Bloomington, US: Indiana University.

Murphy, M. A. (1998), *The Life of R. F. Mackenzie: A Prophet Without Honour.* Edinburgh: John Donald.

Neill, A. S. (1912a), Editorial. The Student, 03.01, pp. 295f.

— (1912b), Editorial. The Student, 01.03, pp. 315f.

— (1912c), Editorial. The Student, 08.03, pp. 335f.

— (1912d), Editorial. The Student, 04.12, pp. 148f.

— (1912e), Editorial. The Student, 10.05, pp. 355f.

— (1912f), Editorial. The Student, 28.06, pp. 403f.

— (1915), *A Dominie's Log.* London: Herbert Jenkins.

— (1917), *A Dominie Dismissed.* London: Herbert Jenkins.

— (1919a), *The Booming of Bunkie.* London: Herbert Jenkins.

— (1919b), Psycho-Analysis in Industry. The New Age. A Weekly Review of Politics, Literature and Art, 4.12, p. 69.

— (1920), Psychology of the Flogger. *Education For The New Era* 1(4): 113f.

— (1921/1922), The Abolition of Authority. In New Education Fellowship (Ed.), *The Creative Self-expression of the Child.* London: New Education Fellowship.

— (1921a), *A Dominie in Doubt.* London: Herbert Jenkins.

— (1921b), *Carroty Broon.* London: Herbert Jenkins.

— (1921c), Hellerau International School. *The New Era* 2: 32f; 220f.

— (1921d), The Outlook Tower. *The New Era* 2: 155–8.

— (1922), Education in Germany. *New Era* 3: 57–8.

— (1923), *A Dominie Abroad.* London: Herbert Jenkins.

— (1924), *A Dominie's Five.* London: Herbert Jenkins.

— (1926), *The Problem Child.* London: Herbert Jenkins.

— (1928), Summerhill. *New Era* 9(34): 70f.

— (1931), My School Days. *Scots Magazine* 15(1): 7–13.

— (1932), *The Problem Parent.* London: Herbert Jenkins.

—(1934), Summerhill. In T. Blewitt (ed.), *The Modern Schools Handbook*. London: Gollancz.

—(1936), *Is Scotland Educated?* London: Routledge and Sons.

—(1937), *That Dreadful School*. London: Herbert Jenkins.

—(1938a), A Warm Defence of Reich. Dagbladet, 25 June.

—(1938b), *The Last Man Alive: A Story for Children from the Age of Seven to Seventy*. London: Herbert Jenkins.

—(1939), *The Problem Teacher*. London: Herbert Jenkins.

—(1945), *Hearts not Heads in the School*. London: Herbert Jenkins.

—(1946), Shaw and Education. In S. Winsten (ed.), *G. B. S. 90: Aspects of Bernard Shaw's Life and Work*. London: Hutchinson.

—(1949), *The Problem Family*. London: Herbert Jenkins.

—(1953), *The Free Child*. London: Herbert Jenkins.

—(1958), The Man Reich. In P. Ritter (ed.), *Wilhelm Reich*. Nottingham: Ritter Press.

—(1960a), *Summerhill: A Radical Approach to Child Rearing*. New York: Hart Publishing.

—(1960b), My Scholastic Life. *Id Magazine* 2 (Sept): 2–4.

—(1960c), My Scholastic Life- 2. *Id Magazine* 3 (Oct): 3–5.

—(1960d), My Scholastic Life - 3. *Id Magazine* 4 (Dec): 3–4.

—(1961a), My Scholastic Life - 4. *Id Magazine* 5 (Apr): 3–6.

—(1961b), My Scholastic Life - 5. *Id Magazine* 6 (Jul): 8.

—(1961c), My Scholastic Life - concluded. *Id Magazine*, 7 (Oct): 8.

—(1962a), *Summerhill*. Harmondsworth: Penguin.

—(1962b), Summerhill. Co-educational boarding school from 4 to 16. In H. A. T. Child (ed.), *The Independent Progressive School*. London: Hutchinson.

—(1963), A Dirty Word. *Id Magazine* 11: 19–23.

—(1964a), Recollecting Homer Lane. *Anarchy* 4: 144–6.

—(1964b), Using the Extra Year. Or Daydreaming of Freedom. Times Educational Supplement, 14.02, p. 363.

—(1966a), *Freedom not License!* New York: Hart Publishing.

—(1966b), Obituary: Jonesie. *Id Magazine* 16: 3.

—(1967), *Talking of Summerhill*. London: Gollancz.

—(1969), Introduction. In H. Lane (ed.), *Talks to Parents and Teachers*. New York, NY: Schocken Books.

—(1972a), *Neill! Neill! Orange Peel! A Personal View of Ninety Years*. London: Weidenfeld and Nicolson.

—(1972b), Freedom Works. In J. Hall (ed.), *Children's Rights*. London: Panther.

Neustatter, A. (2011), Summerhill school and the do-as-yer-like kids. Guardian newspaper, Friday 19 August (http://www.guardian.co.uk/education/2011/aug/19/summerhill-school-at-90).

Newman, M. (2006), When Evidence is Not Enough: Freedom to Choose versus Prescribed Choice: The Case of Summerhill School. In D. Kassem, E. Mufti and J. Robinson (eds), *Education Studies: Issues and Critical Perspectives*. Maidenhead: Open University Press.

Noddings, N. (2003), *Happiness and Education*. Cambridge: Cambridge University Press.

Nussbaum, M. (2000), *Women and Human Development: The Capabilities Approach*. Cambridge: Cambridge University Press.

Ollendorf, I. (1969), *Wilhelm Reich: A Personal Biography*. New York: St. Martin's Press.

Ornstein, A. (1977), Critics and Criticism of Education. *Educational Forum* 42(1): 21–30.

Overy, R. (2010), *The Morbid Age: Britain and the Crisis of Civilisation, 1919–1939*. London: Penguin.

Papanek, E. (1970), In H. Hart (ed.) Summerhill, For and Against. New York: Hart Publishing.

Pearson, H. (1961), *Bernard Shaw: His Life and Personality*. London: Methuen.

Pedley R. (1963), *The Comprehensive School*. Harmondsworth: Penguin Books.

Peters, R. S. (1962), Moral Education and the Psychology of Character. *Philosophy* 37(139): 37–56.

Peters, R. S. (1966), *Ethics and Education*. London: George Allen and Unwin.

—(1967), (ed.) *The Concept of Education*. London: Routledge and Kegan Paul.

—(1981), *Moral Development and Moral Education*. London: G. Allen and Unwin.

Philpot, T. (1985), A. S. Neill on Bertrand Russell. *Russell: The Journal of Bertrand Russell Studies*, Winter5: 146–9.

Phillips, D. C. (1987), *Philosophy, Science, and Social Inquiry*. Oxford: Pergamon Press.

Placzek, B. R. (ed.) (1982), *Record of a Friendship: The Correspondence between Wilhelm Reich and A. S. Neill 1936–1957*. London: Gollancz.

Popenoe, J. (1970), *Inside Summerhill*. New York: Hart Publishing.

Potter, J. (undated), That Dreadful Educationalist: Answering A. S. Neill's Critics. http://spinninglobe.net/spinninglobe_html/dreadfulneill.htm (accessed 4 July 2011 11:41).

Potts, A. (2007), New Education, Progressive Education and the Counter Culture. *Journal of Educational Administration and History* 39(2): 145–59.

Powers, T. (1971), *Diana: The Making of a Terrorist*. Boston, MA: Houghton Mifflin Company.

Punch, M. (1972), How Free Is Summerhill? Times Educational Supplement, 4 Jan, p. 7.

—(1974a), The Sociology of the Anti-Institution. *British Journal of Sociology* 25(3): 312–25.

—(1974b), Some Problems of Research and Evaluation in Alternative Education. *Paedagogica Europaea* 9(2): 101–18.

—(1986), *The Politics and Ethics of Fieldwork*. Beverely Hills, CA: Sage Publications.

Purdy, B. (1997), *A. S. Neill: "Bringing happiness to some few children"*. Nottingham: Educational Heretics Press.

Rafferty, M. (1970), In H. Hart (ed.) Summerhill, For and Against. New York: Hart Publishing.

Ravitch, D. (2000), *Left Back: A Century of Failed School Reforms*. New York: Simon and Schuster.

Readhead, Z. (2006), Summerhill Today. In M. Vaughan (ed.) *Summerhill and A. S. Neill*. London: Open University Press.

Reich, W. (1969), *The Sexual Revolution: Toward a Self-Governing Character Structure* (trans. Theodore P. Wolfe). New York: Farrar, Strauss and Giroux.

Reich, W. (1983), *Children of the Future*. New York: Farrar, Straus and Giroux.

Rossman, M. (1970), In H. Hart (ed.) Summerhill, For and Against. New York: Hart Publishing.

Rousseau, J.-J. (1762), *Emile*. London: Dent.

Russell, B. (1916), *Principles of Social Responsibility*. London: Allen and Unwin.

—(1926), *On Education*. London: Allen and Unwin.

Russell, Dora (1967), What Beacon Hill School Stood for. *Anarchy* 7: 11–16.

Saffange, J.-F. (1985), *Libres regards sur Summerhill* [A Fresh Look at Summerhill]. Berne, Switzerland: Peter Lang.

—(1994), Alexander Sutherland Neill. *Prospects: The Quarterly Review of Comparative Education* 24(1/2): 217–29.

—(2000), Alexander Sutherland Neill. Prospects-English Edition, 24(1), 217–30.

Schumpeter, J. A. (1954), *History of Economic Analysis*. New York: Oxford University Press.

Schweitzer, A. (1923), *The Decay and Restoration of Civilization*. London: Black.

Scotland, J. (1969), *The History of Scottish Education* (2 volumes). London: University of London Press.

Segefjord, B. (1970), *Summerhill Diary*. London: Gollancz.

Selleck, R. J. W. (1968), *The New Education: the English Background 1870–1914*. London: Sir Isaac Pitman and Sons.

—(1972), *English Primary Education and the Progressives, 1914–1939*. London: Routledge and Kegan Paul.

Sen, A. (1998), *Freedom as Development*. New York: Knopf.

Sharaf, M. (1994), *Fury on Earth: A Biography of Wilhelm Reich*. Cambridge: Da Capo Press.

Sims, H. (2000), *Inspecting the Island*. Ipswich: Seven Ply Yarns.

Skidelsky, R. (1969), *English Progressive Schools*. Harmondsworth: Penguin.

Small, R. (1987), Franz Kafka at Summerhill. *Educational Theory* 37(2): 179–83.

Smith, M. (1983), *The Libertarians and Education*. London: George Allen and Unwin.

Snell, R. (1975), St. Christopher School: 1915-1975. Letchworth: Aldine Press.

Snitzer, H. (1968), Living at Summerhill. New York: Collier Books.

— (1983), A. S. Neill Remembered. *Educational Leadership* 41(2): 56.

Sowell, T. (2002), *A Conflict of Visions: Ideological Origins of Political Struggles*. New York: Basic Books.

Spring, J. (1975), *A Primer of Libertarian Education*. New York: Free Life Editions.

— (2006), *Wheels in the Head: Educational Philosophies of Authority, Freedom, and Culture from Confucianism to Human Rights*. New York: Routledge.

Stachura, P. D. (1981), *The German Youth Movement, 1900–1945: An Interpretive and Documentary History*. London: Macmillan.

Stanley, A. P. (1845), *The Life and Correspondence of Thomas Arnold - Volume 1*. London: Fellows.

Steedman, C. (1990), *Childhood, Culture and Class*. London: Rutgers University Press.

Stewart, W. A. C. (1968), *The Educational Innovators - Volume 2: Progressive Schools 1881–1967*. London: Macmillan.

Stinton, J. (2005), *A Dorset Utopia: The Little Commonwealth and Homer Lane*. Norwich: Black Dog Books.

Stronach, I. (2002), *The OFSTED Response to Summerhill's Complaint: An Evidence-Based Appraisal*. Manchester: Manchester Metropolitan University.

— (2005). Progressivism against the audit culture: The continuing case of Summerhill School versus OfSTED. Unpublished manuscript.

Stronach, I. and Piper, H. (2008), Can Liberal Education Make a Comeback? The Case of "Relational Touch" at Summerhill School. *American Educational Research Journal* 45(1): 6–37.

Suissa, J. (2010), *Anarchism and Education: A Philosophical Perspective*. Oakland, CA: PM Press.

Summerhill School (2004), Where the whole school deals democratically with issues. http://www.summerhillschool.co.uk/pages/issues.html (accessed 12/11/12).

Sunstein, C. (2005), *Why Societies Need Dissent*. Cambridge, MA: Harvard University Press.

Swartz, R. (1982), John Dewey and Homer Lane: The "Odd Couple". Among Educational Theorists. *The Journal of Educational Thought* 16: 181–90.

Smith, M. C. (1984), Student Choices and a Standardized Curriculum Reconsidered. In M. C. (ed.), *Proceedings of the 1983 Annual Meeting of the Midwest Philosophy of Education Society*. Chicago, IL: Midwest Philosophy of Education Society, pp. 63–78.

—(1999), Homer Lane and Paul Goodman: Two Often Forgotten Socratic Educational Reformers. In M. A. Oliker (ed.), *Proceedings of the 1997–1998 Midwest Philosophy of Education Society*. Chicago, IL: Midwest Philosophy of Education Society.

Tetlock, P. Peterson, R. S., McGuire, C., Chang, S. and Feld, P. (1992), Assessing Political Group Dynamics. *Journal of Personality and Social Psychology* 781(63): 403–25.

Tetlock, P. (2005), *Expert Political Judgment*. Princeton, NJ: Princeton University Press.

Thomson, M. (2006), *Psychological Subjects: Identity, Culture, and Health in Twentieth-century Britain*. Oxford: Oxford University Press.

Ullrich, H. (2008), *Rudolf Steiner*. London: Continuum.

Van der Eyken, W. and Turner, B. (1969), *Adventures in Education*. London: Allen Lane.

van Petten Henderson, S. (1957), *Introduction to the Philosophy of Education*. Chicago, IL: University of Chicago Press.

Vaughan, M. (ed.) (2006), *Summerhill and A. S. Neill*. London: Open University Press.

Viola, W. (1936), *Child Art and Franz Cizek*. New York: Reynal and Hitchcock.

Viola, W. (1944), Child Art. London: University of London Press.

Waks, L. J. (1976), On the Political Conception of Free Education. *Curriculum Inquiry* 6(1): 73–82.

Walmsley, J. (1969), *Neill and Summerhill, A Man and his Work: A Pictorial Study*. Harmondsworth: Penguin.

Washington, P. (1993), *Madame Blavatsky's Baboon*. New York: Schocken Books.

Wells, J. C. (1985), *A. S. Neill and the Scottish Tradition in Education*, Unpublished Masters Dissertation, University of Edinburgh.

Whitbread, N. (1972), *The Evolution of the Nursery-Infant School*. London: Routledge and Kegan Paul.

Who's Who (1972), London: A. and C. Black.

Wills, W. D. (1964), *Homer Lane: A Biography*. London: George Allen and Unwin.

Wingate, W. (1919), *Poems*. Glasgow: Gowans and Gray.

Wooldridge, A. (1994), *Measuring the Mind: Education and Psychology in England, c. 1860 - c. 1990*. Cambridge: Cambridge University Press.

World Education Archive, letter Ensor to Yvonne Moyse 3/12/67.

Zellinger, M. (1996), Summerhill Heute: was ist aus Neills Erziehungs experiment und was aus ehemaligen Schülern geworden? [What happened to Neill's educational experiment and what happened to former students?] Unpublished Diploma Dissertation. Austria: University of Salzburg.

Appendix I: Reading Neill and Summerhill

Neill's somewhat idiosyncratic representation of his life and ideas has been a theme running throughout this book, so I will not repeat these discussions here. Suffice to say, serious students ought to balance their reading of Neill's books with something more sober. With regard to the former, I recommend starting with the Dominie series, which traces Neill's life from a frustrated Scottish teacher to a celebrated educational writer. They are well written, funny, and historically fascinating. It would be a grave error, though, to follow Neill's American publisher Harold Hart in assuming that all the stories are true!

A sensible next step would be to go straight to "Summerhill," the book that made Neill an educational "celebrity." It is, in fact, a collection of material from a range of earlier sources. However, whatever its origins, the book succeeds in presenting a clear and attractive introduction to the principles of Summerhill School. Next, the reader might wish to find out more about the founder of that school, in his own words. Neill's autobiography—"Neill! Neill! Orange Peel!"—is, as might be expected, very entertaining. It was published when Neill was 90 years old, and is a remarkable document of societal, political, and educational changes. It was, of course, written by an author who never let facts get in the way of a good story or a valuable lesson, so the usual disclaimers apply.

There is currently only one comprehensive biography of Neill: Jonathan Croall's "Neill of Summerhill." It is a very good biography, but it is all the more valuable in light of its subject's fondness for "necessary fictions." Ray Hemmings' "Fifty Years of Freedom" draws out the relationships between Neill's life and his evolving theories. Hemmings' book is unusual because it was written by a former teacher at Summerhill, but it manages to avoid the perils of many of the other "insider" accounts, of which hostility to any form of criticism is the most pervasive.

Neill and Summerhill have received a fair amount of attention from academic writers, which is unusual for so-called alternative or radical educationists. I am only aware of one "insider" account of Summerhill in thesis form. It was written by Danë Goodsman, who has the distinction of having being a pupil, parent, teacher, and trustee of the school (and her mother attended, too!) It is probably the best account of what it is actually like to go to Summerhill. The fullest philosophical treatment is probably John Darling's PhD thesis. David Carr's articles, cited in the reference list, and Robin Barrow's book "Radical Education" are also worth reading: the former shows how Neill's ideas connect to broader educational themes; the latter provides a strong critique of Neill's ideas). Axel Kühn's thesis is also a useful source of information about Neill's publications and their reception, although only to those able to read German.

Appendix II: Neill and Summerhill Chronology

This chronology offers a brief summary on the dual lives of Neill and Summerhill. To some extent, it tries to build upon and update Matthias' (1980) rather idiosyncratic earlier chronology of Neill/Summerhill. Another source on information was Hussein Lucas' (2011) "insider" account.

1883   Alexander Sutherland Neill is born on 17 October in Kingsmuir, Forfar Scotland.

1897   Neill leaves School and works as a clerk and draper's assistant.

1898   Neill begins a 4-year period assisting his father in Kingsmuir School as a pupil teacher.

1903   He fails the entrance examination for teacher training college.

1905   Neill teaches briefly at Bonnyrig near Edinburgh.

1906   Neill passes the first part of the Acting Teacher's Certificate.

1906   Neill starts teaching job at Newport near Dundee. While teaching here, Neill attended classes at the University of St Andrews.

1908   Neill passes Second half of the Acting Teacher's Certificate and the University Entrance Examination, and enters the University of Edinburgh. He begins by studying agriculture, but switches a year later to English.

1910   Neill takes over the editorship of the Edinburgh University *Student* magazine. He also writes his first published article, appearing in the *Glasgow Herald*.

1912   Neill graduates from the University of Edinburgh. He starts work at a publishing house in Edinburgh, hoping to establish a career in journalism rather than teaching. Later that year, Neill is transferred to London by his employer.

1913   While living in London, he joins the Labour Party.

1914   When the publishing house went out of business due to the outbreak of war, Neill is forced to return to teaching as acting Headmaster of a school at Gretna Green, on the Scotland-English border.

1915   Neill publishes "A Dominie's Log." Its focus is Neill's life and work at Gretna.

1916   Neill writes "A Dominie Dismissed," a largely fictional account of a teacher (obviously Neill) being dismissed from Gretna School and returning to the community as a cattle man. In fact, Neill is not dismissed from Gretna school; he leaves his teaching post after a year and a half to join the army.

1917   Neill receives a commission with the Royal Scots Fusiliers. While training at the Royal Artillery School in Trowbridge, Wiltshire, Neill meets Homer Lane, whose Little Commonwealth in nearby Dorset becomes a great source of inspiration for him. Neill visits Lane at The Little Commonwealth as frequently as he can during 1917. After a medical discharge late in the year, Neill joins the staff of King Alfred School in Hampstead, London, a famous progressive coeducational school of the day.

1919   Neill writes the novel "The Booming of Bunkie."

1920   Neill leaves King Alfred School to take up the coeditorship of *Education for a New Era* journal with the Theosophist Beatrice Ensor. *New Era's* first journal appears in January 1920. While working on the journal, Neill writes "A Dominie in Doubt," which is an account of his developing educational thinking and experiences. He also completes another fictional and humorous book, "Carroty Broom."

1921   During a tour of Europe on behalf of *New Era*, Neill is invited to start a new international school in the garden city of Hellerau, near Dresden, Germany, within a complex of buildings run by the Dalcroze movement. He writes "A Dominie Abroad" in 1921, which as the name suggests, focuses on his experiences on the Continent.

1923   After a series of disagreements with Mrs Ensor, Neill's co-editor on *New Era*, Neill is forced to resign his editorial position.

1924   Neill is forced to leave the International School and move to a small village in the Austrian mountains called Sonntagberg. While living in this village, which becomes a miserable experience, Neill writes "A Dominie's Five," a fictionalized account of the experiences of five of his students. Neill is forced to return to England with his new wife, Lillian, and they start a new school in Lime Regis in the south of England, called "Summerhill."

1926   While in Lime Regis, Neill writes "The Problem Child," his first extended account of the relationship between psychoanalysis and education.

1926   Neill and his wife buy a large house in Leiston, Suffolk, and brings the name Summerhill with him.

1932   Neill writes "The Problem Parent," which is primarily concerned with the home and the role of parents in children's development.

1936   Neill writes the polemic "Is Scotland Educated?"

1937   Neill writes "That Dreadful School," his best-known book at the time. It offers the fullest account of the Summerhill philosophy and practices. The book is widely and positively reviewed, and does a great deal to raise the profile of Summerhill and Neill.

1938   Neill writes "The Last Man Alive," a book written specifically for young people.

1939   Neill writes "The Problem Teacher." This book discusses issues of gender and sexuality, and how they might influence the school and politics.

1940   Summerhill moves to Wales for 5 years during World War II. The British army moves into the Summerhill buildings in Leiston.

1944   Lillian Neill dies in Wales. Neill writes "Hearts Not Heads in the School."

1945   Neill marries Edna May Wood (known as Ena). The newly married couple and the Summerhill students return to Leiston later that year.

1947   Neill and Ena have a baby daughter, Zoë.

1949   Neill writes "The Problem Family." The book draws upon his experiences of bringing up Zoë within a philosophy of Reichian self-regulation.

1953   Neill writes "The Free Child," which continues Neill's account of the development of his daughter Zoë.

1960   Neill writes the US edition of "Summerhill: A Radical Approach to Childrearing." This is his most famous and influential book, although it is a compilation of extracts from earlier books.

1962   The UK edition of "Summerhill" is published.

1966   Neill writes "Freedom – Not License," a sequel to "Summerhill."

1967   Neill writes "Talking Of Summerhill," which is essentially a commentary on "Summerhill."

1972   Neill publishes his autobiography, "Neill, Neill, Orange Peel."

1973   At midday on 23 Sunday September, Neill dies of pneumonia, less than 1 month before his 90th birthday. Five days before this, at Neill's request, Ena had taken over as headteacher of Summerhill, in time for the new academic year.

1983   Croall's biography is published.

1985   Ena passes responsibility for Summerhill over to their daughter Zoë.

1997   Ena Neill dies.

1999   English government seeks to close Summerhill.

2000   Tribunal dismisses the government's cases, and supports Summerhill's future.

Index

Abbotsholme School   29
Adler, Alfred   37, 42, 57
adults   2, 39–40, 43, 47, 57, 76, 103,
    107, 113–14, 116, 122, 128–30, 137,
    143–4, 149, 154 *see also* parents
aggression   66, 137
aims, of education   24, 47, 91, 105,
    140, 161
Aitkenhead, John   153
anarchism   81, 111
Arnold, Matthew   16
Arnold, Thomas   110
art   43, 48, 50, 102, 126, 140
attendance, class   2, 12, 89, 125, 130,
    141–3, 153–4, 160
Auden, W. H.   24
authority   3, 128–35

Baer-Frissell, Christine   45, 48–51
Barrie, J. M.   9
Barrow, Robin   116, 129
Beacon Hill School   48, 60
Bedales School   29, 48, 87, 153
Berlin, Isaiah   148
Bernal, J. D.   83
Bettelheim, Bruno   79
Blair, Tony   89–90
Blunkett, David   90
Booming of Bunkie   36
buildings   6, 50, 83
bullying   6, 78, 131
Burke, Edmund   110

Calvinism   4, 8–9, 56, 69, 110,
    115, 121
capitalism   62, 67–8
Carr, David   23, 117–19, 122
Carroty Broon   8, 36
character-analysis   64, 72

character-moulding   28, 51, 112,
    126–7
child-centred education   158
children
    being on the side of   27, 111
    development of   19, 29, 32, 34, 39,
        43–4, 61, 72, 111, 119, 122, 129,
        137, 140
    interests of   3, 5, 41, 122–7, 135, 142,
        148
    problem   28, 55, 58, 63, 115,
        119, 123
    psychology of   27, 37, 64, 72, 75, 79,
        138
Coué, Emile   39, 47
craftwork   24, 44, 48, 50
Croall, Jonathan   56, 58, 83, 135, 139,
    141
Curry, William   48, 70, 163

Dalcroze Movement   34, 44–5, 50
dancing   12, 44, 99, 101–2
Dartington Hall   48, 163
de Condorcet, Marquis   110
delinquency   24–7, 57, 115, 119
democracy   18, 88, 133, 154, 164, 169
Dewey, John   24, 37, 42, 80, 151, 155,
    158, 169
D'Holbach, Baron   110
discipline   11, 13, 21–2, 26–7, 34,
    62, 105, 112, 118–19, 130, 138,
    147, 154
Dominie Abroad, A   41–2, 48, 53, 138
Dominie Dismissed, A   20–2, 35, 41
Dominie in Doubt A   36–7, 124
Dominie's Five A   55
Dominie's Log A   5, 18–21, 23, 27, 29,
    35, 40, 56
Duane, Michael   85, 153

emotions   47, 58, 64, 76, 78, 116, 199,
   123, 124, 137–40, 155
Ensor, Beatrice   34–5, 38–42, 45–8, 107,
   111, 115–16, 123, 157
examinations   6, 30, 70, 89, 91,
   140, 147

family   8–9, 17, 36, 49–50, 58, 62, 65–6,
   71–2, 74, 84, 88, 135, 144
fascism   60
fear   5–6, 9, 11, 26, 41, 95, 102
Federalist Papers   110
Ferrière, Adolphe   107, 124
Free Child, The   75, 78, 80
freedom   3, 128–35
Freedom – Not License!   81, 83
Freud, Sigmund   23–4, 37, 42–3, 53,
   59, 61, 63, 65, 71, 75, 77, 80, 110,
   113–14, 116, 119, 123–4, 137–8
Friedman, Milton   110
Froebel, Friedrich   32, 37, 114,
   158, 169
Fromm, Erich   80, 139

Galbraith, J. K.   110
games   99–100
Godwin, William   110–11, 113
Goodman, P.   79, 81, 155
Goodsman, Danë   131–5, 141–2, 147,
   162
Gretna School   17–18, 20–1, 44, 59, 67,
   84, 131
guilt   56, 115, 121

happiness   3, 122–7
hate   30, 62, 67, 111, 121, 123
Hayek, Friedrich   110
Hearts Not Heads in the School   62, 70–1
Hobbes, Thomas   110, 117
Holmes, Edmond   33–5, 37
Holt, John   107–8, 157–8
homesickness   10, 76, 88
humor   22, 36, 98, 103, 112

Ibsen, Henrik   16, 20, 85, 162
Illich, Ivan   107, 153, 158

indoctrination   47
inspections   78, 82–4, 88–90, 92
intelligence   141
Isaacs, Susan   42, 61
Isherwood, Christopher   24, 26
Is Scotland Educated?   59

Jesus Christ   78, 121–2
Jugend movement   51
Jung, Carl   29, 34, 37, 42, 53, 138

Lane, Homer   22–31, 36, 38–9, 41,
   52–3, 56–7, 63–4, 67, 73, 78,
   110–14, 117, 121–3, 130, 137–8,
   158, 160, 163
Last Man Alive   55
learning   3, 136–48
libertarianism   xiii, 56, 81, 156–7
Little Commonwealth   26–9, 36, 38,
   122, 130
love
Lyme Regis   55–6, 61

Mackenzie, R. F.   71, 84, 153
MacMunn, N.   32
Malthus, T.   110
masturbation   56–7, 123
Mendelssohn, Peter de   51–2
Montessori, M.   23, 25, 34, 37–9, 42, 44,
   47, 61, 153, 158, 169
moral training   43, 51, 67, 111–12,
   118–19, 122, 155
Muir, E.   8–9, 50, 54
Muir, W.   50, 54

nature, human and child   24
Neill, Alexander Sutherland
   at Bonnyrig   11
   at Gretna   17–21, 44, 59, 67,
      84, 131
   at Hellerau   44–50, 54–5, 88
   at King Alfred's   29–31, 37, 44,
      52, 87
   at Kingskettle   11–12, 17, 36, 59
   at Kingsmuir   5, 10–11, 17
   at Leiston   58ff, 72–3, 100

at Lyme Regis   55–6, 61
at Newport   12–13, 18
as public speaker   47, 78
as pupil-teacher   6, 10–11
at Sonntagberg   54
as university student   13–16, 50
as writer   3, 16–18, 20, 35–6
Neill, Ena (née Wood)   72–4, 85, 87
Neill, George   5–7, 9–10, 17, 19, 32
Neill, Lillian (née Neustatter,
   aka 'Mrs Lins')   44, 48–9, 55,
   65, 70–1
Neill, Mary   5, 8
Neill, Zoe Readhead   72, 75–6, 84,
   87–9, 120, 142, 153
New Educational Fellowhip   23,
   34–5, 37, 39–43, 46, 48, 61, 105,
   124, 158
New Era, The   35–48, 55, 76, 121
"New Psychology" The   23, 27, 37,
   40, 52, 59, 119, 124

original sin   38–9, 59, 110, 117, 1
   20, 154
Owen, Robert.   110

Paine, Thomas.   110
parents   59, 75, 78, 123, 129, 137
payment-by-results   8, 32
Pestalozzi, Johann Heinrich   158
Peters, R. S.   117–20
Piaget, Jean   42
play
Problem Child, The   56–8, 79–80, 112,
   138
Probem Family, The   2, 62
Problem Parent, The   59, 80
Problem Teacher, The   61, 65
progressive schooling   1, 7, 13, 23–4,
   26, 28–9, 32, 35, 37, 39, 41–2, 47–8,
   58, 61, 71, 87, 105–7, 123, 130, 153,
   155, 158, 163
psychoanalysis   23, 29, 36, 40, 49, 53, 61,
   66, 80, 119, 121, 137, 149, 154
punishment   18, 30, 34, 41, 46, 110–12,
   123, 132, 135

radical education   1, 25, 50, 80, 107–8,
   122, 151–3, 155, 157–8, 163, 168–70
Reich, Wilhelm   61, 63–72, 74–5,
   77–80, 110–11, 113, 120–1, 137,
   156, 161, 163, 168
religious instruction   9, 29, 121
risinghill School   85
Rogers, Carl   113
Rousseau, Jean-Jacques   33, 110,
   114–16, 151–2, 158
rules   29, 40, 81–2, 99, 118, 128,
   131–3, 135
Russell, Bertrand   38, 57–61, 83, 141,
   163
Russell, Dora   48, 60–1, 107, 158
Russia   68, 121

science   126–7, 144, 159
self-control   117–19
self-discipline   18, 135
self-government   18, 34, 36–8, 40–2,
   46–7, 60–1, 63, 130–1, 154, 160
   at King Alfred's School   29–30
   at The Little Commonwelath   25,
   27–31
   at Summerhill   63, 98, 127,
   130, 160
self-hate   123
Shaw, George Bernand   16–17, 20, 67,
   73, 82, 110
Skinner, B. F.   23, 136
Smith, Adam   110
socialism   44, 51, 58, 67
Sowell, Thomas   108–16, 136
Spock, Benjamin   72, 151
sport and games   13, 100, 140
Stekel, Wilhelm   24, 65
Steiner, Rudolf   33, 37–9, 153, 169
Summerhill School *see also* Lyme Regis
   authority at   2–3, 15, 60, 62, 66, 128,
   131–2, 134, 144, 146–7
   campaign to save school   88–93
   Lessons   2, 89–90, 93, 98, 125, 136,
   141–4, 146–7, 153–4, 160
   Private Lessons ('PLs')   28, 93, 97,
   115, 137

School Meeting 60, 76, 82, 90, 132
sex at 65, 67
swearing at 76
teaching methods at 144
Summerhill 3, 80–1, 83, 122, 139, 153, 155, 159
Sims, H. 95–103, 133

Talking of Summerhill 99, 131–3, 135
teaching 3, 136–48
That Dreadful School 60, 80, 121

theosophy 34
Tocqueville, Alexis de 110

Veblen, Thorstein 110
Voltaire 110

Wells, H.G. 16
Wills, David 38
woodwork 136

Zutt, "Prof" 50